POST-WAR CHURCH BUILDING

AN EXAMPLE OF MODERN STAINED GLASS
From the Hardman Studio

POST-WAR CHURCH BUILDING

EDITED BY

ERNEST SHORT

Author of *The House of God*

With contributions by

SIR CHARLES NICHOLSON, Bt.
JOHN ROTHENSTEIN
STANLEY ELEY
N. F. CACHEMAILLE-DAY, F.R.I.B.A.
GEOFFREY WEBB
ALBERT A. HUGHES

HOPE BAGENAL, F.R.I.B.A.
COLONEL BERTRAM SHORE
FRANCIS C. EELES, O.B.E., D.Litt.
ANDREW FREEMAN, B.Mus. (Cantab.)
JUDITH D. GUILLUM SCOTT
LLEWELLYN E. WILLIAMS, A.R.I.B.A.

LONDON
HOLLIS AND CARTER
1947

MADE AND PRINTED IN GREAT BRITAIN BY WILLIAM CLOWES AND SONS, LIMITED, LONDON
AND BECCLES, FOR HOLLIS AND CARTER, LIMITED, 25 ASHLEY PLACE, LONDON, S.W.1

First published 1947

Contents

Acknowledgements

The Editor and Publishers are grateful to the Central Council for the Care of Churches, the Bromsgrove Guild, the Warham Guild, and various architects, artists and craftsmen for permission to reproduce examples of their work, and to the photographers who have given permission for the reproduction of copyright photographs

List of Illustrations

Foreword ✍ ✍ By the GENERAL EDITOR

A CHRISTIAN CHURCH is more than a building and its designer more than an architect. Something of the poet must be added. His task is to create a symbol, and he must ever have in mind the full purpose of his building, always remembering the particular denomination concerned. These essays upon the planning and furnishing of a modern church have been written by craftsmen and others well versed in the practical problems involved, which include important considerations arising from the collection and spending of what may well be very limited funds. Just because each contributor is well-instructed in his special branch, what is written will have added worth because there is the underlying recognition that every structure which is to be worthy of the designation "church" must be recognisable as a very House of God. This can only mean that it should have beauty of design and goodness of material comparable with the final values which we enshrine in the idea of the Godhead.

In a very real sense the planning, building and furnishing of a new church is an act of worship. When churches are built to mend the destruction wrought by the years of war and meet the needs of changing social circumstances due to economic reconstruction following the War, church builders will have to approach their tasks in this mood of dedication. So to be fully worthy a church should carry the imagination of worshippers back through almost two thousand years of Christian history, embodying the idea of a vast chain of prayer and thanksgiving, a chain, moreover, in which the worship of to-day is by no means the final link.

The building may be a small church as lovely in design, material and craftsmanship as that of Thomas Garner and G. F. Bodley at Hoar Cross, a metropolitan cathedral as majestic as the designs of Sir Giles Scott for the Anglican cathedral at Liverpool, or a Christian Centre as carefully planned as that Sir Giles designed to replace the war-ruined cathedral of Coventry. On the contrary, the building may be a relatively humble suburban or village church in which the architect is strictly limited by the funds available; nevertheless, because of its high and enduring purpose, there should be no second best in design or craftsmanship. When C. Harrison Townsend designed the village church of St. Martin, Wonersh, near the hamlet of Blackheath in Surrey, he was content to convert an old cottage into a vestry and to this he added his church, just over sixty feet long and no more than fifteen feet high. Necessarily, the proportions of the structure were not noble, but they were fully adequate to the needs of the little community and that sufficed.

So much by way of preface. For the rest this book has the purely practical purpose of helping parish priests and zealous laymen who may be entrusted with the task of collecting funds to build a new church or restore an old one. Not a few people will recognise the need for guidance, seeing that the building will not only serve immediate needs, but also, happily, carry on the tradition of church building which makes many English churches things of beauty which succeeding generations have delighted to enlarge and embellish. War-time destruction has made it certain that many new churches will be called for, an almost equally important consideration being the desirability of readiness to meet the needs of changing industrial populations. Factories in the post-war Britain will not necessarily remain in the over-weighted industrial centre of to-day. Garden cities will arise and each will need its quota of churches. It is an inspiring, but also a disturbing thought, that such a metropolitan suburb as Becontree, with its 25,000 houses and flats, needed ten parish churches, when it was planned by the London County Council after the first World War. The calls upon the energy, versatility and skill of architects and decorators will be on an even greater scale during the coming years of peace, ranging from the smallest chapel of ease for a few score of worshippers, to large parish churches seating 1,500 or 1,800. Some 14,000 churches, monasteries, convents and other ecclesiastical buildings have suffered damage in Great Britain and Northern Ireland. The whole matter of church building calls for careful thought, and readers will do well to ponder the considerations put before them by Sir Charles Nicholson, based as they are upon an unrivalled experience of diocesan architecture. The same may be said of the sections upon church bells and the towers to contain them from the pen of Mr. Albert Hughes, whose contacts with church bell foundries date back to before the Armada, his firm having had its beginnings in 1570. And I would add very special thanks to Dr. Francis C. Eeles, of the Central Council for the Care of Churches, who has been generous with advice and practical help from the inception of this book. He has also contributed the section treating an all-important aspect of church-building, that is, raising the funds. It may be added that the publications of the Incorporated Church Building Society, at present under the chairmanship of Sir Cecil Harcourt-Smith, give full details of building between the two World Wars. With the authority of more than a hundred years of useful endeavour, the Society is also in a position to assist the building, enlarging and repairing of churches and dedicated mission rooms with technical advice and money grants.

Architect and Committee

As has been said, a primary consideration facing those who contemplate a new church is cost. Directly the problem is faced, it must be plain that the primary essential is stability and sound construction. Accordingly, chancel arches and exterior turrets, towers and steeples may well be regarded not as essentials but as charming accessories. Here, a difficulty at once suggests itself. Any architect of worth will desire to see a fully complete design associated with his name, and, if possible, a building in which he has had a considerable voice in the furnishing and embellishment. Very seldom will an architect of the post-war period come upon the opportunity vouchsafed to J. D. Sedding in Holy Trinity, Sloane Street, London, when he was permitted to wed the metal work of Alfred Gilbert and the pictorial art of Burne Jones to his personal conception of a modern church. What an architect, as well as the committee commissioning him, must remind themselves continually is that they are not creating for a decade but for generations yet unborn. Good material and sound construction are the first considerations.

In this connection it is a comforting thought that many an English church has gained much of its interest and charm from the accretions of time. Now a nave has been re-roofed or a choir rebuilt and, if taste and sound craftsmanship have been displayed, the new work has enhanced the beauty of the old. Some charming embellishments to post-war churches may safely be left for later addition. Indeed, there can be no other decision if the embellishments are likely to be at the expense of sound walls, windows and roofs. Committees are apt to be strongly influenced by picturesque plans, so the truly wise and wily architect will not place undue temptation in the path of the uninstructed. Though decoration may add much to a church and even redeem a building from ugliness, the first thing to be ascertained is whether the due proportion of part to part asserts itself. In this lies excellence, and, as has been said, it is not necessarily a matter of spending large sums of money. The committee must select an architect who knows his job, and then trust him.

There are those who profess the belief that church building is a lost art and belongs to bygone ages. With the coming of a machine-age, some of the craft skill which used to beautify cathedrals and churches has been lost. But never let it be thought that there is not professional skill in abundance, and to this may be added a growing interest in the subject among clergy and laity which promises to make the best efforts of the church architects more profitable than at any time during the past four hundred years.

Certain problems which might conceivably arise from the war damage done to churches will not be discussed in these pages. It has been suggested that a church, say in Plymouth, Coventry or other suffering area, should be left as ruins as a fitting memorial to symbolise a city's grief. This idea was sufficiently condemned by Sir Herbert Baker, when he quoted the Kipling lines:

"If thought can reach to Heaven,
On Heaven let it dwell,
For fear thy thought be given
Like power to reach to Hell."

As Sir Herbert wrote, "a war-blasted church left in ruins would surely lower our remembrances of the sacrifices of the second World War to the Inferno where hate and revenge dwell."

Again, there are problems of town planning, such as those associated with London City churches or St. Paul's, where an imposing forecourt and restful grassy areas are proposed by the City of London's Town Planning Committee, for the better display of Wren's masterpiece. The matter is very interesting, involving as it does the control of building heights, so as to preserve vistas displaying Wren's majestic dome and the widening of Ludgate Hill to provide a ceremonial approach to the west front, but it is not within the scope of our book.

Nor is it proposed to discuss the market value of the site of a ruined church and the possibility of this being sold with a view to the erection of churches where they are more needed. Such matters involve considerations outside the experience of builders or decorators. Again, it will suffice to chronicle the interesting plans for rebuilding Coventry Cathedral which Sir Giles Scott prepared. Alas, they came to nought. The lesson to be learnt from the unhappy episode is that the less interference there is with the considered plans of an architect of proved genius the better. Happily, the partnership of the Free Church in the scheme continues, so that the new cathedral will be a Christian Centre of service for the community as a whole. The old cathedral was little more than a large parish church, and it is proposed that the post-war church shall be on a considerably larger scale. In the cathedral close, connected with the cathedral, will be a Chapel of Unity and a Lady Chapel. The Chapel of Unity will help towards a richer fellowship, while the community centre for Christian service should extend and deepen the contribution of all churches to the life of the people. In the words of the President of the Coventry Free Church Federal Council, "together we press on to make our city more nearly a city of God." This aspect of church planning is one which has always interested Mr. Cachemaille-Day, who has contributed a section to this book regarding the layout of the whole site upon which a church and its allied buildings may arise.

Tradition versus Originality

An overplus of originality is seldom desirable in any building which may have to face centuries of use, as thousands of village churches in Britain have done in times past. We tend to tire of architecture which is not firmly based upon the traditional needs of worshippers, whether cleric or lay. The dictum of Le Corbusier to the effect that a house is "a machine which has to be lived in" has a wider application to business premises and dwelling houses than it has to churches, just because the symbolic element in a church is insistent upon finding expression. The beauty to be found in an efficient machine is not nearly related to the beauty we seek in a church.

Reinforced concrete as a building method was only invented in the nineties of the last century, and it has yet to develop its tradition in connection with either the aspiring and mystical appeal of the Gothic style or the order-loving charm of Wren's renaissance architecture.

M. Perret, after the first World War, designed a highly original church in Paris, dedicated to St. Joan of Arc, the material being reinforced concrete, but this volume is not concerned with such experiments, interesting as they are. While not denying architects opportunities for promising innovations in design and ornament, it will be well that both architects and those who commission them should remember that there is little room for experiments in building materials and methods which have not been well tested. An overplus of enterprise is to be discouraged where public money is being spent upon communal needs. Nevertheless, this amounts to no more than a warning. It is to be remembered that the rectangular Gothic plan with transepts is by no means the only building tradition with a long Christian history. The early Armenian churches were based upon a dome above a square plan and Wren himself gave this plan a modern application in St. Stephen's, Walbrook. In this connection Mr. Hope Bagenal's article upon acoustics in churches and their relation to planning is highly suggestive. Very properly he emphasises the part "a preaching place" should have in a modern church, particularly in times when the task of expounding Christian truths is added to the more personal and individual acts of worship.

The actual structure as set out in an architect's design entails numerous problems over and above the preliminary one of seating accommodation, and in this connection it is worth while recalling that it is easy to spoil an architect's design by overcrowding nave and aisles with benches or chairs. Not every congregation will fill a church. Only enough seats should be in place to meet the needs of an average congregation. The extra seating accommodation can be brought from an adjacent storeroom, and this should be provided for in the original plan. Such a storeroom may well be more important than an imposing bell tower, though the experience of Mr. Albert Hughes may deserve consultation before a decision is made.

Precisely the same considerations apply to the vestries in a parish church. These should not only be comfortable but, if possible, sufficiently spacious to allow of small meetings, such as those of the Church Council, which cannot conveniently be held in the church itself. Spacious, well-ventilated and properly heated vestries for clergy and choristers are a primary, not a secondary, consideration in church building. Again, there is the position of organ and choir stalls in relation to the all-important matter of congregational singing. In a properly organised church service, there may well be women as well as men and boy singers. In such matters architects, as well as those who commission them, will welcome guidance from the Reverend Andrew Freeman.

Church Furniture and Decoration

Thus far, we have been concerned with the structure of the church which is to be. Other considerations associate themselves with its decoration. Again, insistence must be laid upon the truth that church furniture and church decorations have symbolic significance as well as material uses. In both an Anglican and a Roman Catholic church, the altar will be the centre of a sacred rite. Tertullian it was who described the Mass as the Drama of the Pious, and under this conception the altar is the place where the mystery of mysteries is enacted. It will be for the architect to determine the size of altar or communion table so that it shall appear worthy of its high office and not be dwarfed in relation to the rest of the chancel. Sir Giles Scott carried this thought so far in planning the rebuilding of Coventry Cathedral, that he placed his altar in the centre of the congregation; in other words, he proposed to build the new cathedral round the altar. Commenting upon the scheme, the Provost of Coventry pointed out that a further object of the change is to confront the people, worshippers and visitors alike, with certain ideas which are of paramount value for the destiny of mankind—namely, the reality and priority of God in all human life, the essential character of God as self-giving love, the Holy Communion as the deepest source of true community, and the hallowing of man's daily work and craft by the offering of it to God in worship. These are beliefs common to all Christian communions. We simply think that they are better emphasised by an altar table visible to all at the centre than by one partially hidden from sight at the far end of the church.

From the architectural standpoint, a central altar allows of a lantern tower above the altar, with a richly decorated roof and well-lighted windows in plenty, as well as affording an unobstructed view of the altar to the congregation. Plainly, this is impossible in a church with the normal Gothic aisles, transepts and sanctuary.

This brings to mind the candlesticks, monstrances and other furniture which the sentiment of Christendom tends to associate with the altar, regarded as the focal point of Christian worship. I am not thinking of such objects as the amazing 15th-century censer in the Treasury of San Antonio, Padua, or the vast Tabernacle of Adam Kraft in the Church of St. Lawrence, Nuremberg. Neither forethought nor money will produce such masterpieces to order. Nevertheless, careful selection should ensure the installation of something of enduring value which, without such care, might prove worthless. In the smaller suburban or village churches, it may well be that local craft should be sought, in preference to more imposing objects of wholesale manufacture. I can call to mind a delightful series of carved Angels, dating from mid-Victorian times, which add significance to the altar space in a small parish church near Lichfield. The carver belonged to the parish and his skill does not suggest that of a professional sculptor, but he made a thing which even a casual visitor to the church remembers with pleasure and those who see it Sunday after Sunday may well regard with affection, remembering that in a sense it is by one of themselves.

This use of local craftsmanship is capable of many variations. When Randall Wells designed his church at Kempley in Gloucestershire, it was a condition of the contract that the labour should be local. In fact, the church was built without a contractor. The roof timbers were cut on Lord Beauchamp's estate nearby, and the stone tiles were specially quarried by the workmen upon Lord Beauchamp's estate. Similarly, when Lever Brothers built the church of Christ Church, Port Sunlight, all the building work was done by the firm, local red sandstone being used. Again, in Rivington Church, Lancashire, it is an added delight to note that altar table, reredos, panelling and altar rails are of old Cheshire oak. Only a very small part of general church furnishing can be done by such efforts. Always, the major part will fall to those who make a business of designing and manufacturing such things. Much experiment with materials and designs is called for if the multitudinous needs are to be met, and this necessarily calls for considerable capital commitments. Nevertheless, the work of local craftsmen, willing and anxious to beautify their own place of praise and worship, has an appeal of its own in certain circumstances.

Mr. Geoffrey Webb and Miss Judith Scott have contributed authoritative articles upon the altar and its furniture in the church usage of to-day, with special reference to the building of churches in the post-war period.

A single object may give character and thus add dignity to a building which, in other respects, is almost featureless. St. Stephen's, Coleman Street, London, which was destroyed by bombing in 1940–41 was far from being a Wren masterpiece, but it included a carved Jacobean altar table of real quality and a large east window, reproducing the Rubens' *Descent from the Cross* in Antwerp Cathedral. The window was only of 19th-century manufacture but had quality enough to add distinction to Wren's simple rectangular plan.

Our generation has already seen a marked revival in the public interest regarding the treasures of religious art and architecture which have survived from past centuries. Following upon the Ancient Monuments (Churches) Committee which reported to the Archbishops of Canterbury and York in 1914, Advisory Committees were established in every diocese, and all applications for alterations and additions to the fabric or ornamentation of parish churches are referred to them.

Salving the Art Treasures of the Church, published in 1945 by The Central Council for the Care of Churches, should also be consulted. It treats of numerous problems arising from churches and chapels in *blitzed* areas.

As a consequence of the heightened interest in the work of times past came a new interest in the religious art of our own day, and it is this interest which our book seeks to enforce and sustain. All denominations call for the support which modern art can give to church building and the arts allied with it. The movement from Victorian realism to the symbolism which characterises much recent painting and sculpture, in itself, should foster a revival of religious art, if only because a closer alliance between craftsmen and the several denominations gives promise of a more assured market for imaginative work. And not only painters and sculptors. Wood, ivory and metal workers of all kinds should find fresh outlets for their talents.

There are designers in Britain to-day with talent in plenty to satisfy such demands, an example being Benno Elkan's Old and New Testament candelabra in Westminster Abbey. The first was given to the church by anonymous donors and placed at the head of the Nave in the opening months of the War of 1939, while the dedication of the second candelabrum happily synchronised with the United Service of International Christian Witness held at Whitsuntide in 1942. Each candelabrum stands six and a half feet high and has the form of a fan-shaped tree, the branches of which carry the figures of the sculptor's symbolic vision. Thus, in the centre of the New Testament candelabrum are the Virgin Mother and the Holy Child and upon branches on either side figures representing the Magi and the adoring Shepherds. A devotional hour can be spent identifying the figures upon the two great pieces, and who will say that this is not, in truth, an act of worship?

Some of the churches to be built may well be adorned by objects from war-damaged buildings and thus add historical associations to objects of Christian significance. Altars, screens, wrought-iron grilles and similar tributes to the Dead of the Allied Armies in two great wars, are other forms in which a chance gift may add dignity to a new church, large or small. Examples are the altars and altar screens which Sir Robert Lorimer and Walter Tapper designed for York Minster, in memory of the sacrifices suffered by Yorkshire regiments between 1914 and 1918. For a metropolitan cathedral, high professional talent is called for, but local craft might well be employed for work in villages up and down the country. Nor is it desirable that these war memorials in churches should *always* have a military application. A statue of the patron saint, for example, may have more abiding meaning than the figure of a khaki-clad soldier, standing with rifle reversed. Remember the little lead figure of St. Christopher which Mrs. Spooner added to the west front of her husband's church at Haslemere.

As with structure, so with the decoration and furniture of a church. The symbolic import must ever be borne in mind. The Council of Trent in the decree *De invocatione, veneratione et reliquiis sanctorum et sacris imaginibus* explained what the cult of images should mean to Christendom, laying emphasis upon its value as a means of example. The dictum of the Council is reiterated in the 25th chapter of the *Rituale Romanum*, in a prayer used at the time of the dedication of a picture, and few Christians will quarrel with its teaching :—

"Almighty and Everlasting God, who art well pleased that the likeness of Thy

I. THE NEW TESTAMENT CANDELABRUM AT WESTMINSTER ABBEY
By Benno Elkan

2. CENSER IN THE CHURCH OF ST. ANTHONY, PADUA

Saints should be made manifest in painting, so that as often as we behold them with our bodily eyes, so often may we resolve in our hearts to imitate their holiness of life, vouchsafe we beseech Thee to bless and sanctify this picture. . . ."

The *Rituale Romanum* is only reiterating the thought with which this introductory essay began. A church, its altar furniture, its coloured glass windows and its decoration all have symbolic value, as well as the worth which arises from sound craftsmanship and good material. For the rest, the problem of the church-builder is to provide comfort and convenience for a congregation of determined size, within the limits circumscribed by strictly limited funds. The committees who seek to spend wisely and to good purpose must face this final test. By its capacity to lift the creature to his Maker and Redeemer will their effort to beautify a Christian church be judged.

Introduction ∾ By JOHN ROTHENSTEIN

Director of the Tate Gallery

IN THE SOMBRE LIGHT of subsequent events, one of the saddest documents in our history is an account of England, and particularly of English churches, written about the year 1500 by the secretary of the Venetian ambassador to London. This account reveals the wonder of a citizen of one of the most beautiful of cities at the number, size and opulence of the churches not of London only, but throughout the whole country.

The world had nothing to show more splendid, he reported, than the shrine of Edward the Confessor in Westminster Abbey, unless it were the shrine of St. Thomas in Canterbury Cathedral. In particular he was amazed by the magnificence of the objects of craftsmanship with which these churches were embellished.

"In a single street leading to St. Paul's," he wrote, "there are fifty-two goldsmith's shops, so rich and full of silver vessels, great and small, that in all the shops in Milan, Rome, Venice and Florence put together, I do not think there would be found so many of the magnificence that are to be seen in London . . . above all are their riches displayed in the church treasures; for there is not a parish church in the Kingdom so mean as not to possess crucifixes, candlesticks, censers, pattens and cups of silver; nor is there a convent of mendicant friars so poor, as not to have all these same articles in silver. . . . Your Magnificence may therefore imagine what the decorations of those enormously rich Benedictine, Carthusian and Cistercian monasteries must be." *

In little more than a generation a great part of this beauty had perished. Of what survived much was destroyed by the Puritans of the 17th century. The relatively little which survived two such virulent outbreaks of iconoclasm the 18th century neglected, and the 19th—with results incomparably more disastrous— "restored." Thus of the beauties which moved the Venetian to admiring wonder only minute vestiges remain to us, and these grown grey and sterile. It is true that in the course of these centuries much has been added. The genius of Wren blossomed with prolific brilliancy; but even within living memory many of his churches have been demolished in order that their sites should be sold. The 18th century built churches with extraordinary distinction, but relatively few

---

* From *A Relation of the Island of England* (Camden Society), quoted in *Thomas More* by R. W. Chambers (Cape, 1935).

I

in number. Many of these, too, have been demolished, and of what survived until 1940 much was ravaged by the Nazis, one of whose objects was the destruction, where annexation proved impracticable, of the art of their enemies.

No great nation has destroyed so preponderant a part of its own artistic heritage as ours. A responsibility, therefore, of unique gravity now rests upon our town-planners, architects, artists, craftsmen and patrons. There is so much to be done, and that by a generation which cannot in justice be called a generation of great builders, and among whom fine artists and craftsmen are not sufficiently numerous to perform the tasks that should be required of them. It is plain then that we can ill afford mistakes.

The responsibility borne by all those concerned with the erection of new churches is especially heavy, for the church is not only the House of God, but as a prominent building it is one which inevitably contributes largely to the beauty or the degradation of the neighbourhood in which it stands. For many centuries, a church was, as it ought to be again, the natural focus for the artistic genius of a people. Christianity is not a distillation of man's creativity but the gratuitous gift of Divine condescension, yet (or rather therefore) it solicits and inspires men's total response, and demands that the quality of this response be as perfect as possible; so that it should call out every "natural" perfection. Furthermore, since human nature is in general of a piece, and what goes on in one part of it intimately affects what goes on in another, you cannot afford to isolate a man's religion from his æsthetic quality. For this last concerns his sensibility and therefore affects his imagination; and the quality of his sensibility and his imagination affects both his religion and his normal quality, and upon these therefore the effect of the tin roof or the pink-and-white tawdriness can only be to degrade.

No one would claim that the church any longer plays any such glorious part as of old, for there has taken place during the past centuries a catastrophic decline in the quality of ecclesiastical art patronage. The Church, once the most inspired and most munificent patron of art the world has seen, the patron of Giotto, Jan van Eyck, Bramante, Piero della Francesca, Leonardo da Vinci, Donatello, Michel-angelo, Raphael, Titian, El Greco, Bernini and Rubens, now, with rare exceptions, extends her patronage to the most meretricious and sycophantic architecture, painting, sculpture and craftsmanship that she can procure.

An immense opportunity now confronts us, but a pessimist will dwell (and not without justification) upon the decadence of architecture, the rarity of fine painting and sculpture, and the fact that craftsmanship—notwithstanding heroic efforts to revive it—shows hardly any signs of life; and he will conclude that the responsibility is too heavy for us, that the opportunity calls for achievements altogether beyond our powers.

If then we are not to fail we must compensate for scarcity of genius by making constructive and generous use of all available talent, and by taking clear and careful thought before any project is undertaken, and above all by the most scrupulous honesty of purpose.

The Puritan Outlook

The first function of a church is, of course, the protection of the altar (or communion table or pulpit or whatever may be the focus of worship or principal object of reverence) and of the congregation from the weather, but any building specially dedicated to the performance of religious rites, however simple, is of necessity a work of art. In their dread lest anything should interpose between the soul and its Creator, certain extreme Protestants have sometimes failed to recognize this necessity, and behaved as though it were possible to dispense altogether with the arts. The most austere place of worship, even if all traditional symbolism is excluded, in fact inescapably involves the arts of masonry or bricklaying, of woodwork, of metalwork, and of printing. The choice therefore between art and no art cannot arise : there exists only the choice between good art and bad. The puritan, wishing to endow his chapel with the character of gravity and of severe simplicity should not attempt to ignore the arts but should rather employ them with all the sensibility and intelligence at his command in order that the building should be the noblest and the most exact symbol of the religion associated with Calvin. There is perhaps no religious building so absurd, on account of its incongruity with the spirit of the worship which it serves, as the Calvinist chapel which apes one or other of those grandiose styles which the early Calvinists so passionately repudiated as reflexions of the pomps and vanities of this world. Chapels of this kind, tawdry travesties of Roman basilicas and even of luxurious pagan temples, are not uncommon, but the prevailing defect of Nonconformist chapels is a particular and noxious species of gloominess, acrid and shabby, often celebrated in fiction. This gloominess arises in part from the Manichean doctrine that earthly beauties are but snares for the soul, but even this doctrine cannot be effectively enforced by an acrid and shabby gloominess any more than a bore can be convincingly portrayed in a novel as a person about whom it is boring to read. For the spiritual beauties of the renunciation of earthly glories and delights to be expressed in visual terms, their visual equivalents must be found. Ugliness and gloom can in no case serve this purpose. But Protestants of such unyielding opinions have become less common of late years ; indeed the growth of an enlarged and less exclusive—if also, perhaps, a less intense—outlook among the Free Churches, has been one of the conspicuous features of recent religious history.

In the best, indeed in numerous Nonconformist chapels, these equivalents have been found. Many villages and most towns contain chapels which, by their reticent and sober dignity, provide an exact reflection of the doctrines which are preached within their walls. Some of the most notable of these are to be found in the great cities of Northern England, monuments mostly of that heroic moment in Nonconformist history when John Wesley and others came to comfort the wretched workers in these teeming industrial camps, when the Church of England displayed hardly a trace of that social conscience by which it is now distinguished, and when the Roman Catholics had scarcely emerged from their long struggle for bare survival.

Architects of future Evangelical places of worship possess, in such buildings as, say, the classical Unitarian Upper Chapel in Sheffield, and the elegant Gothic Baptist chapel in Cheltenham, admirable examples which require merely to be modified to bring them into harmony with altered conditions. Nor do the best of these chapels provide lessons for one denomination alone. After a heavy air-raid on London in 1941 I had occasion to express to a Roman Catholic Assistant Bishop of Westminster my regret at the destruction of the Church of the Holy Apostles, in Claverton Street, Pimlico—a charming but plain little Georgian style church with a white, galleried interior, one of the best churches in the diocese—but my description of it at first conveyed nothing to him. After some thought, however, he exclaimed, "I know the place you mean: but we bought that from the Methodists!" Cardinal Mundelein, Archbishop of Chicago, built his own church in frank imitation of the Congregational Meeting-House at Lynn, Connecticut.

The principal reason for the existence of large numbers of good Nonconformist chapels is that the problems which they pose are relatively simple. Protestantism has always made its strongest appeal through the ear: "Hear, that thy soul shall live" has been its ministers' constant exhortation. The Nonconformist church must therefore constitute the best possible auditorium, and, on account of the reserve in the Protestant attitude towards visual beauty, the part which it may play in worship is severely circumscribed. Innumerable occasions of error are thereby avoided.*

The Power of Symbolism

Of all religious bodies that which, during the past hundred years, has been guilty of the largest number of errors in the building and embellishment of places of worship, is the Roman Catholic Church. But among the several causes for her failure, the chief derives from the very loftiness of her ideal as to the part which the arts should play in worship. This Church has always held, in principle, that only the most beautiful architecture, sculpture, painting and craftsmanship are worthy of dedication to the service of God, and that works of such an order are true intimations of the Divine Glory. Such confidence in the arts the history of

* The principles underlying post-war church building in the Methodist Church are discussed in detail in *The Methodist Church Builds Again*, by E. Benson Perkins and Albert Hearn, published in 1946 by the Epworth Press. The book includes a number of plans and building models, suited for very varied needs.

the Church abundantly justifies. At the beginning of the Middle Ages the Roman Catholic Church was confronted by the formidable undertaking of making her complex and unfamiliar teachings acceptable to a Europe without a popular common language, divided by continuous war and nearly illiterate. To the almost miraculous success of the undertaking the artist contributed hardly less effectively than the priest, for, under ecclesiastical direction, he created a sublime imagery which transcended dynastic strife and the barriers of language and which even the illiterate everywhere were able to understand. All Christendom at last could see its Saviour, and be present with Him in His Mysteries. It was not a rigid imagery, but one which developed with the increasing complexity of man's vision. The great religious artists from Giotto to El Greco evolved a succession of symbols which embodied for each generation its profoundest intimations concerning the relation of man to the Persons of the Trinity.

Of the power of religious symbolism one of the most memorable instances is related of the 19th-century congregation of a Danish Protestant church. As the worshippers passed along the aisle they invariably turned and bowed towards a white space on the wall at one side. For this practice they were able to give no reason, except that the custom had always been observed. Its origin, however, became apparent when a thorough renovation of the building brought to light, beneath the whitewash of the stretch of wall in question, a pre-Reformation painting of Our Lady.

For just so long as the exalted Catholic conception of the consecration of the arts to the service of religion remained, in effect, a relation between inspiring patrons and artists of vast resource, it gave rise to religious art of unsurpassed splendour, but when both the quality of patronage sharply declined and artistic genius and talent became less widespread, there took place a lamentable change. At last the disparity between conception and accomplishment became immeasurable, and the great tradition collapsed and almost disappeared. But in spite of the prevailing meretriciousness in the architecture, and still more conspicuously in the embellishment, of contemporary Roman Catholic churches, the interior architecture of Westminster Cathedral furnishes triumphant proof of the continuing power of art to serve religion.

The most obvious cause of the lamentable effect produced by great numbers of Roman Catholic churches is their overcrowding with shoddy mass-produced objects of piety. These objects have one attribute to recommend them—an attribute which exercises a particular attraction in the lean days which follow the conclusion of the war—namely, cheapness. As a suit of clothes made to measure costs more than one ready-made, so does a work specially commissioned cost more than one which is mass-produced; there is, however, no reason to suppose that to embellish a church with a few authentic works of art would prove more expensive than to clutter it up with mass-produced objects of piety. And it is a commonplace that a few works of art, harmoniously disposed, give an effect of solemnity and reverence, and that a disorderly profusion of tawdry mass-produced objects is, on the contrary, gravely distracting. It is often, perhaps generally, the case that these objects are imported from abroad, and a church filled with foreign objects of a manifestly inferior kind inevitably gives an impression both deplorable in itself, and unwise, as implying a tacit waiving of the claim that the Roman Catholic Church is identical with the ancient Catholic Church in England.

The Problem of Light

I have treated of certain considerations affecting Nonconformist and Roman Catholic churches before making any reference to the Church of England because each of these two represents an outlook more sharply defined and more consistently held than that of an established Church of which comprehensiveness has been a steadily pursued ideal. The Church of England may be said to include—so far as is consistent with the rejection of Papal Supremacy and the retention of the Episcopal form of government—every shade of religious opinion. It has need therefore of the widest variety of churches ranging from those to which men go to participate in a sacrifice, to those to which they go to hear a sermon. The one will therefore have the altar for its centre, and the other the pulpit. The one will incline to darkness, especially in the region of the altar, as symbolising the mysterious nature of God. As Donne wrote:

"Churches are best for Prayer which have least light."

The other will incline to light precisely as encouraging a proper emphasis on the real Humanity of the Incarnate Word.

I have referred to the need for each church to embody the convictions and the traditions inherent in the form of religion which it serves, and this has led me to dwell upon the distinctions between the two great fundamental attitudes towards religion which divide the western world. But the overriding problem of the styles in which new churches should be built is the concern of all religious bodies alike.

Implicit in the styles of a vast mass of church buildings in both Great Britain and America is the heresy that Christians look exclusively to the past for their inspiration. No attitude could be more manifestly at variance with the spirit of the Christian past itself. For if we examine the beginning of our Faith we find a Saviour speaking little about the past but proclaiming a Kingdom under the image of a tree, already planted but quick with life to grow and develop throughout the centuries, and Christians intensely aware of the glory of the divine life that is theirs in the present, and looking forward impatiently, very often, to its consummation in the future. And we find, in these early centuries of our era, a Christian Church which, through her Fathers and in other ways, selects without disquiet or discomfort from the best elements of contemporary culture whatever she thinks

6

will serve to clarify the Revelation committed to her custody or enhance the dignity of her worship.

Ecclesiastical architects appear for the most part to have forgotten that, according to our Faith, through the Incarnation was accomplished, in the life of grace, a salvation that is nothing less than the "divinisation" of men in Christ, no honourable activity of the human spirit excluded; a redemptive work to which an unworthy response is made by any timid inhibition of natural creative activity in set patterns just because these patterns have the authority of custom. Indeed, in the last resort, such an inhibition is to immobilise certain particular moments in the life of the Church herself, and to stunt the full glory of the growing tree. By their pedantic preoccupation with "period" styles, by employing forms which they have not animated but simply copied, numerous ecclesiastical architects, therefore, have shown themselves to be quite at variance with the authentic Christian spirit.

"To be concerned with period design," declared Professor Lethaby, "is not only irrational in itself, but it blocks the way to any possibility of true development. . . . To go on building . . . in the cocked-hat and brass candlestick style is not only rather imbecile play-acting, but it destroys rational growth. We have to put an efficiency style in place of this trivial, sketchy picturesqueness."

This is not to suggest that architects should give any attention to the ingenuous plea put forward by certain of their Continental confreres that, just as a house should be a machine for living in, so a church should be a machine for worshipping in. It is generally agreed (as mentioned earlier in this introduction) that the first function of a church is to protect altar, pulpit and worshippers from the weather, but a building which did no more than this would be a poor-spirited place and scarcely entitled to the name of church. A more naïve or a grosser instance of the Mechanical Fallacy one would be hard put to it to find. Of this fallacy Geoffrey Scott, in the wisest contemporary treatise on architecture in our language, said:

"The art of architecture studies not structure in itself, but *effect* of structure on the human spirit. Empirically, by intuition and example, it learns where to discard, where to conceal, where to emphasise, and where to imitate, the facts of construction. It creates, by degrees, a *humanised dynamics*. For that task, constructive science is a useful slave, perhaps a natural ally, but certainly a blind master."

The architects of our new churches should not, therefore, refrain from making the fullest use of the traditional styles, always provided that every fragment that is imitated is brought into the closest harmony with the life of the new building. Whistler truly observed that "nature contains the elements, in colour and form, of all pictures, as the keyboard contains the notes of all music. But the artist is born to pick, and choose, and group with science, these elements, that the result may be beautiful. . . ." In the same way existing architecture may be said to contain a vast repertory of forms (though not, as nature does, all possible forms) from which the architect, too, is born to pick and choose, in order that the result may fulfil the

7

three conditions of good architecture, according to the famous definition of Sir Henry Wotton, namely, Commodity, Firmness and Delight.

Certain of the architects of our century, dazzled by the possibilities offered by newly-invented materials, have envisaged a new and original architecture "unfettered" by the architecture of the past. But these men have "misunderstood the very nature and meaning of originality, and of all wherein it consists" as gravely as certain contemporaries of Ruskin, whose indictment of them is applicable to many of their successors of to-day.

"Originality of expression," declared Ruskin in *The Seven Lamps*, "does not depend on invention of new words; nor originality in poetry on invention of new measures; nor, in painting, on invention of new colours or new modes of using them. The chords of music, the harmonies of colour, the general principles of the arrangement of sculptural masses, have been determined long ago, and in all probability, can no more be added to than they can be altered."

But in drawing upon the past for the elements of a living style, architects and craftsmen would do well to consider with the utmost care the limitations imposed upon their choice by present circumstance. Our poverty in craftsmanship should severely limit the use of any highly ornamental style, in particular Gothic, except in its later and simpler manifestations. Baroque architecture, too, the glorious incredibility of which, Claudel has said, is so magnificent a tribute to religion, should be drawn upon with the utmost circumspection, for in the words of Mr. Goodhart-Rendel, "It is a tribute which we have neither the skill nor the means to pay."

The architects of our post-war churches have an almost illimitable repertory of traditional forms into which they may infuse new life. Or, provided that the Mechanical Fallacy does not deceive them, they may, if they so desire, by drawing inspiration from the mechanical forms evolved by the industrial age, legitimately create "The Temple of Mars" pictured by Chaucer:

> "Wrought all of burned steel
> Every pillar, the temple to sustene,
> Was tun-great, of iron bright and sheene."

*　　　　*　　　　*　　　　*　　　　*

Ecclesiastical Art and Craft: the Lost Tradition

Although there has been for rather more than a century a marked decline in church architecture, this decline has been slight and fluctuating compared with that to which church art and craftsmanship have been subject. It has been justly observed that while many of our churches, more especially the ancient ones, are beautiful, they contain little that is beautiful, and much that is ugly. The present condition of ecclesiastical art and craftsmanship is due in part to circumstances outside the control of the churches. But not entirely, for another grave heresy has been implicit in the generality of ecclesiastical patronage, namely, that religion is a simple matter, which it is possible to make manifest in terms so commonplace that not even the spiritually dead can misunderstand. It is this heresy which has been so largely responsible for the notorious "repository" art—the art which mocks, by its simpering inanity, the sacred persons which it purports to represent, and the not less notorious "ecclesiastical" style, which is among the shabbiest by-products of the industrial age. Every Christian knows that his religion is not simple, but infinitely complex, and that its innermost truths—not without compelling reason known as its "Mysteries"—have ultimately baffled the wisest among men. If therefore the Gospel of Christ is to be made effectively manifest once more through the art and craftsmanship of the churches, the "Mysteries" must cease to be presented to the people in the guise of platitudes.

*   *   *   *   *

A tradition has indeed been lost. But some may say, as many have in fact argued, that what is lost is more than a tradition; we have lost, they think, the things that make a tradition possible, and among these things the prime requisite is a certain homogeneity of culture. This is not an age of faith but of secularism, according to this account; and in such an age there is small hope for Christian art. However willing, and in all other respects able, the individual talent may be, its exercise is twisted or paralysed through the turn given to its sympathies and modes of thinking and feeling by the "atmosphere" in which it has been nurtured. It is a glum argument, and its conclusion should be that the churches should await with folded hands for the day when circumstances have changed and ideals of Christian art are once more practicable.

So runs a common judgment. Its defeatism is apparent, and this alone, perhaps, should be enough to rule it out of court; for it should appear how alien is such an attitude to the spirit of the Christian Church as it is informed by its dogma and as it has on countless occasions manifested itself in history. But as an argument it is vulnerable to other criticisms as well. Its plausibility would appear to depend on what might not ineptly be called the "panoramism" of its survey of the history of art, a panoramism that leaps to a generalisation that takes no account of the recalcitrance of many particulars. What common factor, for instance, is there between Fra Angelico and the Roman School that would enable one to say that thus and not otherwise must a man express himself if his work is to merit the title of *Christian* art? Or what, for that matter, is to be made of the later achievement of Georges Rouault—or who can say, on the evidence of his early period, what superb Madonnas and Child we might not have had from Picasso? But, however plausible, the dispiriting argument is fallacious.

9

To say, as a rough historical generalisation, that achievements in the arts (whether in painting or in sculpture or in literature) are conjoined with such and such other features of the cultural environment, is one thing; to say that these features are *conditions*, in any strict sense, *i.e.* that the possibility of the achievements depends on their presence, is another; so that if it is presented as a conclusion from the first generalisation, it is a fallacious conclusion. And it is all the more fallacious in that the cultural features on which the artistic achievements are believed to depend are thought of as produced (and, perhaps, even maintained) independently of the artists; whereas it is surely a characteristic of the history of the arts that it is artists themselves who contribute most of all to the conditions requisite for their own appreciation and, indeed, for their own activity. And this criticism is not side-stepped by saying that at present what militates against Christian art is not merely a declension in standards of art, but the atrophy, through ignorance and secularism, of the Christian sense; for, although Christianity is a revealed, historical religion, it is so little alien to art that it evokes and perfects the deepest and most abiding of human longings and sentiments; and of these the most ineradicable are man's religious longings. But however abstract may appear what has just been written, surely it is patent that there is something grievously wrong with an argument that uses the fact that in the past good religious art and Christian culture went together as a canon by whose application all effort after good Christian art is, in the present, declared to be idle and foredoomed to failure, on the ground that we must wait till we are assured that such art is possible before we are ambitious about its being attempted. This is the ultimate defeatism, to be inert in the belief that we know what is possible not from what we do but from what, antecedently and on general grounds, we think we can do. Indeed, we may take an analogy from individual psychology: however much a man may say that he was bound to act as he did, it is not until he has acted and can look at the motives which he gave weight to, that he can say it.

This is not to deny that in the commissioning of more ambitious works of art, like mural paintings and sculpture, ecclesiastical patronage should not have to ponder long and take the best advice it can command, and then be courageous. But courage, like wisdom, is justified of her children, and the wall-painting now being carried out, by Mr. C. Mahoney, in the Lady Chapel of Campion Hall, Oxford, and the Madonna and Child recently completed by Mr. Henry Moore, at St. Mark's, Northampton, are monuments respectively to the enterprise of Father M. C. D'Arcy, S.J., then Master of Campion Hall, and the Rev. Walter Huffey, and examples from which many may take heart.

The Great Adventure: A New Church

By STANLEY ELEY

Prebendary of St. Paul's Cathedral

"A church for us all and work for us all
And God's world for us all even unto this last."

The Rock: T. S. ELIOT.

TWO DIFFERENT THINGS stir up our deepest sense of pride. We may justly be very proud of something intrinsically beautiful which has been handed on to our keeping by the loving care of the past; but we become even prouder of those things which we have had a positive share in creating or acquiring. Thus in most homes we see articles of beauty which have come from the homes of our parents or ancestors side by side with those which we have purchased with our own savings or created by our own skill.

So for a parish or congregation, a church which has been built by past generations is rightly regarded as a sacred trust, particularly if it be of real architectural merit. Even those buildings of little or no merit, many belonging to the worst type of Victorian architecture, have the power to stimulate the pride of those who worship in them.

But the greatest joy of all is to be able to say, "This is our own church: we helped to build it. We shared in its planning, we sacrificed for its cost, we saw the Foundation Stone laid, we were present when it was set apart for God's use."

The purpose of this essay is to describe various ways in which this building of a church may be achieved, and to contrast the ways of the past with those of the present.

In the long distant past when many of our most glorious architectural treasures were built, the social conditions were so different from those of to-day that we shall expect to find that when a church was required in any place the people set about their task in a different way from that of the present age.

The land for the church would nearly always be given by a landowner in the neighbourhood, and usually he or she would provide a substantial part of the cost of materials and labour. But though the people might not be able to furnish much money for the church, they would give their skilled labour and time. The church might be built as an offering of either thanksgiving or penance by king or nobleman. The whole financial method of building was so different: there were no architects in our modern sense, no contracts with tenders and specifications and quanti-

11

ties. The great churches of the remote past grew. Some took a very long time to complete. The magnificent pre-Great Fire Cathedral of St. Paul in London took 200 years to build.

At a later period we find a variety of methods of raising the necessary funds for building, as well as a great development in the differentiation of function between surveyor or architect and builder. But still we note the special place of the skilled craftsman in the economy of church building. We have not space to do more than briefly enumerate the ways of raising the money, for we are primarily concerned with the problem of raising the funds for building a church to-day.

We find a continuous succession of generous lay people who paid for the whole cost of churches in various parts of the country.

In some places the cost of the church was largely provided by a church rate levied on the inhabitants of the parish by the vestry or churchwardens.

In others local subscriptions were raised over a period of years.

Occasionally, though rarely, Parliament set aside money for building churches. At the close of Queen Anne's reign a large sum was thus voted and part at least of this sum was actually provided for building churches.

After the great victory of Waterloo, again state funds were used for building what are known as the Waterloo Churches.

These official ways of providing funds by a rate or by a parliamentary grant applied only to churches for the Church of England, and the Roman Catholics and Nonconformist bodies had all along to rely on private initiative.

And, as the 19th century advanced, the Church of England had to rely almost exclusively on two methods for building its churches. We say almost, because there is a third method which has provided funds for new churches in areas where they are badly needed. Under the Union of Benefices Acts it is possible for a church to be demolished in a place where it is no longer needed and for the site to be sold so that the proceeds of the sale may be used for the erection of a church elsewhere.

In the main, however, the Church of England and other religious bodies rely now either on large private benefactions or on the efforts of the many to provide churches. Large private benefactions have become much fewer during this century, although there have been notable examples of munificent gifts. Some of these gifts have been to provide family memorials, and some have been made by land-owners who, having sold their land for building estates, recognise that they have not thereby parted with all responsibility. In allowing a building estate to be developed a landowner has encouraged a large population to settle there and has thus created the problem of providing for the spiritual needs of these people. This is something for which he is responsible quite as much as the builder who erects the houses, but unfortunately it is becoming increasingly rare for a landowner or builder to recognise any responsibility in the matter.

In rare instances, we shall see later, the estate developer himself gives a site for the church but he is usually concerned only to build and sell his houses and then pass on to do the same thing elsewhere.

When municipal authorities develop estates they cannot use ratepayers' money to provide churches and can sell the sites for the churches only on a strictly economic basis.

So for the most part the official authorities of the church and the people in a housing area themselves are left to cope with the task.

Between the Two Wars

Here let us notice a great difference between the development of housing estates in the years before 1914 and in the years between the great wars.

For the most part, before 1914 housing areas grew up much more slowly and provided homes for a different section of society than in later years. A comparatively few houses were built at one time and were occupied generally by people who had reached some measure of financial security. Further, it is important not to ignore the fact that amongst such people there was a far deeper interest in religion and desire for churches than can be found in housing areas to-day. The low cost of living and almost negligible income tax made it possible for people living in these new houses to give larger sums than are possible to-day, and, of course, the cost of building was very considerably lower.

Consequently the major part of the cost of the erection of a new church was found in the locality and needed only a small supplement, as a rule, from the central resources of the Diocese or of the denomination concerned. There were a few exceptional estates—those erected for the artisan section of the population—where this description does not apply, but such provision for artisan dwellings was usually made near to the place of work of the occupants and thus there was nearly always a church already in existence.

The spiritual needs created by immense increases of population in the inner suburbs of our great cities, as for example in Stepney and Islington in London during the nineteenth century, had already been met by the erection of churches with funds raised largely by subscription from the more affluent section of the population. Bloomfield, Bishop of London, is said to have consecrated 200 new churches in his diocese during his episcopate from 1828 to 1856.

But after the 1914 war the whole situation changed radically and an entirely new problem had to be met. There had been no building of new houses for five years, and there was an acute shortage of houses. The older suburbs had been almost completely built over and consequently it was necessary to go to what was then the fringe of the country in order to find suitable sites for houses. Thus very quickly large tracts of country were acquired for building estates both by local authorities and by speculators.

13

These new housing estates, which in twenty years covered nearly all Middlesex and all those parts of Kent, Surrey, Essex and Hertfordshire which adjoin London, differed from those of pre-1914 days in several very important ways.

They developed quickly. In as little as twelve months sometimes, a large area of farm land was converted into a busy little township. They developed as a whole and not in small sections, except in a few instances. The site was planned with roads, shops, schools, cinemas, banks and public houses, as well as row upon row of houses, mostly identical in size and very nearly identical in appearance.

The population which rapidly filled these houses was a very different type from the pre-war suburban dweller. In many of the Local Authority or Council Estates, as they are called, the people came from over-crowded parts of Inner London and were for the most part wage earners, and they did not earn very high wages. Many of them had no security at all, and when unemployment became widespread, its evils were to be found in these Council Estates. Separated, in their new homes, from both their work and their old haunts, life was extremely difficult for many of these people and the expense of travelling to work was a very considerable drain upon slender resources. Many families found the cost of maintaining a small house, with two rooms downstairs and three up, much heavier than that of the tenement dwelling from which they had come. The possession of a small garden, more open outlook, and far better conditions for the children, were for many of the better families adequate compensations for these additional financial burdens.

In passing, it should be noted that the local authorities nearly always made provision in their plans for open spaces and for church sites.

These Council estates, however, represent only part of the development between the wars.

Building contractors and estate developers found a great opportunity for expansion. Several factors contributed to this. The construction of large arterial roads from our great cities or in some instances, as by-passes to them, the erection of large new factories, in London the extension of tube train facilities and the increasing urbanisation of England, all made the demand for houses more and more insistent. The mechanisation of many building processes, and the rapid expansion of building society facilities also speeded up the development of housing all round the cities and towns of England.

These "private" schemes varied in quality, but few of them are really satisfactory. In many places the lay-out is bad, the design of the houses is poor, the provision of open spaces is inadequate and the general impression is one of muddle and ugliness.

The houses on these estates were mostly built for sale, and a vast number of people became owners of their own houses, but they were not people of security and some substance. The building societies and builders combined to advance nearly all the purchase price, and most of the occupants of these houses could look

BISHOP HANNINGTON MEMORIAL CHURCH, HOVE

Architect : Edward Maufe, A.R.A.

Building Contractors : James Longley & Co. Ltd., Crawley, Sussex

SUGGESTED DECORATION FOR SANCTUARY

*Decorative Art Guild, Ltd., London, S.W.*1

forward to twenty years of mortgage repayment and interest, coupled with unknown liabilities for repair and maintenance during that time. An ever widening extension of the facilities for hire-purchase combined with the importunities of "tally" men and sales agents, tempted numbers of families to further commitments for furniture and household requirements, often far beyond their real capacity to pay.

Thus it will be seen that a very large number of people who settle into new housing areas in our generation have little financial security and for the most part no capital resources. Times of financial depression hit them very badly, and in some instances have produced real distress.

As an example of the extent of the problem with which the churches have been faced since 1914, the County of Middlesex is perhaps the most significant. Prior to 1914 this County contained a number of small villages with rather delightful but tiny ancient churches, some of which held only a hundred people. Separating these villages there were substantial tracts of country. Rapid improvements in transport facilities, and the extension of factories, especially for the lighter industries, attracted the speculative builders, who bought up large areas of the best market gardening land in the south as well as other areas and proceeded to develop these estates very rapidly. The result was that between 1919 and 1939 no less than 800,000 people were added to the population of the county. This is a population half as large again as that of Leeds, and if we remember that Gloucester has 50,000 inhabitants, it will be seen that a population nearly as large as that of Gloucester was added to the county each year. Thus an acute problem was created for all the churches and the Church of England alone had to face the provision of clergymen, sites and buildings for some sixty new parishes. The Roman Catholics and the various denominations had also weighty new responsibilities to bear.

Before passing to the methods adopted to provide for the spiritual needs of the people, we would emphasise two other factors which considerably affect the problem. The rapidity with which these areas were developed and the fact that their population came from all over England, attracted by the fresh location of industry, made it almost impossible to create any local patriotism. When an area develops slowly new-comers not only absorb the traditions of the place and acquire local feeling, but are themselves absorbed within a community already existing, however small it may have been. But these enormous increases of population completely swamped the older inhabitants and the invaders had little or no common interests upon which to found a community sense. This absence of local feeling made the development of religious, cultural and educational interests very much more difficult than it had been in the past.

It should also be remembered that during this century there has been a marked drift away from organised religion, and thus the number of potential supporters for a church has considerably decreased and the churches have been forced into a far more missionary attitude in the new housing areas than ever before. It is

3

scarcely exaggeration to say that before 1914 the demand for a church came from the people, whereas to-day so often the church has to create the demand by pioneer evangelistic work.

The New Parish

In what follows we shall attempt to describe the normal method of developing a new parish, mainly from the point of view of the Church of England, which works on the parochial system and thus tackles the problem in a way which differs from the methods of other bodies in certain respects; but a good deal of what will be said is common to all religious bodies.

When an area is marked out for development it is essential to secure a site as soon as possible, and for this purpose central resources are needed unless the vendor of the estate or the purchaser is willing to give the necessary land for the church. The selection of a site is clearly of the utmost importance, and it is necessary to approach the developer at the earliest possible moment. The site should be, so far as possible, situated at the natural centre towards which the people of the area will gravitate for purposes other than that of going to church. The church should be near the shopping centre, or the school, or the railway station so that people will see it as they move about during the day. In all probability the cost of securing such a site will be larger than that of land which is more hidden away, but the additional expense will be abundantly justified. Up to 1939 around London the price of a suitable site varied from £1,500 to £2,500. Occasionally a site cost even more. This provides for about an acre to an acre and a third, and on a site of this size a church, hall and parsonage house with a reasonable garden and fairly spacious lay-out can be built. If the central authorities of a church are obliged to acquire a number of sites in a comparatively short time, it will usually be necessary for an appeal to be made in order to raise the money required. The Diocese of London, for example, between 1918 and 1939 had to expend about £80,000 on sites, and in addition, about five sites were given to the Diocese. Where an estate is being developed by the local planning authority, in London at least, there has been the closest co-operation between the authority and the churches in the matter of providing the necessary facilities for Christian worship.

The next step is to provide a building in which services can be held. As soon as a priest in charge or minister has been appointed he will need some centre in which to gather the nucleus of his future congregation. For a time he may have to be content with any large room he can secure, or if the weather be favourable, with a marquee, but it will not be long before he requires a permanent or semi-permanent building. Generally speaking in recent years it has been found that even if funds be available it is not wise immediately to erect the permanent church, which of necessity must be fairly large and involve considerable costs of up-keep and maintenance. The congregation at first will probably be insufficient to give the impression of real vitality in a large building or to provide the necessary means for its up-keep. Further, the close association of the spiritual work of the churches with the social activities of the people makes it imperative, especially for work among young people, that there should be a hall in which the various clubs and other activities can meet. It may be necessary for the first building which is provided to be a dual purpose one, but when the building is of this character, it is essential that there should be at least some portion of it which is set aside exclusively for worship. The size of this part of the building will vary in accordance with the emphasis laid on week-day worship by the church concerned. In many areas recently there has been a growing desire to have, alongside the hall, a building, even if very temporary in character, which is used exclusively for worship. The cost of pro-viding a suitable dual purpose hall, which can eventually become the parish hall when the permanent church is built, was, before the war, from £3,200 to £4,500. For this sum it was possible to build a hall to hold some 250 people with a chapel at one end and a stage at the other. The chapel holding some forty people becomes the chancel on Sundays and on week-days is separated from the hall by folding doors. In addition, there can be two class-rooms, vestries, kitchen and lavatory accommodation. Such a building becomes an admirable parish hall at a later stage in the development of an area, but meanwhile has to serve as both church and hall. An alternative plan is to build two semi-permanent or even temporary ones either of wood or some pre-fabricated material so that one can be used exclusively as the church, and the other for social work. In this case the cost before the war would probably have been some £2,000. Here again it is the central authority of the church which must face the burden of providing the buildings, although the area concerned may well be asked to accept some portion of the cost as a debt to be re-paid over a number of years.

Generally speaking, it is not wise to burden a new congregation with a substantial debt for the first building or group of buildings because it is important to set before the congregation as soon as possible the permanent church as the main objective, and the burden of a substantial debt may well sap the energies of the people. It is never as easy to secure money for something which is already built as it is for some-thing which will not be built until those concerned have raised at least a proportion of the cost.

Building Begins

Let us now imagine that the housing area has its site and a sufficient provision for services and other work. In the case of the Church of England there will be a resident priest-in-charge, and in sufficiently large areas other religious bodies will also have a resident minister. Starting usually with a small nucleus of people, he will have to develop all the normal life of the church, and, as we have said above, by evangelistic enterprise create a demand in the neighbourhood for the permanent church. In some areas there will be fairly rapid growth in the congregation. In others progress will be slow, but there will come a time when the people will begin to press their minister with the question : "When are we going to have our church?" At this stage the real adventure begins, and those who have had any share in the building of a new permanent church will understand how exciting this adventure can be. It is of the utmost importance that from the very outset the people should feel that they have a very real share in all that concerns the planning and erection of what will be their own church. At the same time their enthusiasm needs to be guided by the experience of those at the centre who will have a large share of responsibility in all that concerns the future church.

The following is a convenient plan of operation : a Building Committee should be appointed from the congregation to act as the representatives of the congregation, to consult with the Central Authority, to interpret the desires of the congregation and to initiate and sustain local enthusiasm for the project. Discussions should then take place between the Building Committee and the centre with a view to the appointment of an architect. Here, obviously, central experience will be of the utmost value, and it is sometimes possible for the Building Committee to be taken to see a number of churches erected by living architects so that they can form some opinion as to the type of building which they would themselves desire to have for their area. A very delightful and instructive evening can be spent by the Committee at the offices of the Central Authority inspecting photographs and generally discussing the problem of the new church. These discussions will include such matters as the number of seats to be provided, the vestry accommodation, the position of the organ and choir, the provision of a tower or spire, if financially possible, the type of architecture, traditional or modern, and so on.

After these visits and discussions agreement will be reached that Mr. X shall be approached with a view to his becoming the architect of the church, but before he can be approached some estimate must be made of the money which will be available for the new church.

The Building Committee and the Central Authority together decide that a church to seat 450 people is necessary, with adequate vestries for the clergy and choir and that the maximum cost including furnishings and fittings but excluding the organ, shall be, let us say, £14,000. This sum could, in 1939, have provided a reasonably spacious building in brick or concrete with simple but good furnishings. Many churches were built between 1920 and 1940 at considerably less cost. Some cost as little as £9,000 for 400 seats, but from a considerable experience of this work we would deprecate an attempt in future to build cheap churches. Lavish expenditure, even if funds be available, can scarcely be justified when other needs of the Church are considered, but if the building is to be a really worthy one to

18

hand on as a heritage to future generations, then there must be a perfection of workmanship and especially of finishings which cannot be obtained if the cost is pared down to the barest minimum. Such reduction in cost is very unfair to the architect and, taking a long view, it is not in the best interests of the congregation. Obviously architects should be encouraged to explore the possibilities of modern methods of construction and fresh materials but the church is being built not for one generation but for posterity.

Doubtless at this stage the vexed question of "modern" or traditional will be thrashed out. Conservatism is a marked characteristic of most suburban congregations in matters of art if not of politics, and on the whole this attitude exercises a salutary influence on the choice of a design. "We want our church to look like a church." This is sure to be the first comment when the matter is raised and we believe that this expresses a sound point of view. This is not to say that a new church must necessarily be in the Gothic or Renaissance style, but that it should be obviously a church and not a town hall or cinema or factory. There have been some notable churches built in recent years which satisfy this condition while at the same time by their strength of line and simplicity of treatment they are very clearly in the "modern" style. The period between the wars did not, however, produce a style in church architecture comparable with the marked styles of the Renaissance or Waterloo or Gothic revival periods. It was largely a period of experiment.

With some fairly clear idea of the cost the Building Committee has to decide with the centre how much shall be the portion which the parish or area is asked to provide. Here it is impossible to lay down any standard, but it can, we think, be fairly assumed that very few parishes could raise more than £4,000 towards the cost of the new permanent church before the war. With money values changing and wages rising the figures will probably be different in the future but a fair proportion for most areas is from one quarter to one fifth of the cost. It is generally assumed that the organ is an extra for which the parish must be responsible. In some areas, too, some at least of the furnishings will be provided by special individual gifts.

Ways and Means

So we will imagine our parish faced with the task of raising £4,000, and in the minds of the small but keen nucleus this must be raised in a very few years so that the church can really be built and not be a mere dream for the future. There are two classes of potential givers. There is that staunch band of keen and devoted churchpeople who will not only have to give themselves, but be the means for collecting from the other class, those who are vaguely interested in having a church but who, as yet, have little association with organised religion, except perhaps for baptisms, weddings and funerals.

It cannot be too strongly emphasised that the mainstay of any Church Building Fund should be direct giving. Sales of work, bazaars, concerts, fêtes may have their place in the social and economic fabric of the parish, but even if they be accepted and used as a means of raising money, they should be supplementary to a proper scheme for raising regular systematic contributions from the largest possible number of givers.

The following is a method which has been proved extraordinarily effective in many parishes.

A meeting is summoned of all churchpeople and is addressed by the clergyman in charge and usually by a representative of the Central Authority. In the broadest possible outline, for no details are yet available, the project of building a church is put before the meeting. A number of photographs of churches recently built may be exhibited and questions invited. Then volunteers shall be called for, who will be prepared to take a street or portion of a street and canvass every family to secure regular subscribers. They must be prepared to make weekly calls. This is especially important in an area where the people are weekly wage earners. Contributions are to be invited of from 1d. per week upwards and cards should be printed so that a proper receipt can be given each week or month as the case may be. From the outset the task of the collectors should be presented as a task of first-rate spiritual importance. The collectors for the "Church Builders' Scheme" are a band of men and women who, if rightly used, will be not only builders of the material fabric of the church but in a very real sense builders of the spiritual Church of God in their parish. They will by their many contacts acquire a great deal of useful information concerning children who do not come to Sunday School, older children and adults who have lapsed from Church membership, sick and distressed persons, and those who would welcome a visit from the clergyman but are too shy to ask for it.

The collectors or messengers should be solemnly enrolled in the temporary church and blessed for their most important work. A competent and enthusiastic secretary is indispensable. Upon him or her will rest the real burden of making the effort a success. When the preliminary visitation is completed a further meeting should be held at which the prospects can be assessed. Thereafter monthly or quarterly meetings should be held at which money is paid in and further supplies of cards, etc. obtained, and periodically these meetings should include prayer and an address so that the spiritual importance of the work remains always in the forefront.

Quite astonishing results can be achieved by this method. In one area in the suburbs of London where, in a population of 7,000 people, the average wage of the householder in 1937 was barely £3 per week and where all the crippling burdens of hire-purchase weighed very heavily, in one year nearly £800 was raised by this Church Builders' Scheme.

Plans and Contract

When, by this means and others as supplementary to it, about half the required sum is in hand, the time has come for definite plans to be drawn by the architect and he may be invited to attend a meeting of the Building Committee and discuss the whole problem with the members, or if possible they can go to his office and discuss it there, thus having an opportunity of seeing pictures of his work and, in some measure, sensing the atmosphere in which he works. It is essential that a representative of the Central Authority should attend this meeting. This meeting is usually a most thrilling and entertaining one. If he be skilful the architect can win their confidence and double their enthusiasm. The questions of cost, style, furnishings, organ and arrangement of accommodation will all come up again. After a time he will complete his rough sketches and will be ready to meet the Committee again. He will have a block plan of the site and of the actual building and rough elevations and, if possible, a perspective. He will explain how he has tried to meet the various requirements and give some idea of the material he proposes to use. Concurrently his sketches will be discussed with the Central Authority and if they are approved in principle by the local and central representatives, he will produce more detailed plans, such as can be exhibited and explained to a larger meeting.

At this stage, a large meeting of all the collectors and as many contributors as possible should be summoned and the architect should be invited to attend and explain his pictures. Properly handled this meeting can be the means of arousing a fresh burst of enthusiasm for the new church, and if a small picture of the interior and exterior of the proposed building is afterwards sent to every contributor there will be a marked revival of interest.

The working drawings are now prepared, quantities are written and tenders are invited. The Building Committee meets to hear the result of the tenders. Another exciting moment. "Can we do it for the money?" If the lowest tender is within the figure, all is well, but if there is an extra £500 to £1,000 to face, there are anxious moments. Most architects have some economies up their sleeve which will not materially affect the design. But usually a really keen Committee will say: "Oh, but we must not spoil it for £500. Somehow we will raise the extra." It is not wise to press them beyond a very few hundreds. It is better, if possible, to make some economies.

The contract is signed. Here a word of caution is necessary. It should be impressed most clearly upon the architect that no extras are to be incurred without specific authority. As the work proceeds some variations are inevitable, but they should be discussed and approved at each stage. Care should also be taken to see that in the contract the items for heating and lighting are based on firm estimates and not on mere guesses. All such items, known in the contract as P.C. items, should be firm figures. Instances have occurred in which several hundreds of pounds have been added to the cost owing to the neglect of this precaution.

At last the first lorry load of materials and tools arrives, and trenches are dug for the foundations and each day the Church Builders on their way to work or school note progress. Soon the walls appear above ground and the time has come to lay the foundation stone. This should be made a most solemn occasion, and if rightly used should be the signal for a fresh burst of enthusiasm amongst the Church Builders.

Before 1939 an average-sized church took about twelve to fifteen months to build and during this time meetings of the Building Committee will be required from time to time to discuss various details and especially those of furnishings. Most people require education in the use of colours and it will generally be found that there is a predominant opinion in favour of blue for furnishings. This colour in most modern churches is cold and hard, and red and gold should nearly always be used at least in part to lend richness and warmth to the severity of the architectural form. No trouble should be spared to secure the intelligent co-operation of the Building Committee in the choice of colour and of designs for furnishings.

Furnishings

Many people argue, and with considerable force, that the furnishings provided for a church when it is first opened should be the minimum necessary for public worship, and simple in character. This policy provides an opportunity for future generations to add to the equipment of the church and to replace some of the more simple articles with more costly and elaborate ones, either as memorials or to mark some outstanding occasion. Whether the furnishings be simple or elaborate it is always desirable wherever possible for them to be designed by the architect to fit into the rest of his work. When the furnishings are being considered there will be some, even in comparatively poor parishes, who wish to give from their savings the cost of a particular article, and the Building Committee will sometimes have to be very firm and at the same time tactful in insisting that any such gifts should be designed or approved by the architect. There are many ways in which individuals can be encouraged to help with the furnishings of a church in addition to what they are already doing as Church Builders: for example, if the church is to be seated with chairs, and this is nearly always necessary owing to the fact that seating with pews costs at least three times as much as chairs, families may be asked to give one chair, and children may be asked to save and present one hassock each.

For many new churches the cost of providing really suitable choir stalls, pulpit and reading desks well designed and made by craftsmen from oak or teak will be prohibitive. It is far better to have such fittings plainly built of less expensive wood

3. EXFORD CHURCH, SOMERSET
By Reginald Bell

TWO SIMPLE AND INEXPENSIVE MODERN TREATMENTS

4. TENTERDEN, KENT
By Christopher Webb

5. STRAND UNITARIAN CHAPEL, MANCHESTER
By Martin Travers

and beautifully painted in rich colours. These fittings can easily be replaced in later years.

Building in Whole or Part

Before we leave this discussion of the cost of a church and how it should be met, it may be well to refer to the question which so often perplexes a Building Committee. Funds are limited and there is an urgent need for a permanent church. The cost of building is beyond the resources available and it is suggested that a part of the church should be built immediately and the remainder when further funds become available. It is obviously impossible to give a dogmatic answer to the question as to whether this is a wise policy in the circumstances. Conditions vary in the parishes concerned and for some parishes the erection of a portion of a church as a first stage in the adventure may be the right policy. It remains true, however, that in some parts of the country there are far too many "splendid fragments." The Sanctuary and Chancel and some three or four bays of the Nave and Aisles have been built and a temporary West end of wood or corrugated iron has remained for as many as forty years awaiting the time when the remaining two or three bays can be built and the Narthex and West door and porches added. In one particular instance the completion of the church was estimated to cost some £10,000 to £15,000 before 1914, and to-day the cost of this work would probably be in the neighbourhood of £50,000. Generally speaking, if a church is to be erected in sections by far the major part of the church should be built in the first stage, leaving only a comparatively small burden to be faced after the consecration of the building, and if there is any reason to believe that completion will be delayed for a number of years, then any temporary work should be of such a character that it will last quite easily for say twenty-five years, and will from the outset harmonise with the completed portion. Otherwise the temporary work gives constant trouble and expense to the congregation. There are, of course, some designs which readily lend themselves to being built in sections, and what we have said does not apply in such instances.

The finances of the building of a church, if it is completed in one operation, should envisage little debt outstanding at the consecration and a reasonable possibility of clearing off any debt within three or four years. Inevitably when the church is consecrated, enthusiasm will wane, and also the congregation will find that the heating and lighting and cleaning of the new church is a serious item in the parochial budget.

We began by quoting some words from T. S. Eliot's pageant play, *The Rock*:

> "A church for us all and work for us all
> And God's world for us all even unto this last."

Those who have a share in planning the erection of a House of God and sacrificing to secure its completion, so that it may stand for generations as witness to the claim that this world is God's world, will have taken part in a great adventure and will be able to look with just pride upon something beautiful to hand down to the loving care of others.

Church and Community ∽   ∽   ∽

By N. F. CACHEMAILLE-DAY, F.R.I.B.A.

THE UNDERLYING PRINCIPLES OF POST-WAR BUILDING

THERE IS EVIDENCE that the general public still considers that a church ought to have higher qualities of design than are required in other buildings, though any building in the architectural sense should receive the same care in design, because all buildings, whether public, domestic or commercial, form part of the elements which constitute a civilisation. There are, however, qualities of permanence, both in appearance and construction, which properly speaking belong to a church, because a church is not built to last only a century, nor is the purpose for which it is built a purely temporal one, changing with the changing times. It stands for something which is at one and the same time eternal, yet demands a suitable expression or style in each succeeding age. Therefore it is a right instinct to expect something rather different in a church.

Yet the respect which most people subconsciously have for an ecclesiastical building has led to very incongruous results in the cities and towns of this country, particularly since the industrial revolution.

This can be illustrated if a comparison is made between any 19th-century industrial town of moderate size and an ancient city, such as Canterbury or York, where there may still be seen a fairly complete picture of domestic, commercial and ecclesiastical life, as understood by the civilisation of the medieval days. The various houses, shops, colleges and churches of the old cities, dominated by the cathedral, all form a unity, and one does not get the impression that those who built these cities regarded religion as a special matter for eleven o'clock on Sundays and having very little connection with daily life.

The modern industrial town has quite a different appearance. It is not only the ugliness and the smoke which constitute the difference, but rather the different values attached to its various buildings, showing quite clearly that there is no longer much sense of a unity in people's minds : the church, the factory, the shop, the town hall, etc., all being card indexed for their separate functions, with the result that the town looks a haphazard and irregular growth, without any real design or plan behind it. Very often in these sprawling industrial towns, there will be found a well-designed church, generally Gothic in style, erected about the same time as the surrounding factories ; but the whole effect is one of disappointment, because the church does not seem to be natural or regarded as natural, nor does the beauty of the church (and one trusts the beauty of the worship that goes on inside) seem in the least to affect the ugliness of the other buildings.

The birth of a new social consciousness, both in political life and religion, has already begun a work of healing, so that factories built to-day are many of them well designed and worthy buildings, and there are numerous examples of fine churches, looking like churches, but at the same time expressing in their design the idea that the same people who built the factory and work in it, might conceivably worship in the church and might also have themselves built it. In other words, one can see the beginning of a promise of unity in the civilisation of this age, which may in time produce new towns, which have the same beauty, though quite different in architectural style, as those of the past.

Fixing the Principles

It will be the object of the succeeding pages to try to define in more detail what is meant by this. There is a danger perhaps that at first sight the general public with its admiration for old churches might be led to suppose that this is a plea for factory-built churches, or churches looking like factories. Actually, such a criticism is very generally levelled at any modern building, church or otherwise, which is new in design and may have lost some of the picturesqueness of the past ; but when a modern building is a factory or perhaps business premises, the man in the street shrugs his shoulders and generally does not care what it looks like. It only looks like what he expects to see. But when it is a church or a house that is in question, then he minds very much, and generally hankers after the past.

Much of this point of view is gradually being eradicated by the facilities for studying architecture and the arts generally, which are being given by the Royal Institute of British Architects and numerous other societies, both through lectures and exhibitions, and by the B.B.C. In this way the critical faculties of the public are being trained, and it is gradually understood that the eternal elements of beauty in architecture come first of all from good planning, good proportions, sound construction, and fine but not necessarily elaborate detail. One has only to think of the great cathedral of Albi to see how a transition between the ordinary conception of medieval church architecture and a possible new development in style to-day might come about. This cathedral is built in brick and it has that kind of simplicity and grandeur which result from scale and proportion and do not depend on ornamental elaboration, although it is by no means devoid of ornament.

On the other hand it is possible to have a church containing much ornament, and very likely good ornament, but which is badly planned and badly proportioned, and in this case it cannot be said that the ornament saves the building, but only perhaps that it makes it tolerable. It is to be hoped that as economic recovery gradually takes place, there will be funds available to employ good artists and craftsmen in their several capacities to fill our new churches with beautiful decoration. But the first need is that the churches should have the elementary qualities of good architecture—scale, proportion and a proper appreciation of space; for this last is a primary quality of architecture in the sense of abstract beauty.

The churches and cathedrals of the past took many years to build, and throughout the ages there were constant additions and further decorations; altars, chapels, chantries, etc., being incorporated in them. A living religious life will be certain to result in similar additions to our modern churches in the future.

It is impossible as yet to form a final judgment of what the effect of the war will be on the ecclesiastical buildings of the future, but it is clear that various factors enter in, such as:

1. The result of air raid damage to buildings.

2. The new Education Bill in relation to schools.

3. Any regulations there may be in connection with the building of parsonage houses. (It seems certain that there must be a serious attempt to embody in the houses erected for the use of the clergy the many improvements in equipment and possible changes in construction likely to develop in ordinary housing.)

4. The great changes in social consciousness, which are already being exemplified in the Church's growing desire to identify herself with the important questions of housing, education and proper recreational facilities for the people, and to see religion as a matter of daily life and not purely a spasmodic attendance of the services of the church on Sundays.

5. New requirements in the planning of the church and its surrounding buildings to meet the growing consciousness that the centre of all the Church's life and its power to exert an influence on society as a whole lies in the sacraments. (The increasing habit of holding a Parish Mass or Family Communion service at a reasonable hour on Sunday morning, usually at nine or nine-thirty, followed by a breakfast in the adjoining hall, is one of the chief things which will affect future planning of churches and indeed has already done so to a considerable degree in the period between the two wars.)

All these developments will affect the planning of future ecclesiastical buildings.

Between the Two Wars

First of all it must be observed that great progress was made in the planning and building of churches between 1919 and 1939, and most of the above developments

27

except those directly caused by enemy action, were on the way to come about; the special effect of the 1939–45 war will be to cause a vast speeding up both in conceptions and actual building activities, as soon as the absolutely essential needs for the erection and repair of houses have been met. These must take first place; but the period during which attention is being given to these needs will be no more than enough to enable various ecclesiastical authorities to organise their schemes and to arrange for the preparation of plans, thus taking the necessary preparatory steps to enable this great work of reconstruction to begin.

The two most noticeable developments between 1919 and 1939 were, first, that the building of new churches became a "democratic" activity, and most churches erected during that time were paid for out of the pennies and shillings of relatively poor people, rather than being, as so often before, individual gifts of beneficent donors, such as those who built many of the magnificent churches of the last century. The result of this more communal effort was to bring about the necessity for relying on simplicity and proportion and fairly cheap materials like brick and concrete (rather than stone) to achieve the dignity of a church; and there are numerous outstanding examples of churches, both in this country and abroad, built under the influence of economic necessity, which achieve architectural distinction. It seems unlikely that this necessity will cease; in fact the very wording of the agreement reached between the Churches' Main Committee (including all denominations) and the War Damage Commission, that the hundreds of destroyed and damaged churches should be chiefly characterised as either "plain repair" or "plain substitute building", emphasises this.

The second development was the realisation by all Christian denominations that the custom of building a church on one site, a hall sometimes separated by two or three streets on another site, with the vicarage possibly quite a long way away from the church on yet a third piece of land, was most unsatisfactory; and it had become usual for the ecclesiastical authorities with the advice of their architects to purchase sufficient land in one piece for the erection of a church, vicarage and hall, and possibly the school, and then to require that as far as possible this group of buildings should be planned as a unity, even if built in sections. As a rule the first building erected was the church hall, which became ultimately the hall when the adjoining church was erected; and very often the building of the hall was soon succeeded by the erection of the vicarage, as it is extremely difficult for the priest-in-charge or vicar of a new district to carry out his parochial duties satisfactorily if living in lodgings some distance away from his church or hall.

It will be easy to see how this great improvement in organisation is likely to be extended by new developments already mentioned, such as the Parish Eucharist, together with the increasing necessity for providing club and recreational facilities. When the sacramental life becomes the centre of activities such as communal breakfasts, lectures, games, study circles and a community interest in the arts, all these fall into their right perspective. It is by no means certain how far the Church herself ought to cater in her own buildings for all these activities, but it is quite obvious that she must either do so herself or come into closer relationship with community centres, village colleges and similar organisations which are endeavouring to meet these educational and recreational needs.

With this vision before us, and it is indeed a vision, such as there has never been in this sphere since medieval days, it will be unnecessary to go into arguments about style and detail. A great vision usually brings a great response in the arts. With a democratic spirit and a unity of organisation extending right down from the central committees of the dioceses to the individual parishes, the solution of this problem will arise out of the plain necessity of the case combined with the resulting vision of the architect, always provided he is given adequate freedom.

The Principles in Practice

The creation and gradual development of a new district or parish can be a great Christian communal adventure. Experience has shown that there can be no separation between the spiritual leadership of the priest, the enthusiasm of the people and the ability and technical skill of the architect. A new parish is an adventure in which all these people must combine.

It has been sad to notice in some cases in the past, where there has been a really living spiritual life in a new parish, that the buildings are not worthy of the work that is being done; but this does not often occur. A really vigorous life has nearly always produced the right architect. But there is another aspect of the case, which is even more unfortunate: when a church and other ecclesiastical buildings of merit have been erected and there is no life to fill them. These buildings, for all their architectural qualities, are even more desolate than the ruins of an ancient abbey, because whereas in the latter case the spirit of centuries of worship still clings to the stones, these other new buildings have never had any spirit put into them at all, and are really still-born.

It is important, therefore, to consider the sort of co-operation which has been found necessary to bring about a living organism in a new district, and these steps can be illustrated in a simple way by diagrams. Let us assume an imaginary case. A new housing development is proposed perhaps on the outskirts of an existing town, to populate, let us say, 15,000 to 20,000 people—a very likely number for post-war development in the case of many towns. The diocese in which the town is situated will (it is to be hoped) first of all in co-operation with the local authority and the town planning expert acquire a site centrally situated for the formation of a new parish to serve the proposed houses. To do this in a satisfactory manner it has been realised by most diocesan authorities that the advice of an architect, who is experienced in the requirements of ecclesiastical buildings and parochial life, is essential at this very first stage of the negotiations, though it may not follow as a matter of course that the same architect carries out the work.

It is the architect's business to know how much land is necessary for the proposed buildings, so that all the units which are required for this particular parish can be accommodated in an adequately spacious and well-planned manner on the one site. This includes the question of the size of the church building itself. Most churches, for instance, recently have been built to seat 500 people, though sometimes seating accommodation for 400 has been regarded as sufficient. A church should be neither too small nor too big for the congregation which may be expected. If too big, then the people are lost in a great space, in which they do not feel at home, and if too small—the answer of course is obvious. On the other hand, the idea of just having enough room to pack in a sufficient number of pews or seats is, one is thankful to say, a Victorian nightmare of the past. The determination to block up every little bit of floor space in a church with a useful object is not the way to approach the planning of a church. There is a beauty in spaciousness, and a spirit of pure utilitarianism makes it impossible for churches to be designed in a dignified manner. As mentioned previously, even the man in the street does not expect a church to be a purely utilitarian building.

The architect therefore knows almost at once the probable dimensions of the right church for the site, and he will study the site and draw a block plan showing the church, orientated whenever possible, though sometimes this requirement is not insisted on, if the site makes it difficult. Next he will outline the block plan of the hall, which may be separate from the church, or continuous with it, or be connected to it by a covered way or cloister; the latter arrangement often gives an opportunity for a pleasant church garden. This is a point which should not be forgotten in these days, when it is quite usual to have quiet days, retreats or day conferences, when people meet together for worship, have meals in common and need also a space in which they can walk about in silence, or during a conference continue the discussion of the points raised in the meetings. It is important that the spirit which existed in medieval days in monasteries, the feeling that the services of the church and the problems of daily life should be united again, should also have an expression in the way a parochial group of buildings is planned.

Then the architect will consider the best position for the vicarage, first having found out if it is to be of a larger or smaller type, and remembering that it is essential to keep the vicarage a little away from the hall, where noise from Boy Scouts or even Girl Guides may make it difficult for the vicar to pursue his studies; but that it should at the same time be in an accessible position for the vestry entrance of the church, if not actually connected.

The planning of church vestries was entirely inadequate in past centuries and even up to comparatively modern times. But the vestries need to be planned on spacious lines, for it is very often a great help to the priest, who may have a large

6. CHRIST CHURCH, ALERT BAY, BRITISH COLUMBIA
By J. E. Nuttgens

7. PART OF THE SOUTH WINDOW, LIVERPOOL CATHEDRAL
By James H. Hogan

and sometimes noisy family, to be able to use his vestry for seeing parishioners, more or less in the nature of a second study. Sometimes a parishioner may prefer to come to the vestry and see the vicar quietly rather than to have to go to the door of the vicarage and be ushered in ceremoniously to the vicar's room. Then, in addition to a communal garden associated with the church, the vicar will require his own garden and space for a garage.

If no school buildings are contemplated on the new site, in all probability the hall will require additional rooms for separate classes in connection with Sunday School, and for week-day engagements, such as lectures, Boy Scouts, Girl Guides, Mothers' Union and the innumerable other activities which go on in a healthy parish.

Utilising the Site

It will be seen from this preamble about the buildings associated with the parish, how extremely important it is that the site should be properly chosen, be large enough, and that a possible arrangement for the different units should be visualised right from the beginning.

Church architects have sometimes been appalled with the sites that have been offered them, probably purchased years before, finding them entirely inadequate for the requirements which afterwards were seen to be necessary.

This first step is generally a matter for the diocesan authorities and throughout the Church it is now being done very well. The appointment of the priest-in-charge is also a matter for the diocese, and the necessity for the choice of the right man has already been emphasised, as on him depends in the long run the success or failure of the whole thing.

The choice of the architect is generally a matter of common agreement between the diocese and the newly appointed priest-in-charge or vicar. If the architect, when appointed, can at an early stage have at least a little experience of the corporate life of the new district and meet a number of the people (perhaps attending one or two services in a temporary hut), it undoubtedly imparts the right spirit of communal adventure from the beginning and unites priest, people and architect in one purpose with full mutual understanding.

While considering the arrangement of the various buildings on the site, there are many quite practical details upon which an experienced architect will be able to advise, and which have the effect of keeping down costs. There is, for instance, the all-important question of drains. The hall and vicarage will both have lavatories, and probably the church will also have some lavatory accommodation in connection with the vestries, unless it is possible to make use of the hall lavatories by a suitable arrangement of the buildings on the plan. It is surprising how much money can be thrown away on drains, if a wasteful arrangement of the units is

4

adopted, causing long lengths of drains and numerous extra man-holes. The fall of the land is a factor which conditions the right lay-out of the drains, and affects their cost and therefore also the cost of the buildings. Hundreds of pounds can be saved by dealing with such problems sensibly and carefully. This is a point of real importance and it is easily forgotten, because the drains are not a feature that meets the eye. Their arrangement cannot be altered once the buildings are erected.

Having considered the ultimate planning of the site, it will be possible for the Diocesan authorities to erect a temporary hut of semi-permanent construction for the initial services and meetings on some part of the site, where it will not interfere with the future buildings. It would be most unfortunate if the hut were erected on the very spot which was afterwards found to be the best position for the hall, which is usually the first building of a permanent nature to be erected; hence the necessity for a clear idea from the beginning of the ultimate arrangement of the site.

The Church Hall

The semi-permanent hut or shed will probably have to remain for a year or two, and in any case will be very useful for some time after the hall has been built, because it is usual to design a hall which is partly church and partly hall. Sometimes there is a sanctuary seating as many as fifty people, separated from the hall by single, or better still, double folding doors that exclude sound, and this chancel or sanctuary is never used for anything else except for services. The platform is often planned at the other end of the hall, so that on Sundays the folding doors can be opened and the whole area used for services, the platform being available to accommodate the choir and piano.

It is needless to say how valuable it can be to have a hut available as well as the hall. A play can then be rehearsed on a Boy Scout evening, and in multitudinous other ways competition between various organisations is avoided. Sometimes it may be felt that it is better not to allow smoking in the place used for worship, especially shortly before a service.

It must be decided in the first instance with regard to the hall whether a Dancing and Occasional Stage Play Licence is to be applied for, even though perhaps this will not be taken out until the church is built and the whole of the hall can be given over to recreational purposes. The reason for deciding this in the first instance is that most Councils make the granting of licences conditional on stringent requirements as to exits, steps, notices, lavatories and so forth, and these measures ought to be taken in the original planning and design of the hall.

Most halls have a small kitchen for the preparation of light refreshments. Reference had already been made to a movement of importance in the shape of a Parish Eucharist on Sunday mornings, generally about nine or nine-thirty, followed by a united breakfast. The purpose of this excellent development is to maintain the unity of family life and make it possible for mothers to bring their children and accompany the fathers to Holy Communion, whereas otherwise they would probably have to stay at home to get the breakfast. Also the hour of nine or nine-thirty gives most people some extra rest in the morning, and also makes it possible for the wife to attend the chief Sunday service and have time after it for the cooking of a proper Sunday dinner, which is an important matter in the family life. After the service, others can be free to do more or less what they like; golf and gardening now come into their right perspective as excellent Sunday recreations.

If this scheme is adopted in a parish, it becomes particularly important that the hall should either adjoin the church or be connected with it by a covered way, as already suggested. There will also have to be suitable storage space for trestle tables and chairs. It may also be found that the kitchen ought to be a little bigger than is sometimes planned; because proper arrangements for the serving of a meal should be provided.

There may well be another reason for arranging that the church and hall should form one group of buildings. If this is done, a combined heating system can sometimes be installed, and by careful consideration, the amount of heat required, either in the church or the hall on different days, can be adjusted, in view of the fact that in a live parish the hall and subsidiary rooms will be in use every day, whereas in some churches there are not many services during the week. Difficulties often arise in connection with the heating of a church, where the heating is only put on during the week-end. This is natural where the church is not used during the week, but it is never satisfactory. The building is inclined to get damp, the heating system is not given a chance to display the best results, and cases have been known where the boilers have been cracked for the simple reason that they have been over-stoked on Saturday night, in order to make the church warm enough for Sunday morning.

In many instances the diocese finds the money for the building of the church hall, in order to help the new parish to get together its own organisation quickly with the ultimate idea that when the time comes to build the church itself, which is the crowning outward expression of the parish's spiritual life, the people of the new district can themselves raise a large part of the funds necessary for its building. It has been found from experience that it is not as a rule a good thing for a church to be built in a new housing area without the people themselves having contributed anything towards the cost. The building is not valued in the same way as when it has been erected out of the small savings due to the personal desire and affection of the people for what they are doing.

It is surprising and interesting to note that it is not only the smaller churches built between the two wars which will be largely paid for by comparatively poor people; instances could be quoted where the architect has had an opportunity to express his ideas, with economy of course, but without being really stinted, when the necessary funds have almost all been collected in small sums from parishioners of a by no means wealthy class.

The Vicarage

After the building of the hall it is often thought desirable to regard the vicarage as the next most important unit of the whole parochial lay-out. The priest-in-charge will very likely have been living either in a small house on the estate, perhaps some distance from the church hall or even in lodgings, and in order that the effective work of the parish may proceed with greater efficiency, it is time that he had his own house on the church site.

The cost of the building of the vicarage is very largely borne by grants from the Ecclesiastical Commission, and the regulations, both as regards the types of plan and construction are published and need not be commented on here in detail; but as mentioned earlier, it may be expected that there will be revisions in view of the many new ideas on the planning of houses, especially as regards the kitchen and bathroom units, and possibly in connection with construction, heating, plumbing, etc.

There are one or two particular points which experience suggests might be stressed in connection with the planning and design of a vicarage. It must be remembered that as a rule a parson and his wife are to some extent partners in the working of a parish. The parson's wife has sometimes been described as an unpaid curate, and it is certain that the devoted work which she does has in the past not always been sufficiently recognised; it is to be hoped that in the future recognition will at least be given her in the very practical way of planning the vicarage in such a way as to reduce her domestic work to a minimum.

The large unwieldy vicarages of the past, when the vicar had his horses and probably four or five servants, are of course fast disappearing, and the more or less compact type A or type B vicarage built in recent years is a great improvement; but there are many things which are becoming usual in houses of the same class amongst the laity, which might well be adopted in vicarages.

Arrangements for the serving of meals as between the kitchen and the dining room could well be improved. Double-sided dresser fittings of special design have been planned in some cases and this might well be more frequently done in vicarages to save walking to and fro from one room to another. An ordinary hatch is not enough, and in any case is in many respects not very desirable, as it does not really give much help and lets all the smell from the kitchen through into the dining room. The double doors of a dresser fitting would be better than this.

There has been a great advance during the war in ideas in connection with the provision of heating and hot water, all of them in the direction of economy and the saving of work. Many quite small houses now have fitted basins in most of the bedrooms; why not a vicarage? The additional extra cost is inconsiderable as compared with the comfort and help that they give to the vicar's wife. Everybody knows that the stipend of a priest was insufficient before the war to enable him to live except with a considerable financial strain all the time upon him. Now that the value of money has decreased so much, it seems difficult to know how a parson will manage, and domestic service, even if it were available, will probably be beyond the means of the average clergyman.

Leaving the question of the parson's wife and as it were her part of the house, it should also be remembered that the vicarage is, so to speak, the priest's place of business. The front door bell or knocker of a vicarage is never left long in peace, for in addition to parishioners and others who may wish to come and consult him about spiritual matters, he is constantly being asked to fill in forms and sign papers, to try to assist people in distress (all of whom go first of all to the vicarage), to make arrangements for baptisms, marriages, funerals, etc., to witness documents and carry out many other voluntary duties.

His study therefore ought to be planned conveniently in relation to the front door unless, as sometimes happens, there is to be a separate entrance into the study; and there should be a suitable waiting space and lavatory accommodation, all conveniently planned in relation to the position of the study, as quite likely someone will arrive to see the vicar, while he is already talking to someone else in the study. Reasonable sound proofing is, of course, another most necessary thing to be considered.

There are pros and cons about the advisability of having a separate entrance to the study. Some people would like to go quietly to see the priest, as mentioned earlier on when referring to the vestries; others would feel that there was a certain indignity in not going to the ordinary front door of the house. The answer to this question might easily be different in different types of parishes, the point is just mentioned as one that might be thought of when the vicarage is being planned.

By this time, if it has been possible to build both the hall and the vicarage, it is probable that the hall will be found inadequate to meet the needs of the parish. It will no longer be large enough for Sunday congregations, as the most that it usually holds is about 300, and in any case there will be an urgent necessity for the use of the hall entirely for social and recreational activities, so that the building of the church will have become a really pressing matter. Plans have probably already been drawn up, and a considerable part of the estimated cost collected.

As both the hall and vicarage will have been carefully sited in relation to the proposed church, there will be certain definite lines on which the architect will be required to work, even if plans have not already been drawn up.

THE CHURCH AND THE COMMUNITY

There is a great deal which could be said about the planning of churches, but perhaps a few particular points might be considered in detail.

The focal point of a church is, of course, the altar, around which the deepest elements of the Christian faith are centred. It is the visible symbol of the incarnation of Christ. In medieval days the altar was generally situated at the end of a long chancel and very often separated by a screen from the nave. When it became customary in the last century to have surpliced choirs, the choir was usually placed between the people and the altar, and if there was a screen, east of it.

On the other hand, the second and next most important focal point for congregational worship (leaving out for the moment the question of the font) is the pulpit. The preaching of the word is only second in importance to the administration of the sacraments.

Now in the case of the churches with a long chancel and a screen, the pulpit is usually west of the screen and as a rule only the congregation have the benefit of hearing the sermon, whereas the choir, who after all need it just as much, cannot hear at all; this is proved by the fact that in many churches the choir comes down into the nave during the sermon.

There can be no question that there is great traditional beauty about this type of church plan and the love of it is fixed deeply in the hearts of English people. The rood screen not only can be a beautiful thing in itself, but also adds a sense of sanctity and reverential seclusion to the high altar. But there is another side to the question, which is being realised more and more at the present time, and which to some extent is carrying one back to early Christian days, namely, that the altar should not as it were be somewhat removed from the congregation but in the midst of the people, who all have the priestly vocation to assist in the celebration of the Holy Liturgy.

It is right and proper that the choir should be vested, but both from a liturgical and from the acoustic point of view there is much to be said for returning to the 18th-century position for the choir, namely, a gallery at the west end of the church. Alternatively a very attractive arrangement, and one in which the choir is visible to the congregation, is obtained by building a singing gallery at one or other side of the church. When unaccompanied music is sung and conducted by the choirmaster, it is not at all dignified if the position of the choir between the congregation and the altar shows the choirmaster conducting vigorously right in the middle.

There is yet another disadvantage in the usual position of the choir, namely, that at a Parish Eucharist, where most of the adults make their Communion, many people do not like having to pass the choir in approaching the altar. Obviously a well-trained choir will behave properly, but it is a most exceptional choirmaster who can entirely control the facial and other movements of choir boys.

36

The question of the font is one that has seldom received sufficient consideration in churches, at least since the medieval days. Those who know and admire the grandeur of some of the medieval fonts, particularly in East Anglia, standing in the centre of the church at the west end and having a magnificent font cover in the form of a spire-like hanging canopy, or a structure on columns covering the whole font, will appreciate the indignity which has been cast upon the sacrament of Baptism where a small font, which looks as if it had been forgotten till the last minute, is pushed into some corner of the church. Without going into details, because after all such details are questions for the architect in each case, as to the manner in which the complementary dignity of the sacraments of Baptism and Holy Communion can best be expressed in a church, it seems desirable to stress the point that this thought should be considered, when the church is being planned, in the light of these four elements :

Altar.
Pulpit.
Position of the choir.
Dignity of the font.

A new plan and possibly a new architectural expression of the church may arise out of the necessities of the case, both from a spiritual and practical point of view, together with the possible use of new materials, such as reinforced concrete ; for this can be regarded as just as suitable a material for the building of churches as for secular buildings if treated with understanding.

The combined questions of planning for worship, which objective raises the character of a building from the purely utilitarian and arouses a spiritual conception of life, and that of the materials used together with the physical difficulties of the site and available funds, together provide the essential elements for the development of the design and perhaps even the growth of a really living style.

When the word style is used, it implies in this case a design for churches and ecclesiastical buildings which arises out of the fundamentals of the case and exhibits a certain harmony throughout all the buildings erected for the same purpose in the same country and in the same age. There always seems to be something very artificial, almost trivial, in the fact that a church in these days can either be Gothic or Renaissance or look like a building from the East, in fact will take on almost any style, just as one might dress up in any clothes. The building may in itself be fine and give architectural pleasure, but somehow there is a certain unreliability and theatricality about the whole thing. In the great ages of church building, as in the middle ages in this country, there was a recognised and developing tradition. Different abbeys or cathedrals built in the same century had different qualities of proportion and greater or less beauty, according to the ability of the architect ; but they always had something in common, being in fact the natural and therefore

37

true expression of architecture at that time. How such a standard is to be reached again is obviously difficult to foresee, but a direct and unbiassed approach to the problem should gradually lead to a less irresponsible use of past or contemporary styles.

Building Materials

Some authorities have accounted for the development of Gothic architecture as nothing more or less than the attempt to build a stone and therefore fireproof roof over a wide span. The disastrous fires of the Norman abbeys due to their wooden roofs having spurred on medieval men to avoid a repetition of this. We too have had some bad experiences of fires due to wooden roofs during the war, which might not all have occurred if the roofs had been constructed of other materials.

There is probably a certain amount of truth in this statement, but like most categorical statements it goes too far. Undoubtedly a fireproof building was desired by our forefathers, but this is not the whole explanation of their vaulted roofs; the love of gracious lines and excellent detail, the strong sense of craftsmanship, and the way in which architects, painters and sculptors as well as all the other crafts worked together as one whole, imparted to the buildings of those times far more than any purely practical necessity would have called for. King's College Chapel, Cambridge, has a fan vault, but it was not a practical consideration which produced the design, although the essential form may have arisen out of engineering necessity.

This seems to be the answer to functionalism. It is perfectly true that with the use of modern methods of construction, such as reinforced concrete, it is theoretically possible to span almost any width with a flat beam provided it is deep enough and correctly calculated. Therefore the purists say: why make use of an arch at all, or even a curve (except on plan), if the job can be done just as well with a beam? Why have an intervening support in the form of a column, if you can do without a column?

It is easy to see how traditionalism which says a church ought to look like a church, meaning in all probability Gothic, will violently oppose those who regard functionalism as the only method of building which has complete integrity; but by comparison with the attitude of mind which it has been suggested was held by the medieval builders, both functionalism and traditionalism seem to be exaggerations.

Stone is one of the most beautiful traditional materials for monumental buildings in Europe. We have good natural stone and it seems a great pity that this material cannot be used more often for modern churches, but the fact of the matter is that it is too expensive for the average church, and the principal substitute, namely brick, which is also a beautiful material and natural to this country, must as a rule be used.

If a timber truss is not adopted, and either for reasons of design, cost or greater safety from fire it is decided to have another kind of roof, there would appear to be a great future for the use of concrete, and there seems to be no reason why this material should not be used in a gracious manner, neither attempting to copy vault-like medieval forms nor being tied down to a rigid engineering standard.

Furthermore, whatever columns are necessary can be of a very slender nature, and it sometimes seems as though the natural development of a reinforced concrete construction for churches leads one back to the point where Gothic architecture in this country left off, and the Renaissance began, namely, late perpendicular architecture.

It would be too long a matter to go into details about materials, but it seems necessary in view of a certain amount of possible misunderstanding to say that a fine finish can be obtained in concrete, and there is no reason why this material should be regarded as a very crude and rough substance only possible for the most utilitarian buildings. Similarly, of course, an infinite number of beautiful forms and designs can be executed in brickwork, and the variety of colour obtainable is also sufficient to meet the requirements of any countryside; in a stone district bricks of a stone colour can be used, not of course as a substitute for stone, which it would be preferable to use, but perhaps because the stern facts of economics may make this necessary. But the use of colour in the countryside is a point to which it is to be hoped much greater attention will be given in the future than has been done in the past.

The Church School

It is necessary to conclude this sketch of the group of buildings centring round the parish church with some remarks, however fragmentary, about one other building which would in ideal conditions complete it—the church school. It is only too true that in most cases this is at present impossible; the new Education Act presents a whole set of difficult problems for church schools; the ideal arrangement, however, should at least be studied, though none of the subsequent remarks are regarded as in any sense final, but are only in the nature of suggestions.

It is evident that the ordinary regulations of the Board of Education for the building of an elementary or secondary school are as good as the experience of our time can make them; and in this sense any specifically church school will probably not improve on these standards, the chief necessity being that the church schools should not fall below these standards of healthiness and appropriateness. What then constitutes the difference between a church school and any other school? Obviously the fact that specifically religious teaching is given in those schools.

What is the cause of inspiration in our ancient schools and universities which most people who can gain admittance would still like to experience at least for a time? It seems to be a certain quietness of atmosphere which rests upon their chapels, courtyards, gardens; in fact, various qualities in their buildings which are not purely utilitarian.

Something of this atmosphere needs to be imparted to a church school; and whatever this costs in other ways, it will involve no extra financial expense and no loss of efficiency as compared with a secular school. If a church school could be built in connection with the parochial unit, either on the same site or in its immediate vicinity, so that the school buildings also group with the church buildings, this result would be achieved and the church would automatically become the school chapel, and the whole group would express unity.

It might, however, be worth considering whether such school buildings could not be erected in semi-permanent materials for two reasons: first, for the sake of economy and, secondly, because experience has shown that school buildings soon become out of date. This is the opposite case to that of church buildings.

The church and, it would seem, also the hall and vicarage should all be built in the most permanent manner possible, and in the case of churches and vicarages this is required by the Ecclesiastical Commission with the object of keeping down upkeep costs to the minimum; but the opposite may well be the case with regard to the school. There is still no reason, however, why a school built in a different form of construction should not be designed to harmonise satisfactorily with the church and the other buildings; and there is a great deal to be said for the formation of a composite group of buildings expressing the life and spirit of the church as a witness in our new towns and estates.

*   *   *   *   *

In this essay an attempt has been made to analyse the problems which lie before the church architect to-day, and to outline some of the ideals which might inspire his work; ideals which spring out of a genuine recovery in our day of a sense of the church as a community inspired by a living faith. It is this that makes it possible to hope that a truly creative period of church architecture is on the way to birth. The Church is, after all, the same Church which produced the great medieval buildings, developing the Gothic style right up to the triumph of King's College Chapel and the East Anglian perpendicular churches; in the last century it has made a great rediscovery of its own spiritual standards and convictions, and now that it is faced with new problems of planning, and has in its hands new possibilities in building materials and construction, there is hope that a coherent style of church architecture may be developed, which, while refusing any imitative attempts to reproduce the achievements of the past, will humbly and patiently learn from them and so truly carry on the English architectural tradition.

Planning a Post-War Church ꙮ ꙮ

By SIR CHARLES NICHOLSON, Bt.

IT IS LIKELY that for some time to come the repair of damaged churches will be given priority over the building of new ones. In many cases "repair" may amount to rebuilding, perhaps on a new plan and even upon a new site. There will certainly be controversy between people who would like everything to be put back as it was and those who are inclined to welcome the opportunity of making changes.

Where only slight damage has been suffered a policy of conservative repair would certainly seem right, though even then it might not in all cases be desirable to reproduce destroyed stained glass or other ornaments or fittings. In cases where churches of historic or artistic interest have been so seriously damaged as to require anything like complete rebuilding, the desire for exact reproduction will be felt very strongly. But certain questions will have to be settled even if a policy of reproduction is agreed upon. The great majority of churches in England have undergone substantial alterations since they were built; sometimes these alterations have been improvements, in other cases they have been the reverse. To replace everything as it was in 1939 would often mean perpetuating blemishes. On the other hand to restore a church to the condition in which it was left by its original builders, assuming that this can be ascertained, would mean sacrificing improvements as well as the obliteration of blemishes.

Problems are especially likely to arise when the time comes to deal with damaged churches of the Renaissance and later periods. In the case of medieval churches, it is as a general rule impracticable to reproduce the original design of the building for the excellent reason that it is generally impossible to discover it, and nowadays the critics all agree in condemning the attempts of the Victorian church restorers to make old churches look as if they had not been touched since the 14th century or some other arbitrary period.

Blitzed Churches

With regard however to the Renaissance and later churches it is generally possible to ascertain the details of their original architectural features and of their internal equipment, and there has in recent years arisen a tendency to advocate the restoration of some of these buildings to their original condition. This is a natural reversion from the ideas of the 19th-century church restorers who had acquired very cut and dried notions of what a church ought to be like and set to work with the zeal of true reformers to remedy what they regarded as the defects of such buildings as the London City churches.

So successful were their efforts that, in 1939, practically only one of Wren's churches remained in the condition in which he left it; this was the small church of St. Mildred, Bread Street; practically all the others, including St. Paul's Cathedral, had been more or less altered in their equipment or their decoration; or sometimes as at St. Michael's, Cornhill, even in their architectural details.

Because we may consider the Victorians were mistaken in trying to alter the character of Wren's churches in order that they should be made to conform with an arbitrary code of propriety, it does not follow that when a Wren church has been destroyed it should necessarily be rebuilt as a model of 17th-century church architecture. Churches are for use and not primarily for ornament, and although the preservation of old work is most praiseworthy it cannot be claimed that reproduction is on the same footing.

In the case of a destroyed Wren church in London there are certain factors to be considered which it would be pedantic to ignore. Wren built two distinct types of church in the City: the large galleried churches, generally with wooden columns, like St. James's, Piccadilly, and St. Andrew's, Holborn; and the smaller churches without galleries and with stone columns or brick piers, or without any columns at all. With regard to the smaller type of the city churches, these would probably always have a value apart from their architectural excellence, but there seems little demand in the present day for the larger type of galleried church in the City of London, which is no longer a residential locality as it was when these churches were built. Within the City several of these have been destroyed by fire. One of them, St. Bride's, Fleet Street, was probably not intended by Wren to have side galleries and these might be omitted in reconstruction, but others like St. Andrew's, Holborn, and St. Andrew's by the Wardrobe and Christ Church, Newgate Street, were built for galleries and could not be restored in their integrity without them. It would seem questionable whether any restoration should be attempted on the original lines if this involves the deliberate construction of useless reproductions of obsolete arrangements. On the other hand the Church of St. James in Piccadilly has been damaged by explosion, though not by fire. Consequently in this case a restoration of the old arrangements, including the galleries, is practicable and desirable on architectural and historical grounds. And as it happens this church is situated in a district which is less depopulated than the City of London and may therefore still serve a useful purpose in its original form.

The large churches built in the more modern districts of London and in some provincial towns and cities in the early part of the 19th century have always been rather a problem to the clergy and the architects of more recent times. Many of them have been remodelled internally and sometimes transformed into quasi-

Romanesque with a certain amount of success, an example being the work of Street at St. Luke's, Norwood.

In a few cases an intelligent and comparatively inexpensive scheme of decoration has been successful in giving character to these great, gaunt interiors, without the somewhat theatrical expedient of constructing "Hollywood" interiors within their walls. St. Pancras' Church is a good example of what can be done by colour alone, and the handling of the interior of St. John's, Waterloo Road, was a triumph. This most unpromising and depressing church was given an atmosphere of spaciousness and dignity with a minimum of alteration and without changing its identity in any way. There was no suspicion of an attempt to convert St. John's, Waterloo Road, into St. Mark's at Venice. When the work was finished it was still St. John's, Waterloo Road, but its interior had merits which had been unsuspected.

It is interesting to recall that in the Mid-Victorian period, when classical and Renaissance architecture was regarded as worse than pagan, Burges, who was essentially a keen Gothic Revivalist, had to deal with the nondescript interior of a church at Clapton. He remodelled it very successfully on classical lines; rather free classic perhaps, but at any rate accepting the character of the original building and not attempting to transform it into Gothic or Byzantine. Burges also redecorated the Chapel at Worcester College, Oxford, without disregarding the classical character of that 18th-century building.

The reinstatement of old churches and even of those of the Regency period will no doubt give rise to a great deal of controversy, but even more difficult problems may be anticipated in dealing with damaged churches built since 1840. When a building is quite new it may be generally admired on account of its novelty, but in a few years' time the novelty may have worn off and the work once acclaimed as a masterpiece may come to be regarded as a failure or even as an encumbrance. If it lasts longer than a century or so its merits may be re-discovered and its faults overlooked and it may come to be regarded as an antique "period" piece, and societies may be formed with the object of protecting it from vandalism. The churches of the Victorian period, especially the earlier ones, have long outgrown the charms of youthfulness and have hardly as yet reached the dignity of old age, and consequently their good points are apt to be overlooked by the critics of the present day. There is some danger therefore that in the general post-war reconstruction a good deal of comparatively modern work may be destroyed simply because it happens to be comparatively modern in spite of the fact that it may possess considerable intrinsic merits.

It is a healthy sign that we should be dissatisfied with the work of our predecessors; but sometimes we carry our veneration for our ancestors too far. In the good old days little respect was shown for ancient buildings and the older they were the less worthy of preservation they were reckoned to be. So William of Wykeham camouflaged the Norman nave of Winchester Cathedral into Perpendicular Gothic and Mr. Wood of Bath turned Llandaff Cathedral into an Italian temple. But although the old builders were anything but conservative in their treatment of the work of their predecessors and ancestors, they generally had a good sense of economy and made the best use they could of existing buildings, even if they were engaged in bringing them up to date. Thus we find in the choir of Canterbury Cathedral that, when it was rebuilt after the fire of 1174, a very great deal of the earlier fabric was retained and incorporated in the reconstruction. At Winchester, too, much of the Norman masonry was made use of in the 14th-century reconstruction, the details of which were evidently so designed as to make it possible to re-use the old stones with the least possible alteration. Since economy will undoubtedly have to be considered in the post-war reconstruction of our churches it may be hoped that a good deal of Victorian work may be preserved for reasons of necessity, although the merits of Victorian work are not generally appreciated by the rising generation.

Advisory Committees

In reconstructing Victorian churches we are generally likely to be confronted with two facts; firstly, that it is generally possible to ascertain in detail the original design of the building and, secondly, that the fittings, and possibly also the structure, will almost certainly have been considerably altered since the church was built. Who then is to decide what should be replaced and what should not? It seems impossible to discover a formula which will apply equally to every case. There exist advisory committees in most English dioceses, but although the individual committee members are persons of education and taste their decisions do not always convince those who have to deal with the practical carrying out of work. Moreover, the procedure of the advisory committees is often dilatory and unbusinesslike.

There exists also a central council which serves as a sort of "senate" to the various diocesan advisory committees, but the procedure of this body is even more difficult to organise than that of the smaller committees. Then there are the National Fine Arts Commission, a body with rather vague functions, the Ministry of Works and Buildings; and a host of societies like the Society for the Protection of Ancient Buildings, most of them anxious to have a finger in the pie when reconstruction is undertaken.

With all their drawbacks it would seem that the diocesan advisory committees would constitute the most reliable courts of appeal in cases of disputed policy connected with church building or reconstruction, but these committees should be strengthened by technical experts and their procedure should be improved. If they are to function in an efficient manner their work should be carried on continuously and not by monthly meetings only.

The dangers of State interference in the control of church building are unfortunately very great. A promise has been given that the cost of reinstating damaged churches will be made good by the State, and it is therefore obviously right that the State should satisfy itself that there is no misappropriation of funds, that compensation paid should not exceed the value of the property destroyed, and that all such compensation should be applied to the work of reinstatement and not used for other purposes. Beyond making sure of these financial matters the State should leave the direction of reconstruction work to local or diocesan bodies, but it is very likely that bodies such as the Ministry of Works may scent an opportunity to acquire control of church building schemes, which would in all probability have very undesirable results that need not be discussed here, although it may be permissible to say that in this country individual enterprise has generally proved more successful than any system of State control.

The consideration of the initial problems of church reconstruction makes it evident that the best and most experienced professional advice should be obtained by those executive bodies which will be entrusted with the administration of the funds available for the work, and it cannot be too strongly urged that the greatest possible care should be taken in the selection of an architect and that, when the architect has been duly selected, he should be trusted to carry out the work efficiently. No architect will do the best work of which he is capable if he is constantly worried with criticisms and suggestions while a building is in progress, and if the architect understands his work he will almost certainly be able to give a sounder decision upon any matter which may arise during the work than a comparatively inexperienced chairman or member of a building committee. A competent architect will not ignore the wishes of his employers, but he has been trained to foresee difficulties that may arise in carrying them out and to disregard his advice may prove to be a costly and unprofitable kind of amusement.

The problems that are likely to arise in the reconstruction of churches belonging to the Roman Catholic and other Christian communities are less complex than those which have to be solved by those who will have to deal with buildings that are in the custody of the Anglican Church south of the Border, or of the established Presbyterian Church in Scotland, since there are very few ancient buildings of historic interest in Roman Catholic or Nonconformist hands. Nevertheless, some of the churches that will have to be reconstructed were of great artistic merit and had interesting associations although comparatively modern ones. Amongst these, Pugin's Cathedral of St. George at Southwark was one of the most remarkable of his works, although it was not so successful as his cathedrals at Birmingham and Nottingham, or his church at Ramsgate. It may be hoped that St. George's may be repaired by someone in sympathy with Pugin's work and that some unfortunate alterations which were made after his death may not be perpetuated by the restorers. Except, however, in a few cases like that just quoted

45

there should be nothing to prevent the architects entrusted with the reconstruction of Roman Catholic and Nonconformist churches from having a free hand as regards design. It is not unduly optimistic to expect that many of these reconstructed churches will be better buildings than those they replace.

Whatever may be decided in any special case as to questions of exact reproduction or the reverse, it is evident that there will have to be a good deal of church building in new centres of population and in the reconstruction of destroyed churches which possessed no particular interest or merit. It is, therefore, desirable to find out what kind of church is required when building again becomes possible, especially in those cases where the architect has a free hand and is not constrained to reproduce a building that has been destroyed.

Building Costs

It was possible some fifty or sixty years ago to build churches at about a third of the cost of similar work in 1939, and funds for church building were forthcoming without much difficulty. Consequently the Anglican clergy and the British public acquired a taste for rather ambitious, rather ornate, and not always very refined or interesting churches; equipped with towers and spires, containing large organs and expensive marble pulpits and mosaic reredoses, and lighted, or more often darkened, with stained-glass windows. The ideal Anglican town church was seated for from 700 to 1,000 persons, a very usual ratio of church accommodation to population being one to ten.

Roman Catholic churches were built on very similar lines, but except in some large towns where good sized churches had already been provided between the years 1840 and 1860, the Roman Catholic communities were generally rather small ones and did not require very large churches.

The Nonconformists of the later Victorian period built some quite ambitious churches in the fashionable Gothic of the time, such, for instance, as the church in Westminster Bridge Road, London, but as a rule these buildings were over florid in external treatment and their internal arrangements seemed out of harmony with the style of architecture adopted by their architects.

In 1939 the requirements of the Anglican church were not the same as they had been at the end of the last century. Population had decreased in many towns where large churches had been built in Victorian times.

Small country villages with little ancient churches had suddenly expanded into settlements of 10,000 or more inhabitants; none of them with money to spare and many of them indifferent even if not hostile to the Church.

Building costs increased slowly but steadily until 1914, after which they rose steeply and remained at a high level until 1939. The cost of living rose simultaneously with that of building. It will therefore be clear that some very difficult

8. THE GOOD SAMARITAN
By Barillet-le-Chevalier-Haussen

9. CHAPEL OF OUR LADY, DOWNSIDE ABBEY CHURCH. FOUR
RELIQUARIES ARE SET ON THE SCREEN BEHIND
By J. N. Comper

problems have had to be faced, and that architects have had to tax their brains in order to get new churches built at all with the funds available.

Perhaps the strict economy that has been forced upon the church builders has been a blessing in disguise. We have been told on excellent authority that war-time rationing has improved the health of the nation, and the austerity of the most recent churches may well lead those who are concerned with the building of future ones to realise that there are sources of beauty other than that of opulent display. The temptation to build shoddily, however, must be resisted at all cost. It is a temptation which has proved too strong for some of our latter-day architects who are apt to ask why a fourteen-inch wall is not good enough. If funds cannot be found for substantial construction the responsible authorities would be well advised to content themselves with frankly temporary churches or Mission Rooms instead of wasting money upon permanent work that will never be really satisfactory.

The financial difficulties attending the reconstruction of damaged churches and more especially the provision of churches in new centres of population affect the Anglican community more than they do either the Roman Catholic or the Non-conformist bodies for several reasons. In the first place the Anglican Church is entrusted with the care of ancient buildings which must be maintained whether they serve an economic purpose or not. In the second place the Anglican Church property consists largely of legally consecrated sites which cannot be sold without elaborate and costly formalities, and lastly, the Anglican Church is morally bound to provide church privileges for the inhabitants of new settlements whether those settlers demand them or not. The Roman Catholic and Nonconformist communities are under no moral obligation to undertake new responsibilities until a definite demand arises.

It will be of interest to compare the relative cost of church building at intervals during the last half century. Fifty years ago it was generally possible to build a solid brick or stone church of good proportions, but without a tower for from £5 to £10 per sitting. The contract price for the large and imposing church of Holy Trinity at Chelsea, with accommodation for some 1,200 persons, was only £18,000. A stone church, ashlar faced internally, at Torquay, cost about £7 10s. per sitting in 1896 and subsequent years; this included a tower. A very simple brick church at Grimsby cost £3,000 for 500 sittings. Harrison Townsend's charming little church of St. Martin at Wonersh, Surrey, cost only £500 and would hold a congregation of 100. Small churches of about the same size and cost were built near Witney, Oxfordshire, and at Westport on the Irish coast, during the early years of the present century.

In comparison with the foregoing, figures are extracted from a volume published by the Incorporated Church Building Society, which gives illustrations and details of the cost of a number of churches built since 1930. The most expensive of these was a flint-faced building with a central tower which cost no less than £75 a sitting. Other brick churches with towers cost £50 and £36 respectively. Three rather provocative modernist churches cost £40, £37 10s. and £30 respectively. Others of less aggressive character, built in a late Gothic or Renaissance manner, without towers, cost from £20 to £30. It will be noted that the "modernist" churches are quite as costly as those of traditional character.

The method of estimating the comparative costs of different types of church by comparing the outlay incurred with the number of sittings provided is, of course, a very rough and ready proceeding and does not give an accurate idea as to whether the outlay on the building has been wisely expended or not, but it does give a fair idea of the extent to which building costs have risen in the past fifty years, and the idea it gives is not an exaggerated one, for the architects of the more recent churches have been obliged to economise in materials and labour to an extent undreamt of in the 19th century and have been further expected to provide a number of gadgets which have only come into general use in comparatively recent years.

It is important to realise that cheap building is not necessarily economical building, but this should not be made an excuse for extravagance. Possibly it is a sordid thing to say, but there is some truth in it. The test of an architect's efficiency is the value of the building he can produce for the sum which is entrusted to him to expend. This value is of two kinds, the practical asset of durability, convenience and so forth, which one has a right to expect in every building, and the intangible asset of beauty which cannot be attained by the observance of a set of rules, although some such code may help an unimaginative builder to avoid errors of proportion and other obvious faults of design.

Choosing a Plan

The planning of a modern church is far more important than its architectural style, in fact to some extent the plan should determine the style of the building. So it will be well to decide upon the type of plan that one wants to have for one's new church before one troubles one's head about its architectural character.

There are plenty of alternatives to choose from. Churches have been built square and oblong, round, oval, and even triangular. Again, a church may or may not have pillars or towers or vaulting or galleries. What the church builder should aim at is to provide the right kind of church for the people who have to use it. Upon a signpost near Truro one can (or could) read the legend "Come to Good," and following its direction a short way up a delightful country lane one came upon a plain cottage-like "Friends" Meeting House with whitewashed walls, a beautifully thatched roof, an open shed for the friends to tie up their horses in, and a mounting block—everything in good repair and absolutely clean and fresh. One could look in at the clear-glass windows and admire the whitewashed walls and the scrubbed deal

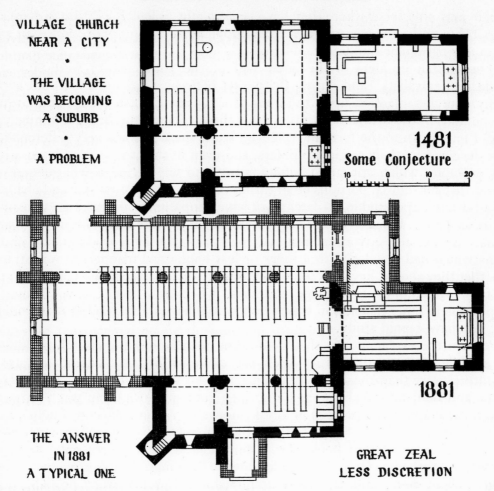

VILLAGE CHURCH
NEAR A CITY
•
THE VILLAGE
WAS BECOMING
A SUBURB
•
A PROBLEM

1481
Some Conjecture

10 0 10 20

1881

THE ANSWER
IN 1881
A TYPICAL ONE

GREAT ZEAL
LESS DISCRETION

benches and appreciate the charms of "Friendship" even if one did not happen to be a "Friend" oneself.

In Truro City the most shapely of 19th-century churches dominates its surroundings almost like a queen seated on her throne, but it has this much in common with the Quaker Meeting House down the neighbouring country lane, in that it absolutely expresses the highest ideals of its builders, which perhaps are not so different from those of the "Friends" at "Come to Good" as some people might imagine.

The cathedral and the meeting house are both satisfactory buildings because both of them are appropriate as well as beautiful. It would not be difficult, though it would be perhaps unkind, to make a very long list of buildings that are either inappropriate or unlovely or both. It is not very profitable to lay down the law about what is beautiful and what is not; some may see beauty wherever they look for it;

49

others may only see it where they have been taught to look for it. But it does seem possible to find some common agreement upon what is appropriate and what is not so in any particular building problem.

The church builders of the latter half of the 19th century were almost all "Gothic Revivalists" and during the period between 1840 and 1865 built a great many churches planned upon the lines of a typical English village church such as one finds in the Midland counties. Now these village churches had in nine cases out of ten grown to the form in which we know them; a form very different from that designed by their original builders, and even in the case of the comparatively few examples which appear to belong entirely to one period it will generally be found that substantial portions of an earlier building of different size and character have been incorporated in the later work which apparently indicates the date of the entire structure. It seems rather illogical therefore of these early Gothic Revivalists to have deliberately advocated as a matter of principle the reproduction of church plans which had developed in a more or less haphazard manner. It was strange, too, that they should have elected to build more or less inaccurate copies of 14th-century Midland county village churches, when they might have turned for inspiration to other districts in which they would have found models that would at any rate have repaid study.

Perhaps the explanation is that the leading men among the church builders of the middle of the 19th century knew the churches of the Midland and Home Counties better than those of East Anglia and the West of England. John Mason Neale and Benjamin Webb were Cambridge graduates. Rickman was a Birmingham man, Pugin was a protégé of Lord Shrewsbury, John Bloxam, Pugin's great friend, was an Oxford don; Matthew Bloxam was a Rugby solicitor and John Henry Parker an Oxford bookseller. Cambridge is about thirty miles from the border of Northants, Oxford about seventeen, Birmingham about twenty-six and Rugby about four, and the Northamptonshire churches were probably very familiar to the enthusiasts of a period when travelling was not so easy as it is nowadays.

The Midland type of village church must not be despised because it has been copied in a mistaken manner and applied to purposes for which it is not well suited. Many of the medieval examples are gems of architecture, others are commonplace, but all were built to satisfy local requirements, which varied at different times and in different parishes.

Victorian Church Builders

Two leading types of churches served as models to the earlier Victorian church builders. The favourite one was that of a nave with aisles, a long rather narrow chancel, less lofty than the nave, and a tower and spire usually at the west end. The other type, less frequently followed, was that of a cruciform church with a central or sometimes a western tower. The architectural detail was generally imitated from 14th-century work. Although these imitative 19th-century churches are seldom successful, either as copies of old work or as examples of church building, there is no reason why their planning and arrangement should not meet the needs of certain parishes or congregations. But the mistake has often been made of trying to meet the requirements of town or suburban parishes with churches such as those depicted on Christmas cards and referred to in Gray's "Elegy."

The average medieval parish church seldom had a vestry, never a heating chamber and never an organ chamber. If it had fixed pews they did not take up the whole floor space; chancels were not stuffed full of "choir stalls." Transepts and aisles were nearly always used as separate chapels. Reproduce the old conditions and the medieval plan will meet your needs, possibly better than any other. But if you start at the wrong end and build your Christmas Card church first and then try to satisfy the ambitions of the clergy and the organist and the choir and the various sections of the congregation, and the old ladies of both sexes, and the local building authority and the ecclesiastical commissioners and the advisory committees and the mourners who want to put up stained-glass windows, and the hot water man, and the electric light man, and strive to do it all with the strictest economy, you may find your path beset with difficulties.

To begin with you may build your long chancel and you will have to fill it with choir stalls of such vast proportions as to convert the floor space into a mere passage. Then you must have vestries, or at any rate one vestry, so you build that on one side of your chancel and block one lot of windows. Next you proceed to build an organ chamber on the other side of the chancel and block up another lot of windows—and when you have darkened the church sufficiently you proceed to fill up the nave aisles and transepts with pews, some facing blank walls, many perhaps never used except at harvest festivals, and finally you try to hide your performances with stained-glass windows and to reveal them with electric light and to satisfy querulous worshippers with a heating apparatus which they accuse of creating draughts.

In building a new church, although the wisdom of our fathers is not to be lightly set aside, it is well that we should not blindly follow their footsteps without realising where they will lead us. This has been recognised by many church builders during the last seventy years who have profited by the experience of their predecessors and avoided many of their mistakes. This is not to say that the general level of church architecture during the last eighty years has been inspiring or even praiseworthy, but it may fairly be said that some of the churches built since 1860 have been both, and that we have reached a time when builders will think carefully upon the question of what they want before they start to build, instead of merrily

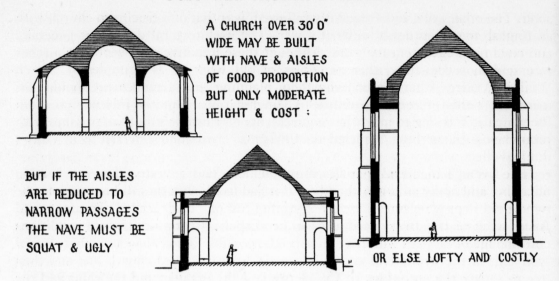

A CHURCH OVER 30' 0"
WIDE MAY BE BUILT
WITH NAVE & AISLES
OF GOOD PROPORTION
BUT ONLY MODERATE
HEIGHT & COST :

BUT IF THE AISLES
ARE REDUCED TO
NARROW PASSAGES
THE NAVE MUST BE
SQUAT & UGLY

OR ELSE LOFTY AND COSTLY

proceeding to build something which they think fashionable but which they don't really want at all.

In considering, therefore, the general layout of a new church we must determine whether we want an auditorium for purposes of instruction; a stage for the display of ceremonies, or a place to say our prayers in, apart from such questions as size and cost and the peculiar requirements of those for whose use we are to build it. In the last few years there has been a tendency to demand an auditorium or a stage, as well as, and sometimes in preference to, a building of devotional character, and in order to satisfy these demands certain churches have been built which are acoustically unsatisfactory, which do not provide an effective setting for ceremonial, and which have very little of the devotional atmosphere. This has often happened in cases where a demand has been made that "every" seat must have an unobstructed "view of the altar and pulpit" and when a considerable number of sittings are required and funds are not unlimited.

The obvious way to satisfy this demand is to build a large hall, possibly flanked with narrow "passage aisles." If a congregation of any size has to be provided for, this hall must be of considerable width, otherwise it will be so long that the back seats will be too far away from the altar and pulpit. And if the cost of the church is limited it will be impracticable to build it very lofty and very difficult to avoid building it very ugly. It is also extremely likely to be unsatisfactory acoustically and will be difficult to light properly. If funds are available and the height of the nave can be made sufficient to give good proportion the effect of a great hall-like church may be very noble. King's College Chapel and Westminster Cathedral are beyond criticism internally, though neither of them happens to be particularly shapely externally. But it is unlikely that many post-war churches will be built on a very generous scale, and even if it were possible to build a church like Souillac in an English town it is doubtful whether it would not prove to be a white elephant, and certainly would not satisfy the desires of those who fondly hoped to fill it with a congregation who could all see and hear everything.

King's College Chapel was designed for a comparatively small congregation, all members of the College. Westminster Cathedral, however, does fulfil the purpose for which it was designed; it gives ample floor space combined with admirable proportions, but it includes a good number of chapels that greatly add to the internal effect without contributing to the open area of the nave, so it can hardly be regarded as a "hall" church pure and simple. Moreover, a reduced copy of Westminster Cathedral would not be likely to reproduce its dignity and impressiveness, nor would it provide for a large congregation except at a very considerable cost. As a matter of fact the experiment has been tried and the results have not been convincing.

The Hall-type Church

Although there may be reasons against laying too much stress upon the advantages of an unbroken floor space in churches of any considerable size, it would be a great mistake in smaller churches to assume that a complex and broken up plan is either necessary or desirable. It is a matter of ecclesiastical policy to decide whether it is better to provide a few large churches in a given area or a number of small ones, but where the latter alternative is adopted a simple

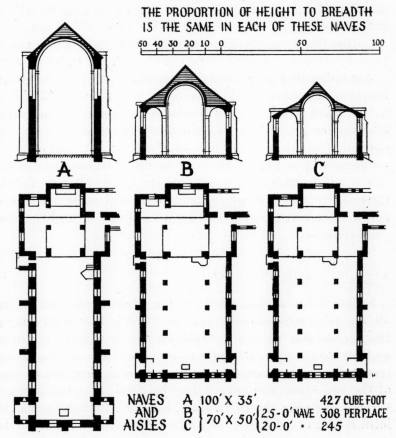

HALL TYPE AND AISLED PLANS COMPARED

THE PROPORTION OF HEIGHT TO BREADTH IS THE SAME IN EACH OF THESE NAVES

50 40 30 20 10 0   50   100

A   B   C

NAVES AND AISLES   A 100' X 35'   427 CUBE FOOT

B } 70' X 50' { 25-0' NAVE   308 PER PLACE
C }   { 20-0'   "   245

type of building is likely to be more satisfactory in every way than a complex one. In a few exceptional cases there may be opportunities of building small churches sumptuously, as Pugin did at Ramsgate and Bodley at Hoar Cross, but as a general rule the church builder is bound to study the art of avoiding wastefulness. To adopt an unnecessarily costly scheme and to carry it out cheaply is waste. To discover the simplest way of meeting your requirements and to spare no expense in carrying out the work in the most durable and seemly fashion is real economy.

There seems to be a limit of size which will determine whether an undivided hall type of church is more economical than a church with aisles. If the comparative costs of different types are compared it will probably be found that, other things being equal, it will be economical to build a "hall type" church to hold anything up to 300 persons; for anything larger than this an aisled building will be found more economical. In the case of very small churches holding less than 100 persons, the hall type is definitely the most economical.

The reason why this conclusion is arrived at is more or less a matter of simple arithmetic. The floor space occupied by each person in that part of the church which is allotted to the congregation is about 7 sq. ft., allowing for gangways, but not including the space required for altar, font, porches, organ, vestries, etc. Accordingly, if the church is to seat 300 persons in its nave that nave will have to have an unbroken area of 2,100 sq. ft.—say, 84 ft. long by 25 ft. wide.

Assuming that an agreeable proportion of height to width is seven to four, the height of this nave would have to be about 44 ft. and this would mean enclosing 308 cu. ft. of space for each person in the congregation. Suppose, however, you are building for 500 and have to provide a floor space of 3,500 sq. ft. A reasonable proportion of length to breadth would be 100 to 35, and if the height is determined in the same way as before, the nave being 35 ft. broad must be 61 ft. high, in which case it will be necessary to enclose 427 cu. ft. of space for each person. Moreover, the cost per cubic foot of the larger nave will be higher than that of the smaller one because the construction will be more difficult and the building will have to be more massive.

Pillars and Arches

Supposing now that we forgo the advantages of an unbroken area, which after all, are more apparent than real, and break it up with one or two ranges of pillars and arches. Say we are to build for 300 it would be practicable to build a nave 40 ft. wide by 53 ft. long and to divide it into two spans, say, of 25 and 15 ft. respectively. In that case the height may be determined by the breadth of the wider of the two spans and would thus be 44 ft. over the greater part of the area and perhaps less over the 15 ft. span, but for simplicity's sake we may assume a uniform height of 44 ft. over the whole area. In this case the height of the nave and

A COMPARISON OF ALTERNATIVE TYPES OF CHURCH

300 PLACES IN NAVE (& AISLE)

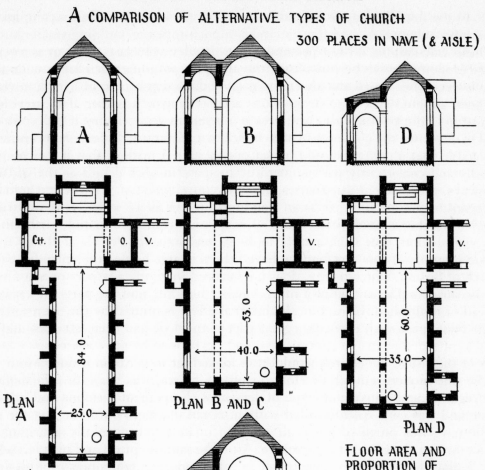

PLAN
A

PLAN B AND C

PLAN D

A
B } 308 CUBIC FEET
C   258 PER PERSON
D   245 WITHIN BODY
      OF CHURCH

FLOOR AREA AND
PROPORTION OF
HEIGHT TO BREADTH
ALIKE IN ALL CASES.
CALCULATIONS APPLY
TO BODY OF CHURCH

the cubic space per person (308 ft.) will be the same as in the case of the undivided nave holding 300 persons, but the cost of the double nave would probably be rather more than that of the undivided one. On the other hand, the double nave being shorter and wider than the undivided one, the congregation would be arranged much more compactly.

If cost were a first consideration the double nave could be built 60 ft. by 35 ft. and the wider span be 20 ft. with a height of 35 ft. and a cubic space of only 245 ft. per person. Calculating the measurements of a nave for 500 persons the area of 3,500 sq. ft. can be obtained in a length of 70 ft. and a breadth of 50 ft. divided into three spans, the central one 20 ft. with a height of 35 ft., or 25 ft. with a height of

44 ft. In the first alternative the cubic space per person will be only 245 ft. and in the second only 308 ft.

These calculations do not pretend to be detailed, but they tend to show that where economy has to be considered the apparent simplicity of a large undivided nave is deceptive. In all the alternatives quoted the same ratio of height to width has been adopted and good proportions are better worth having than mere size. It must not be supposed that cheapness is in itself a virtue; or that it is desirable in itself to cut down the cubic space of a church to a minimum. It does, however, seem reasonable that a church should be set out in such a manner that it can be built soundly and consistently with something to spare in such details as the width of gangways, the space of sanctuaries, and the convenience of vestries and porches.

Regarding a church either as an "auditorium" or as a "stage" it is very questionable whether an unduly large and open nave is advantageous, and, furthermore, it is very seldom that such a nave looks its real size. St. Peter's at Rome is the classic example of this fact but we have others nearer home: the splendid parish church at Boston, Lincolnshire, does not succeed in giving a true impression of its size because its plan is that of a much smaller building and the parts are enlarged instead of multiplied. Here, too, the internal effect is injured by the overcrowding of the floor space with pews. If a great part of the floor had been left open and the pews kept together in the central nave and perhaps in front of the chapels at the ends of the aisles, the church would have looked far larger than it does now.

The fine modern church of Holy Trinity, Chelsea, was built for a fashionable congregation and a luxurious type of service with eloquent sermons and luscious music and was consequently filled with an ocean of chairs until one day the roof of the nave was burnt off in an air raid, fortunately not materially damaging the main fabric or the best of the furniture. After the raid the priest and people, instead of wringing their hands in despair, set to work and got a temporary roof on to the nave and were able to use their church again. But the fashionable congregation had many of them gone off to the wars and it was no longer necessary to fill the place with chairs. The result was that it was at last possible to realise the dignity and spaciousness of the interior in a way one could never do when only small areas of the floor were visible.

Regarding a church as a setting for ceremonial it might at first sight appear that an unbroken hall would best meet the case, but here again there are objections to an unduly long building because people in the back rows of seats are inconveniently distant from the place where the ceremonial is conducted. So that both for seeing and for hearing it is more practical that a congregation should be arranged in an approximately square area than in a long and comparatively narrow one. And if the accommodation of the church is at all considerable, practical conditions of economy, both in first cost and in maintenance, prescribe that the congregational area must be divided into two, three or more spans, unless perhaps the church is built on the plan of a theatre. This would possibly be logical if the only purposes of building a church was to provide a place in which to hear music and sermons and to perform ceremonies.

All religious communities require churches in which these things can be done, however much their doctrine and customs may differ, but very few would be satisfied to build their churches in theatre fashion pure and simple, though experiments have been made in this direction in the cases of the galleried churches of the 17th and 18th centuries (Fig. 1), the circular churches of St. Chad at Shrewsbury,

FIG. I. A GALLERIED CHURCH OF THE 18TH CENTURY.

and All Saints, Newcastle-on-Tyne, and some Nonconformist churches built mostly in the 19th century. Some of these buildings have architectural merit but it is unlikely that they will be taken as models for post-war church building. It is interesting to come across a round church like those at Newcastle and Shrewsbury with their sweeping galleries and curved pews, but one would get a little tired of them if there were more of them. It is true that we get tired of anything if it is repeated too often, but repetitions of a straightforward, ordinary object are not so tiresome as repetitions of an eccentric one. In the outskirts of some of our towns we sometimes find streets of quite commonplace straightforward plain houses or cottages which are by no means tiresome, and in the next street a row of more ambitious dwellings, each with a Moorish arch to its front door and perhaps a half-timbered gable over its bay window, the effect of which is by no means restful. If we are to profit by the mistakes of the speculative builder it may be that post-war church builders will concentrate upon perfecting such traditions of planning and design as have become familiar instead of trying as a matter of principle to devise an entirely new type of design in every new church that is built. Originality is all very well, but sometimes patience and modesty produce the best results.

It must not be supposed that a standard type of church will or should be applicable to all localities or communities, but it is to be hoped that post-war churches will not only satisfy the obvious requirements of clergy and people, but will of themselves inspire those who use them. It is, of course, quite true that one can say one's prayers anywhere, but after all, the church is the one place that is built purely for that purpose, and it is fitting that it should possess dignity appropriate to that purpose. It need not be a particularly costly building although it is incongruous to be content with a cheap church in an opulent district or with a shoddy church in any district, but it should be quite obvious that it is a church and nothing else and, especially internally, it should aim at helping those who use it to realise what it stands for.

That post-war churches will have to be economically built and as a general rule will not justify slight construction which, though cheap at first, is extravagant in the long run, and it is to be hoped that there will be exceptional cases where ample funds are available and architects are equal to the opportunity of spending them wisely. In such circumstances we may look forward to seeing churches built that will bear comparison with Patrington or Shottesbrook or Maids Moreton, or St. Mary le Strand. But the masterpieces will no doubt be created from time to time, and if there were too many of them they would not be appreciated. What is to be hoped for is a general standard of appropriateness and beauty in post-war work, and there is no hard and fast reason why this should not be attained as it has been in the past.

The 19th-century church builders failed because of the poor quality of their every-day "bread and butter" architecture; there were plenty of masterpieces, but they did not seem to have been produced by the brethren of the architects who built red brick churches with brass altar rails for the diocesan church extension societies.

In the 18th century there were few architects and fewer masterpieces, but there was a good building tradition, and the consequence is that the merits of 18th-century buildings have been so evident as to have justified the formation of a "Georgian group" to encourage the study of the area railings and fanlights of Bloomsbury.

CHURCH OF ST. FRANCIS OF ASSISI, STRATFORD, LONDON
DECORATED WITH DURESCO

Duresco Products Limited, Charlton, London, S.E. 7

BRONZE SCREEN IN THE CHAPEL OF ST. GEORGE AND THE ENGLISH
MARTYRS, WESTMINSTER CATHEDRAL

Designed by L. H. Shattock, F.R.I.B.A.
Executed by Blunt & Wray Ltd., London

In an earlier age building traditions were still stronger and architects fewer and every church, whether in town or village, was appropriately designed and honestly built. But much of the designing was crude, and the churches were all of one type in any particular district, and there were only very few masterpieces. Yet where one society has been formed to study 18th-century buildings dozens have been formed to study the architecture and history of medieval churches and scores of books have been written about them.

So it will be well that post-war church builders should learn what they can from the works of their predecessors without attempting to build fake churches of "period" character but without despising the experience accumulated in times past. Above all it is to be desired that the responsibilities of the work should be realised by all concerned with it, that the architect and builder should be chosen for their professional and technical qualifications and not for any local influence they may have, and that neither of them should spare time or trouble or seek personal interest or advertisement in the carrying out of the work; that when expert advice is sought it should be followed, and that neither architect nor builder should be expected to accomplish impossible tasks.

Building the Church: Styles and Requirements

By SIR CHARLES NICHOLSON, Bt.

DURING THE GREATER part of the 19th century most of the church building undertaken in the British Isles and Colonies was carried out in good, bad, or indifferent Gothic, and an immense number of books were written advocating conformity to what their authors regarded as the true principles of church architecture. Much was also written on the subject of civil and domestic architecture and the relative merits of Gothic and Classic for secular buildings. For quite a long time, and practically the whole of the Victorian period, hardly anyone dared to build a church in Classical Renaissance although some experiments were made in Romanesque of various sorts, as, for instance, at St. Barnabas', Oxford. Architectural fashions succeeded each other very quickly during the 19th century. Until the accession of Queen Victoria most of the church building that was undertaken was in the towns, and the churches themselves were great gaunt galleried halls either "Grecian" or "Gothic" in style—the Gothic ones were generally of the perpendicular variety except the very cheap ones which were "Early English"; in neither case were the general arrangements or the design of these churches either Greek or Medieval—they differed only in these architectural details and the choice of style was more or less a question of cost.

Grecian churches with porticoes were the most expensive. St. Pancras' cost £69,000 exclusive of the site and fencing. It was consecrated in 1822. The "estimate" for building St. Luke's, Chelsea, which was consecrated in 1824, was only £20,000, and there does not appear to be any record of the final cost of the work, but the "estimate" for St. Pancras' had been £51,000, so it would appear that the Grecian building cost about twice as much as the Gothic, but it accommodated 2,500 persons, as against St. Luke's 2,000. St. Luke's was one of the most costly Gothic churches of the period.

The cheaper sort were anything but attractive; St. Mary's, Somers Town, cost about £14,000 for 2,000 persons in about 1824, and may be labelled "Early English," but it is worth recording that the church in Regent Street, London, that was known as "Hanover Chapel," which was destroyed at the end of the century, only cost £16,100 for 1,500 persons. It was a Greek building with a stone portico, a small central dome, and two turrets and was the most interesting and attractive of the churches of its period. It was designed by C. R. Cockerell and consecrated in 1825.

From 1837 until about 1859 the fashion prevailed of building churches which resembled medieval ones in plan and arrangement as well as in the form of their doors and windows and so forth. The resemblance was not as a rule very convincing and the models selected for imitation were not well chosen, at any rate for town churches. For various reasons the architects concentrated on the study of 13th and 14th-century village churches, and failed to realise that no 13th or 14th-century builder would ever have dreamt of providing such churches for town parishes of any size. Nevertheless, some of the more thoughtful architects of the 'forties and 'fifties appreciated the importance of designing churches to fit their surroundings, and built distinctively "town churches" in towns and "country churches" in the country, sometimes with considerable success, using as a rule the fashionable 14th-century detail which the critics of the period favoured.

Pugin's churches at Birmingham and Derby, at Nottingham and at Southwark, are all essentially town churches, so are the large Roman Catholic churches of this period by Wardell in Stepney and by Hadfield in Sheffield, and the Anglican churches by Carpenter in Munster Square, London, and Butterfield at Stoke Newington and Huddersfield. During the early years of the Victorian period a good deal of church building was done in country districts, and the old village churches which were favourite subjects of study at the time, made, on the whole, very good models, and in a few cases the smaller churches built from 1840 onwards are quite attractive, although these were the exceptions to the general rule (Fig. 1).

The first of the 19th-century church builders to strike out on fresh lines was William Butterfield who designed All Saints', Margaret Street, London, before 1850 and St. Alban's, Holborn, very soon after. Although both these churches and most of Butterfield's subsequent ones were planned upon lines that differed a good deal from those of medieval churches of similar size, and although they were built of parti-coloured materials in a fashion for which there was only very slight precedent in English medieval architecture, the details of doorways and windows, pillars and arches and so forth, were all based upon English work of the early 14th century, and it is worth while recording that Butterfield adhered through the whole of his long life to the technique he had employed in the building of All Saints', Margaret Street, in the 'fifties.

From 1855 onwards, fashions in church building succeeded and overlapped one another in a bewildering manner—French Gothic, Italian Gothic, mixed Gothic, modern Gothic, church Gothic, chapel Gothic, and back again to English Gothic towards the end of the century, with occasional reminiscences of Continental trips to France and Flanders, Germany and Spain. The result of all this was that a type of church has been evolved in this country which very fairly satisfies the general requirements of an Anglican congregation, and which in some cases has given us buildings that are shapely and dignified and devotional.

Tubney Berks
A.W Pugin 1848.

FIG. I. A SMALL COUNTRY CHURCH BUILT BY PUGIN.

Such churches were, however, the exception rather than the rule, and the common-place work that was carried out in the last half of the 19th century was even more dreary and callous than some of the corresponding work of the earlier Victorian period, which at any rate aimed at beauty though it did not often attain to it.

Such tradition as had been evolved in the Victorian period lasted more or less until the war of 1914–18. The changed conditions of following years produced a whole set of fresh problems for architects to solve and encouraged a spirit of restlessness and adventure among the younger clergy and architects which have produced a number of very queer churches and some very fine ones, sometimes studiously avoiding any tradition, at other times using traditional principles as the basis of modern design.

Thus we have come in these latter days to regard questions of architectural style with more or less indifference, and the violent controversies of the 19th century regarding the respective merits of Grecian and Gothic, English and French and Italian and all the rest, strike us as being rather absurd. Pugin, prostrate in St. Peter's at Rome in an ecstasy of thanksgiving because he thought he had detected a crack in the dome—Ruskin's touching description of a blameless village clergyman designing window traceries by the simple process of arranging autumn leaves on a piece of pure white blotting paper—all seem out of date nowadays, but if we pride ourselves upon pulling up the weeds, we should be well advised to take care we don't pull up all the flowers too.

11. HIGH ALTAR IN THE CHURCH OF
ST. THOMAS MORE, SEAFORD, SUSSEX

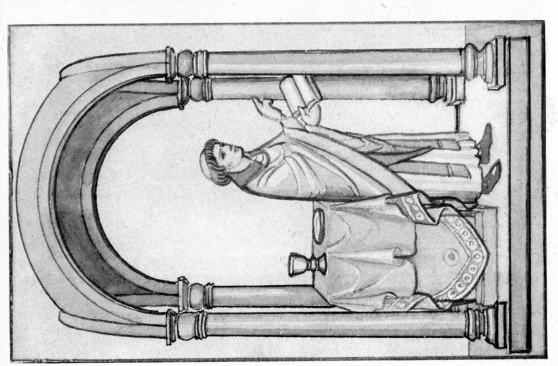

10. RECONSTRUCTED PERSPECTIVE
FROM A 10TH-CENTURY PAINTING

TWO EXAMPLES OF THE ELEVATED TESTER

13. CHURCH OF ST. GEORGE, POLEGATE, SUSSEX. HERE THE TESTER IS
RAISED ABOVE THE EAST WINDOW

12. CHURCH OF THE HOLY FAMILY, MANCHESTER.
A LARGE TEXTILE DOSSAL FURNISHES A BLANK
EAST WALL

It is possible that the whole conception of "style" is mistaken and that the differences of style do not depend on the shapes of arches and doors and windows, but upon the conditions under which building is done. For instance, St. Pancras' church pretends to be Athenian Greek, and St. Luke's, Chelsea, Perpendicular Gothic, but essentially both of these are purely and simply "Regency." And to go back earlier, are there not more similarities than there are differences between Wren's Gothic work and his classic? Before the period of the Renaissance there had been, of course, a succession of "styles" in the sense that the buildings of each particular period differ from those of all other periods, but these differences were only due to such causes as changes in requirements, advances in knowledge, the fluctuations of wealth, the discovery of new materials and appliances. Convenience and magnificence were aimed at by each generation from the earliest times, and each generation of builders tried to improve upon the work done by its predecessors, not always successfully, but there was no conscious realisation of "style" as we now understand it until the study of Classical literature led to a desire to revert to Classical architecture.

This demand for culture was not at first accepted with enthusiasm by British craftsmen. Moreover in England, and incidentally also in Northern and Western France, the Church has always been cautious about accepting new-fangled ideas even though they may have been favoured by ecclesiastical dignitaries. So we find that quite a great deal of 17th-century building, especially in country districts, was more Gothic than Classical in style, and that this was especially the case with regard to church building. Even in London, the only definitely Classical church building that was carried out before the Great Fire, was that done by Inigo Jones at St. Paul's Cathedral and in the building of St. Paul's church, Covent Garden, the other three churches attributed to Inigo Jones, St. Catherine's, Cree, St. Alban's, Wood Street, and Lincoln's Inn Chapel are all more or less Gothic. The 17th-century colleges and their chapels at Oxford and Cambridge are generally of the same character, the earliest of the college chapels that are definitely classical being those of Trinity, Oxford, and Pembroke, Cambridge, both dating from the latter half of the 17th century.

Perhaps the most interesting specimen of 17th-century Gothic church building was the so-called "Charles" church at Plymouth. This was actually built during the "Commonwealth" period, and to all intents and purposes was built on the traditional lines of a 15th-century West Country church. It had no distinct chancel, but was divided into a nave with broad aisles, the pillars and arches and window traceries and doorways were all of a sort that one finds in the 15th-century churches of South Devonshire, and the roofs were of the traditional cradle form. The arches were wider than those of a genuine 15th-century building, moreover, the general proportions were broader and shorter, and the external details are less medieval than those of the interior.

Wren's Gothic church of St. Mary, Aldermary, the towers of Westminster Abbey and the parish church at Warwick, are all more or less Gothic in style—the latter was rebuilt between 1694 and 1704 and the work includes the West Tower and the body of the church; the Chancel and adjacent Beauchamp Chapel being 15th-century work. The church building of the first half of the 18th century was practically all carried out in a plain Classical style except in large towns where such luxuries as porticoes and ashlar masonry could be afforded, but Gothic re-appeared as early as 1763 in the building of the new church at Croome D'Abitot near Pershore, and a church at Tetbury, Gloucestershire, built by Francis Hiorns of Warwick in 1781 is "Gothic."

So the Gothic traditions of church building never quite died out in England except, perhaps, between 1700 and 1760, and even during that half century or so, a certain amount of nondescript building was done in country districts that was more Gothic than Classical in feeling. The result of this survival of Gothic in church work has been to create a distinction between secular and ecclesiastical building which has given offence to many critics. They point out that in Classical times, all buildings were Classical, in Gothic times they were all Gothic, and they cannot see why in the present day we should not build everything in either Classic or Gothic or in some agreed form of modernist architecture.

No doubt it is desirable that a good vernacular style of architecture should be evolved, and that there should be consistency between secular and ecclesiastical architecture, but it is very doubtful whether these ends are likely to be attained as the results of spectacular experiments. It is also rather misleading to ignore the fact that both in Classical times and in the Middle Ages, although there may have been similarities between ecclesiastical and secular buildings, there were also very considerable differences between them.

Pericles did not reside in a Parthenon nor did William of Wykeham lodge his scholars in premises resembling a cathedral nave, or build castles for the king in any but the most up-to-date military fashion. It was not until the 18th century that the people of Berwick-on-Tweed built their town hall after the pattern of a Georgian church with steeple and portico complete, by the way quite a fine thing in itself, although masquerading in clerical trappings. And it was not until the 18th century that British squires discovered the delights of building themselves ruined abbeys or plaster castles to live in.

We do not know very much about domestic architecture in Ancient Egypt or Classical Greece, though perhaps we can guess to a certain extent what they may have been like if we investigate the drawings on Egyptian Papyri, the remains of Roman houses at Pompeii and elsewhere, and some of the early remains of domestic buildings in Syria. Such evidence as we have seems to show that in Classical and Early Christian times, whereas the architecture of temples and churches adhered to a great extent to tradition, that of civil and domestic buildings to an equally great extent disregarded convention. And it was the same in medieval times; though medieval churches were not made to conform to a traditional regulation pattern as the classical temples had been, still, they adhere to certain definite traditional arrangements and architectural character—for instance, a 14th-century church generally had arched and traceried windows. But in a 14th-century house, even suppose it was a stone one, the bulk of the windows would often be square headed, either single lights or mullioned ones; arched and traceried windows would only be used in the great hall and chapel, and the plan of a house would be arranged almost entirely with a view to convenience. Domestic conventions, such as the notion that a house should contain certain rooms for certain purposes, changed very much more rapidly than the traditions which governed church design, and the architectural detail of domestic work was much less distinctive than that of church work.

Thus, although there is more difference as regards general conception between a 13th-century house and a 16th-century one than there is between churches of similar periods, the exact opposite is the case as regards architectural "style." The 13th- and 16th-century churches are entirely different from each other in "style" although very much alike in their essentials, there is, on the other hand, not a great deal of difference between the architectural details of a 13th-century house and those of a 16th-century one, although the planning may be altogether different.

There exists in the present day a certain tendency in favour of avoiding ecclesiastical conventions in church building. To some of these undoubtedly sincere reformers it seems that a distinctively ecclesiastical church building is a hindrance and not a help to his work.

Although one cannot help admiring the enthusiasm and originality of those who search for new methods of contending against indifference, which is nowadays a more serious danger than hostility, it should be remembered that in the "ages of faith" ecclesiastical buildings have always been distinguishable, as far as possible, from secular ones. Furthermore, it is questionable if "conversion" is of much lasting value unless it includes some sort of open acknowledgement which would make it unnecessary to disguise a church as a cinema, or anything else but a church.

Sometimes the studious avoidance of ecclesiastical trappings may have unexpected results. For example, when the Westminster Aquarium was demolished and the site purchased for the Wesleyan Central Hall, it was decided to hold an architectural competition for the new building, and one of the conditions was that this should not be Gothic in style, because "Gothic was inconsistent with Wesleyanism." There is not the least doubt that the condition was a wise one, but the result has been a building with an uncomfortable suggestion of the Paris Opera House—not to mention the Casino at Monte Carlo—which is a very brilliant piece of architecture but not altogether reminiscent either of John Wesley or his brother Charles.

Assuming that one accepts the principle that a church ought to look like a church, there arises the question between tradition and modernism. But there is an alternative to both of these in the cult of negative simplicity—a cult which is attractive because it appears to have the merit of cheapness. Now cheapness is not in itself a bad quality if it means doing without luxuries, but it is anything but desirable if it means flimsy construction. Unless the church builder can afford substantial walls and stout timbers or their equivalents in modern constructive devices, he should, as a matter of principle, eschew all ornament and as a matter of policy would be well advised not to try to build a permanent church but to content himself with a more or less temporary building that could eventually be converted to secular or educational purposes. Granted, however, that sufficient funds are available for substantial construction of a perfectly plain permanent church, or alternatively, an equally plain mission building of less ambitious character, the task of the architect is very interesting one.

It goes without saying that no church or building of any kind is tolerable unless it serves its purpose, and this should be the first article of a builder's creed, but is it not part of the purpose of any building, especially a church, to serve that purpose in a beautiful manner? Costly materials and workmanship, good sculpture, a well-balanced colour scheme may be beyond the reach of a builder, but these are not the only sources of beauty in a building. Proportions, the right use of materials, attention to such matters as the arrangement of floor levels, the pitch of roof and the layout of a site, are more essential to beauty and fitness than any sort of ornament, and in the interior of a church

Wheatley
by G.E.Street

FIG. 2. ONE OF THE SMALLER CHURCHES
BUILT BY STREET.

66

there is always an opportunity for making use of the most effective and least costly of all methods of decoration, daylight.

In the simplest type of churches it is likely that "style" will become less and less pronounced as time goes on; one will hardly notice whether the builder has used round arches or pointed ones or concrete lintels; what will interest one will be the general outlines and colour of the building, its proportions, how it fits its site, how it fulfils its purpose, and how far its designer has been able to get an impression of internal space and dignity.

The unsophisticated builders of village churches in most countries excelled in giving distinction to quite small and unpretending structures so long as they themselves remained unsophisticated. Often the medieval builders, and generally the later builders, were more successful in their simplest work than in that of a more ambitious character. But things are different nowadays. Village builders are no longer accustomed to design village churches, and those who have to design cheap churches in poor parishes or for small communities have been educated in architects' offices or schools of art, where they have acquired knowledge, or rather learning (which is rather a different thing), which they are tempted to air on unsuitable occasions. On the other hand, they may realise the virtues of simplicity and practise them to the extent of affectation—yet many of them have been able to steer clear of the temptations that assailed them on either side, and some of the most successful modern churches have been some of the least ornate or ambitious (Fig. 2).

Often, too, the smaller modern churches in villages or hamlets have a greater effect of dignity than the rather larger ones and are more attractive in all ways, but it must be remembered that there are fewer practical problems to be solved in the building of a small church than there are when one is building a larger one, and it is only in exceptional cases that the building of a very small church is economically justifiable in the present day.

Moreover, although some very charming small churches have been built in modern times, a great many have been built which are very much the reverse of charming. This was especially the case in the Home Counties in the third quarter of the 19th century, when provincial architects were beginning to appreciate the charms of varnished pitch pine and tinted Cathedral glass, and when brasswork was cheap and popular and a "Cathedral Service" was the ambition of most country parsons and their organists. It would be unkind to name the less attractive efforts of the well-intentioned church builders of a past generation, but some of their more successful attempts may be recorded, amongst them Street's church at Farlington, Hants, Temple Moore's at Lake in the Isle of Wight, and Harrison Townsend's St. Martin's at Blackheath, Surrey. And, of course, there are a great many small medieval and a certain number of small Renaissance churches in England which satisfy all the requirements of a small community, and do so in the most beautiful manner, and the same thing is true about the village churches of a good many Continental countries. But the majority of modern churches are built in towns or their suburbs. The demand for village churches has been for the most part responded to in the past, and the present-day problem is generally that of building churches in newly-populated areas or in ancient villages which have undergone "development." Often the financial conditions are very difficult and economy is essential.

The church builders of the earlier half of Queen Victoria's reign were, as a rule, less successful with their suburban churches than they were in some of their town and village ones. Perhaps some of the names given to the suburbs of large cities were misleading. It may have been excusable that an architect designing a church to be enshrined in the groves of St. John's Wood or amongst the dewey meadows of Maida Vale, or the homesteads of Turnham Green, should have thought of heavenward pointing spires and lowly porches and storied windows richly dight.

And no doubt it was natural that the succeeding generation of Victorians should have gone French and Venetian and Queen Anne and Byzantine and neo-classical and functional, sometimes quite successfully, but often otherwise. The more level-headed of the later Victorian church builders such as Bodley, Micklethwaite and others of the old school were content to follow the traditions of Pugin and his contemporaries with this difference that they recognised the unsuitability of certain types of medieval churches as models for new churches in slums or in genteel suburbs, and thus avoided some of the most obvious mistakes of their predecessors. Meanwhile, Pearson was building his vaulted churches, often on quite a large scale, in a style which he made his own, and Sedding, Leonard Stokes, and Bentley were experimenting on rather less conventional lines. Between them, these men and some others of like ideas succeeded in building a number of churches that were very well adapted to the purposes for which they were designed, and which, in many cases, were both impressive and beautiful, although seldom very novel or startling. One can be fairly confident that any of these churches will be pleasant to use and pleasant to look at, just as one can be confident that any medieval church is worth while looking at and was suitable for its original purpose. But the satisfactory churches of the whole Victorian period are only a small minority, whereas the medieval churches, at any rate those in England, never fall below a certain standard, although they may be monotonous and sometimes rude and rather clumsy.

In very recent years, roughly speaking since the war of 1914–18, there has been some tendency towards building freak churches, some of them aggressively "functional," others following some recognised "style," Gothic, Romanesque or Renaissance. The functional ones may affect 14-in. walls, egg-shaped arches and plywood or brick furniture—or they may use lintels where one expects to find arches, and arches where one expects to find lintels. The Gothic ones aim at novelty in various ways—some are built squat and broad, others tall and narrow. Sometimes clerestories are built without any windows in them, and sometimes the aisles are without windows. Some are built of brick, stone and timber, others of brick and concrete and steel and papier mâché. So the builders of post-war churches will have plenty of models to choose from, and it will be interesting to see what novelties they will succeed in evolving.

It is rather singular that so many of these definitely unconventional churches should be Gothic in detail in spite of the pronouncements of the many "ex-cathedra" writers who have criticised the Gothic Revivalists, and in spite of the fact that domestic and secular Gothic is scarcely ever attempted deliberately in the present day. This persistence of Gothic convention in church building is, however, no new thing. Both in this country and in France the same thing existed in the 17th and even in the 18th century, except in the big sophisticated cities and on the estates of people of taste and culture. But when the "Gothic revival" started in the 18th century, it began by these people of taste and culture deciding that they would like to live in castles or ruined abbeys, which seemed to them both romantic and genteel. And so the revival of secular Gothic never really took root as a popular movement in spite of the fact that most of the traditions of medieval building persisted in country districts well into the 19th century for all sorts of un-pretending work such as farm-houses, cottages and agricultural buildings. On the other hand, even at the end of the 18th century, the great majority of churches in England were medieval ones and it seemed perfectly natural to every one except to the highbrows that churches should be Gothic.

So when the Gothic revivalists started building churches instead of building castles for the glorification of the feudal classes and the new rich, it all seemed to come quite naturally and the slow-witted Englishman complacently accepted the new Gothic churches just as if there had never been such a person as Sir Christopher Wren, and the attitude has persisted to the present day. This may be very illogical, but it is a factor to be reckoned with and possibly not one to be deplored; things might have worked out otherwise if it had not been the case that church building had almost ceased in England from the time of Queen Elizabeth until the end of the 18th century, with a brief interlude in the latter half of the 17th century.

It will be generally agreed that the buildings of the future should be distinctive and unmistakably work of the post-war period. This will probably be the case whether it is desired or not, since it is fairly certain that building conditions will be very different from those of pre-war days. New materials and constructive methods will have to be accepted, but these are capable of intelligent use and, indeed, may give great opportunities to the architects. Thus if it is decided to build a colonnade instead of an arcade, it can be done without any false constructions by using rein-forced concrete beams in place of arches, and reinforced concrete can be used in constructing substantial vaulted ceilings which do not require buttressing, as well as fire-resisting flat floors, and roofs and foundation rafts, which will in some cases insure a building from the risks of uneven settlements. In post-war years it is likely that there will be a shortgage of building timber, and some sort of rationing of nearly all buildings materials, and it is almost inevitable that the architectural character of post-war churches will largely depend upon what materials will be available.

It will be well if the church builders err on the side of caution in adopting some of the materials and devices which are sure to be advertised after the war is over. In the past a good many architects have had cause to repent of their own credulity concerning the promises made by advertisers, and have learned by bitter experience that false prophets make dangerous guides.

By now, however, we have had sufficient experience to be able to say that reinforced concrete and some other modern methods of construction may be good servants even if they are sometimes bad masters. And if such inventions are made use of, it is obviously desirable to discover an artistic way of doing so. In the case of concrete, for instance, the material is coarse in texture and the forms are produced by a process of casting, so it would not be appropriate to attempt any elaborate detail—neither is any excessive sharpness of outline as a rule agreeable, since it seems to contradict the plastic nature of concrete and to be inconsistent with the coarseness of its texture.

A certain indefiniteness of form suggests itself as appropriate to concrete construction and the different planes or curved surfaces should not intersect each other abruptly. Thus, in a concrete pier or beam, the edges look best if they are slightly chamfered or rounded, and in a concrete vault a plain or ribbed tunnel looks well, and so does a dome or a round arched intersecting groin, but an acute pointed arch or a groined vault of pointed section looks hard and mechanical, as does also a sharp angled, square section beam or pillar. Concrete, in short, should not be treated as if it were freestone or marble, and similar principles should apply to other modern materials. If this is done a characteristic "style" of the later 20th century will come into being without violent or even conscious effort, even if some of our churches are to be vaulted in stone or in concrete and others roofed with timber or possibly steel, and if some are built with pointed arches and others with round ones or no arches at all.

One cannot prophesy what the prevailing style of the future will be, but one can look back at the past and perhaps learn from its failures and successes.

Some very suggestive work was done at the commencement of the Renaissance in most of the "Latin" countries of Europe and in the Norman and Breton provinces of France, and no doubt similar church work would have been done in England had church building not ceased here in the 16th century. In the Continental churches of this class, Gothic and Classic forms are used together; sometimes one fashion prevails, sometimes the other. Often the Classic detail is so simple as to be hardly distinguishable from 11th-century Romanesque.

An extremely interesting modern church inspired by some of these early Renaissance buildings was that of St. Anselm, Davies Street, London, designed by Thackeray Turner—a brick building of excellent proportion and outline, with round arches, traceried windows, and timber ceilings carried upon stone arches. This was unhappily destroyed a few years ago, not by enemy action, but in pursuance of ecclesiastical policy; it was one of the outstanding pieces of church building done in the last quarter of the 19th century.

Regarding the type of plan that is likely to be favoured, it should be remembered that unless funds are available for carrying out an intrinsically costly plan in a first-class manner, it is sound policy to adopt an economical general plan, and to carry it out well. Nothing is so disappointing as an ambitious scheme that has to be starved or scamped. We cannot expect to discover a new type of building every time a church is to be built, and it is probably very undesirable that we should do so, but we can learn from existing buildings what to follow and what to avoid, and experience seems to show that the best models for the churches that are likely to be wanted in the next few years, are planned with extreme simplicity.

The planning of parish churches such as Saffron Walden or Southwold in the East or Bodmin or Kenton in the West country fulfil all the practical requirements of a modern Anglican church, and were recognised as the best models for modern Roman Catholic churches by the school of Pugin and Hadfield. Pugin's church at Derby is on these lines. So are most of the late 19th-century churches by Bodley and the younger Scott and Micklethwaite. The chief deficiency of the medieval examples is the absence of adequate vestries, which is easily corrected in building a new church. There are other types of medieval churches which are beautiful and romantic, but are not good models for such churches as will be wanted in new centres of population. Such are the grand cruciform church at Ludlow, St. Mary's at Oxford with its long aisleless chancel, or Grantham church with its long dark nave, or Dorchester Abbey.

It is not suggested that any of these churches are inconvenient or that one would prefer to see them replaced with differently planned buildings. On the contrary, we can admire them and learn from them, and it is our duty to preserve and to use them; but to copy them, unless in most exceptional circumstances, would be like talking in Shakespearian or Biblical language. No doubt some abnormal churches will be built in the future, but it is not to be desired that they should be copied from older buildings, although old ideas may be embodied in their design.

It may be that the style of post-war churches will not be a revival of any bygone "period" work, but that it will disregard tradition and the lessons that can be learned from the work of past generations. Possibily the most dangerous temptation to be guarded against will be that of indulgence in slovenliness and calling it simplicity, or restraint, or perhaps refinement. It saves so much trouble to dispense with all ornament except the Polynesian variety of sculpture and to design random assemblages of rectangular structures of no particular proportion, and to use strange materials like aluminium and fancy glass-ware; it takes so much more trouble to produce good ornament and sculpture that is decorative without being grotesque and architecture that has character without being affected or aggressive. Most people too will agree that they would prefer churches to look different from secular buildings, and, generally speaking, their arrangements must be governed by the liturgical requirements of those who have to use them; it can hardly be expected that liturgies will be revised in order to suit new types of church buildings.

On the other hand, the modern church requires certain things which we do not often find in medieval or even Renaissance churches in this country and which have been provided for in a makeshift manner in the last 100 years.

The vestry accommodation in an old English church is generally very limited; nowadays ample vestries with lavatories and church cleaners' rooms should be provided as far as possible; again the question of an organ has to be considered, and artificial lighting and heating are essential.

It may be regrettable that the present generation is so exacting as it is, but unfortunately there are a good many people who insist upon having these things, and it is not practicable to disregard the demand for them.

The provision of vestries, etc., is a simple enough problem on most sites, except, of course, that the more ample the accommodation, the greater will be the cost. Organs are a difficulty in many churches, and a good many things will depend upon what provision is made for them. Heating and lighting engineers are often sworn enemies of an architect, and are aided and abetted by co-belligerent members of a congregation or church council.

Regarding the internal arrangement and furnishing of a church, this will of course vary according to circumstances. There appears to be a certain tendency among Nonconformist bodies to equip their churches in a manner not conspicuously different from modern Anglican practice, and there are no essential differences between the requirements of Anglican and Roman Catholic churches so far as their architecture and furniture are concerned. These externals are no longer regarded as badge of orthodoxy among the majority of Christian communities, but there are a few who, like the Salvation Army and the Society of Friends, have no set forms of worship. Others, like the Eastern Christians, have their own traditional methods of church arrangement. Obviously, too, if one builds synagogues or mosques, one has to arrange them appropriately, but the number of these is very small as compared with that of churches, in which there is no liturgical need for unusual planning.

Nevertheless, one is given a choice in building a new church—not a choice between Anglican or Roman Catholic or Presbyterian or Baptist or high church or low church arrangements—but between traditional and modern principles.

There is much to be said for both alternatives, the traditional view is especially identified with Anglicanism, conservatism, and insularity, the modern with the cosmopolitanism of the Roman Catholic Church and the revolutionary or reforming spirit of Nonconformity. There are, however, two distinct schools of modernism, one aims at pure functionalism devoid of style, and studiously disregarding all precedent, the other affecting modernism by reviving the forgotten styles of prehistoric or ultra primitive, or perhaps even savage buildings, and presenting the results as artistic discoveries—often getting away with the goods. Every builder of a new church must make his own choice as between tradition and modernity. If tradition is to be followed, let us make sure that we are not led into absurdities by inaccurate knowledge of the past; for instance, do not assume that the internal disposition of an average Victorian church resembles in all respects that of the medieval English churches which the Victorians imagined they were reproducing. And on the other hand, if we are going to disregard traditional forms, do not let us proclaim our cleverness from the housetops by being aggressively functional or aggressively archaic or by wilful disregard of convention.

There are certain details of church arrangement which are definitely debatable, such for instance as the position of the choir and organ, and there are others which should be dictated by definite liturgical requirements and which are therefore not debatable.

The church builder should master the essential rudiments of church arrangement and study the alternatives that may legitimately be adopted in debatable matters.

Whether we build traditional or modernist churches in the future, it is to be hoped we shall be able to make them look at home in their surroundings. The Victorian builders were, perhaps, too anxious to build "pretty" churches. Perhaps we are nowadays sometimes too fearful of being misled by their example; they were apt to build country churches in towns, sometimes we have built cockney churches in the country. The great majority of churches built during the last half century have, however, been in newly developed suburbs or building estates, and their sites and surroundings have been the reverse of inspiring—corner plots, iron railings, shrubs, notice boards and villas or cottages of gentility with more railings and more shrubs. Of course it would be wrong to give up the whole thing in disgust on account of uncongenial surroundings, but on many of these suburban sites, a building such as a church cannot depend for its effect upon its setting.

On the other hand, the surroundings of every church should largely govern the practical details of the planning so as to ensure convenient access, good light, proper drainage, freedom from noisy traffic, sufficient prominence, the most effective placing of towers, etc. And as a general rule it is best, where possible, to use traditional local materials and types of design ; for example, to abstain from red tile roofs in Cornwall and Cotswold slates in the home counties.

In post-war church building it is likely that there will be a fair amount of reconstruction work in town and village churches. The opportunity of building a genuine village church in an old churchyard is a delightful one, provided all the people concerned in the work pull together. Here the whole design of the church from foundation to roof tree, inside and out, should be inspired by its setting. Here, perhaps, we may legitimately incline to traditional methods of building and principles of design. A country churchyard is hardly an appropriate place in which to display one's cleverness or advertise one's originality. It is not always necessary to fill the whole of the village church, or any church for that matter, with pews or organs and brazen birds, or to adorn it with elaborate ornament of any kind, although rich and costly village churches are sometimes comparable to pearls of great price, and amongst these are some modern, as well as many ancient, examples. But whether the country church is rich or simple, it seems specially fitting that it should be built of local materials and in a manner not at variance with local traditions of design, that the new Cornish church should be Cornish, and the Yorkshire one Yorkshire in character, although it is not advocated that the new work should in either case be indistinguishable from old.

Perhaps the best opportunities a church builder has is when he is dealing with a genuine town site amongst buildings of moderate height and somewhat irregular arrangement. Truro Cathedral is an outstanding example of what can be accomplished on a site of this description. A more deliberate piece of planning is the arrangement of Nash's church in Langham Place, where the alignment of the surrounding streets was designed by the architect of the church with quite exceptional success. Here, however, we come up against the great drawback of town sites, the prospect of surrounding buildings being enlarged or reconstructed in such a way as to swallow up the churches which at first dominated them.

Some of Wren's churches have suffered this fate to a greater extent than the Langham Place church, notably the steeple of St. Magnus the Martyr, near London Bridge. But the most extreme case is that of Trinity Church, New York— a good sized and handsome Perpendicular building with a tall western spire, the weathercock on which looks into the windows of the surrounding skyscrapers, "which," as Euclid says, " is absurd."

The moral seems to be that in town sites it is essential to find out as far as it is possible, what probability there is of the development of the surroundings of a new church. In some places it is safe to build towers and domes that will dominate the neighbouring buildings ; in other cases it may be wiser to avoid competition with them and to concentrate upon the interior effect of one's new church. In any case, it is manifestly a mistake to deliberately build a tower or spire in a town unless

St. Chad's Birmingham
A.W. Pugin (aged 27) 1839

FIG. 3. PUGIN'S CATHEDRAL OF ST. CHAD AT BIRMINGHAM.

one builds a good large one that will at any rate hold its own so far as can be reasonably foreseen.

Sites like the Rock of Durham and the river bank at Stratford-on-Avon are exceptional, but there are many places in which advantage can be taken of some slope in the ground or alignment of roads or other similar circumstance to give character and individuality to a church or other building. An instance of this can be seen in Pugin's Cathedral of St. Chad at Birmingham, built in the first five years of Queen Victoria's reign. The building has been criticised, possibly rather unfairly considering the difficulties the architect had to contend with, and it must be admitted that the principal front with its two spires is not particularly dignified, but the site slopes steeply in a "diagonal" direction, and the surrounding buildings are low; the site is very irregular and the plan of the church follows its boundaries as far as possible, with the result that the apse, with a lofty crypt underneath it, and the flank of the building, pile up in a surprisingly effective manner which has been overlooked by many critics of Pugin's work.

The sites of Liverpool and Lincoln Cathedrals are as imposing as that of Durham, but less dramatic, and most people would say that a hill-top site was the ideal one from the point of view of dignity. Yet the effect of Ely Cathedral as seen from the east is almost, if not quite as imposing as that of Durham from the west, although the hill on which Ely is built is quite a low one. Again the sites of Llandaff Cathedral at the foot of a steep hill, and of Wells Cathedral and Abbey Dore in broader valleys have very definite charms of their own. Post-war builders are not likely to have opportunities of building churches even on the scale of Llandaff or Abbey Dore, but there is this to be learned regarding the sites of new churches, that the more obvious advantages of an elevated and open site as compared with a sheltered and secluded one are sometimes more apparent than real. The essential conditon of a satisfactory building scheme is that the building shall fit its purpose and fit its site, and if the site has a certain individuality and the building conforms to this, the more interesting and attractive the result will be.

As a great deal of the church building of the next few years is likely to take the form of rebuilding upon old sites in towns which have suffered war damage, it is probable that certain questions will arise in connection with town planning schemes. There is likely to be a tendency on the part of town planners to arrange vistas and public gardens and other similar amenities around the sites of important ancient churches whether these have escaped destruction or not. It is possible that this sort of thing may be carried too far, especially in the case of medieval town churches; these were often built in narrow streets and their planning was determined by the limitations of their sites. To obliterate those limitations makes the building unintelligible and may often make it appear ugly by exposing what was never intended to be seen. This is very much the case with Wren's London churches, perhaps even more so than with some medieval town churches which at any rate are generally equally well finished all round, whereas Wren did not pay much attention to the backs and sides of most of his churches, unless they faced a street. Those who know the city of Rouen will recollect the formal square and the public gardens round St. Ouen, and the contrast with the narrow crooked streets round the cathedral, and will acknowledge the perfection of the architecture of St. Ouen (barring its west front), though they may think it stands aloof from the city and misses the friendliness and romance of the less perfect and regular cathedral. Municipal improvements may be all very well in their way but should be accepted with caution when ancient buildings are concerned. Sometimes, however, war damage has revealed beauty in unsuspected places. The most striking instance of this is perhaps the view of St. Paul's Cathedral from the east—possibly the most favourable quarter for appreciating the lines of the building. The preservation of this view would seem quite as valuable as the suggested street of stairs leading from the river to the south transept of the cathedral.

The war has destroyed much that was valuable in and about our churches, but it has also destroyed a good many things which can well be spared with considerable resignation, for example, iron railings and stained-glass windows and slum property. When the time comes to put things in order again, it is to be hoped that enthusiasm will not outrun discretion, and that reformers will not destroy what has hitherto been spared.

Church Acoustics ↶ By HOPE BAGENAL, F.R.I.B.A.

DURING THE 18TH CENTURY the ordinary parish church with its galleries, family pews, lofty pulpit, curtains and coats of arms, had good rather than bad acoustics. How homely and familiar some of these churches that survive appear to us to-day. Had they nothing to be said for them? Was the Gothic Revival right in attempting to sweep away that characteristic interior and all it stood for? If I were to choose a citadel of English religious life I should still seek out some good old unrestored St. Nicholas church in a coast town, where the spirit of the generations—countless mothers with children, seafaring fathers, merchants and their apprentices, soldiers and their girls—still haunt about its shape and about the ancient furnishings. Here are spirits not dead but living: they too have held to their faith and to their country in times of war. It is in fact the spirit of the family in a natural religious form that for a moment pleads against the scepticism of modern life—it is the religion of the middle way, a mysticism and a common sense laid side by side. And not without good argument. From the high pulpit, from which the preacher could command the galleries also, he mitigates the rigours of Evangelicalism with the inspiration of William Law or the fine charity of Thomas Cooper.

But our grandparents changed all that.

Leaning from the pulpit of St. Mary's, with the judges of assize and the University notables settling themselves beneath him, Keble gave out his text: "As for me, God forbid that I should sin against the Lord in ceasing to pray for you, but I will teach you the good and the right way." It is the assize sermon of July 14, 1833, and the Oxford Movement has begun. Now the great Tractarians were great preachers and Newman laid stress on the sermon. But fortunately for them, and for their teaching, the churches they used were, in those early days, still in the auditorium tradition of the previous century so that they were well heard. If their mission had depended on the acoustics of the Gothic Revival church type, later to come into being, it would not have been so effectively heard—might not have been *heard* at all. For in the next generation through the length and breadth of the land the parish churches were restored. The old decent plaster was scraped off the walls, galleries and high pulpits removed, old woodwork scrapped, memorials, curtains, screens, old organ cases, swept away. Doubtless much lumber was got rid of, but the process left the typical church unfurnished and bare. The sound absorbents were removed and the result was the characteristic long reverberation which made for bad preaching conditions. The element of the shrine had been restored,

78

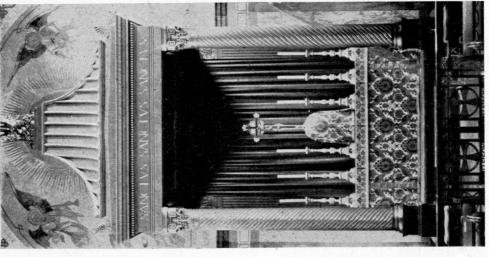

15. ALTAR IN THE CHURCH OF ST. MARY,
HOLLY PLACE, HAMPSTEAD
By A. Gilbert Scott

14. HIGH ALTAR IN THE CHURCH OF THE SACRED HEART OF JESUS
AND ST. JOSEPH AT WARE, HERTFORDSHIRE

Photo by F. S. Doble, Liverpool

16. ST. HELEN, SEFTON, LANCASHIRE

but at the cost of the element of the auditorium. And the new churches were loftier and their reverberation even longer than the existing restored buildings.

Now we must not underrate the Gothic Revival. Space, proportion, a communicating of devotion, these things the great architects of the last century won for us; and the sense of them must be preserved. It has given us great works of art—the churches of Pearson and Bodley and Temple Moore, and Liverpool Cathedral by Sir Giles Scott. The imaginative wealth of enduring Christian worship, luminous in the Middle Ages, was then rediscovered. But also one must not deny the sheer bad art that accompanied the movement and grew out of it. And not only bad but inappropriate and crippling. The bad acoustics of many 19th-century churches are a confession of failure. An Anglican church is not primarily an auditorium; I believe it to be primarily a shrine, yet such is the delicate balance between God's word and His Sacrament that if such a church is not also an auditory it may turn out to be *a nothing at all*.

And now the scene has again changed. Architects have a new problem and a new responsibility. To-day Christianity is a religion in action. It is vital that the words of the New Testament shall be heard. If they can be heard one might say that Christianity is invincible. To-day there are large numbers of people who have not heard and do not know those words. They have heard about them, but have not heard them. A recent writer in the *Spectator* has calculated that not more than ten per cent of the population can be considered practising Christians of any denomination; another notes that: "The work of St. Gregory, who sent missionaries to the English, would seem to need doing again." Therefore essential education in Christianity is necessary—education in the acts and words of Our Lord, in His ideas and in the great interpretations of them. And for this there is a demand. People now as in early Christian times do not go to church to follow the mode: if they go it is because they are asking and seeking. Congregations now may be small, but they are more sincere. And this applies to all forms of Church worship.

And so this—the mission side—cannot be ignored in any new church. We can define our particular problem as restoring the auditorium element without sacrificing the primacy of the shrine. How shall we keep that eternal thing in its central position, and yet also serve the needs of Christian education? We do not want a reaction, a futile swing of the pendulum, but an intelligent synthesis—a placing of the two side by side, and to use our art in making a relatively inexpensive building noble and beautiful.

Preaching Conditions

"Reverberation" is the term given to the duration of a sound in any enclosed space after the source has ceased. Extreme cases are fairly well known—cases such as the Taj Mahal, the Baptistery at Pisa, and to a lesser degree St. Paul's Cathedral. Reverberation varies directly with volume so that the larger the church (other things being equal) the longer the reverberation. For this reason reverberation is often found in churches, especially in those having vaults, domes and deep transeptal spaces. There is, therefore, a good first reason for restricting height and space in a church design, and seeking for moderate proportions rather than for a theatrical height. This was in fact recognised by Wren when he wrote "it should seem vain to make a parish church larger than that all who are present can both hear and see . . . to build more room than that every person may conveniently hear and see is to create noise and confusion." Again reverberation varies inversely as the amount of sound absorption present—that is to say as the amount of curtains, carpets, furnishings, special absorbing linings, and, above all, members of the congregation. Of these absorbing factors, members of the congregation are generally the most effective, and indeed it is a matter of common observation that a full church generally makes for very much better preaching conditions. That is to say the more "absorbent" the church the shorter the reverberation. Now modern hard hygienic wall linings, hard plasters, hard flooring materials absorb very little sound, and we find often extreme complaints of bad acoustics in moderate-sized churches built of hard lining materials to hold 500 or 600 and having present only fifty or sixty people. Good design suggests, therefore, that new churches should not be over ambitious in scale and that some money should be included in the first cost for sound absorbing materials. It suggests also that furnishings such as curtains, tapestries, carpets are valuable; and in fact the beautiful hangings in a church like Thaxted play a functional as well as a decorative part. A tapestry can be as beautiful as a stained-glass window, and can be useful.

A theoretical approach to reverberation as a physical phenomenon exists. It is enough here to say that reverberation is defined as the length of time in seconds taken for a sound of standard loudness to die away to the minimum audible. The standard of loudness chosen is roughly that of the speaking voice. Reverberation can be distinguished from echo. If any one should

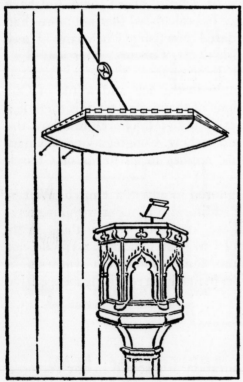

FIG. I. A CONVEX SOUNDING BOARD.

clap his hands in a large empty church he will detect two kinds of response—a sharp clap back, or echo ; and a much longer dying away of the sound, or reverberation. Echo is a single reflection from a remote surface (wall or vault) whereas reverberation is the result of prolonged inter-reflection from a large number of surfaces and may last audibly in a large church for five or six seconds.

Now since the interval between syllables in speech at normal speeds is only one-twentieth of a second, it is clear that an echo just filling up the syllable intervals may make speech unintelligible. A long reverberation causing the prolonging of each syllable for several seconds must greatly obscure speech at ordinary speeds ; and though by speaking slowly, and dissociating syllables, clear speaking can be achieved under such conditions, yet the slowness prevents intimate delivery and restricts the preacher. It is fairly well known that a visiting preacher in St. Paul's Cathedral is warned that his sermon must contain about half the number of words he would utter in a normal parish church. For good preaching in a moderate-sized church reverberation should not be longer by ear than about two to two and a half seconds. In buildings of the Free Church communions, where preaching requirements are emphasised, it ought to be shorter ; in large churches where a tradition of choral music exists it may require to be longer.

We may make a first summing up, therefore, by saying that good preaching conditions require absence of echo and a relatively short reverberation, and add the practical comment that a church of small cube per seat with an open-textured lime plaster, undistempered, some well disposed curtains in folds, and a fibre-board ceiling, may have fair acoustics initially, and therefore require but little outlay on the more expensive sound-absorbing materials.

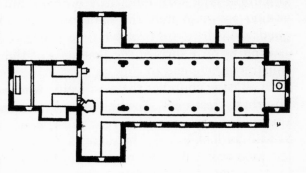

CRUCIFORM PLAN

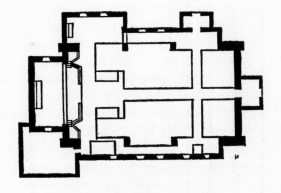

AUDITORIUM PLAN

FIG. 2. CHURCH PLAN TYPES COMPARED.

Some Practical Points

And let us add to this one or two practical points. The higher the pulpit the wider the angle of impact of the sound, and therefore the more effective. But more effective still is the provision of a rear wall behind the preacher's back, and for this purpose a pulpit is well placed on the return wall of the chancel arch or in the angle (Fig. 2, lower plan). This position is better than against a pier of the nave. A "sounding board" is generally useful in lofty churches, but not generally useful in the smaller churches. Its function is both to cut off some of the vertical sound reaching the vault, and also to increase the volume of sound directed upon the congregation by reflection from the canopy. For both these purposes the spread of the canopy must be large; more efficient reflection is given if the ceiling of the canopy be tilted or made convex. (Fig. 1.) Good hearing from the lectern is just as important as from the pulpit, yet how often it happens that the sermon is just intelligible and the lessons not intelligible at all. This suggests that the Early Christian ambones, or equal rostra, at a good height above floor level, offer a solution in a familiar mode. In Fig. 2 is illustrated two types of plan, namely the cruciform type with long, narrow nave and deep transepts; and a broader type, seating approximately the same number. The cruciform does not easily provide good acoustics; the broader type can give good auditorium conditions without ceasing to be a shrine: the positions of the ambones, each with a back wall, are illustrated here and in Fig. 5.

In all large churches the west wall—where there is no gallery—requires a sound-absorbing treatment. Acoustic boards, or tiles, or one of the felt, or asbestos spray treatments, are desirable. This presents an æsthetic problem that must be faced. It will not look exactly the same as the other wall surfaces, however disguised; but the west wall is not *under contemplation* by regular church-goers, as is the east wall and window, and could be treated as a functional unit with appropriate decoration. The lower portion should be hung with curtains in folds. It is worth noting that a useful absorbent for church roofs is the type of "wood-wool" board which can be fixed between purlins and can be distempered without spoiling its sound-absorbing properties. In the case of the felt and spray treatments, paint or distemper is liable to give a crust or shell which spoils the sound-absorbing properties.

Some wall linings provide, naturally, greater sound absorption than others. For instance a lime plaster having a sand-faced finishing coat, not gauged with cement, is better than a hard gypsum plaster. But if the lime plaster be distempered then its slight porosity is destroyed and it loses its advantage. If not distempered it presents difficulties as to evenness of colour where new work comes next the old. This can be met by designing in bays and arranging to finish each bay before breaking off work. If "acoustic plaster" be used technical difficulties arise owing to the dryness of the mix, and a firm having experience ought to be employed. Domes, barrels, and segmental ceilings will require powerful sound absorbents, giving seventy per cent or eighty per cent absorption at least, if the sound focusing effect liable to cause echo is to be noticeably reduced. In designing new churches, domes and barrels ought to be avoided. Segmental ceilings having radius of curvature struck from floor level, or near it, are particularly dangerous and are frequently found associated with serious complaints.

Types of church building easily giving good acoustics are the English Perpendicular hall church, such as St. Margaret's, Westminster (Fig. 3), having a wood roof; the smaller "basilican" or early Christian type; the Wren City church of the smaller variety having a flat ceiling. These parental types are appropriate to-day.

Music Traditions

But the church designer will rightly say that the church at all times has had another function besides a preaching place, and that he must think of "quires and places where they sing." The church as a building has always contributed to purely choral music; and for a good reason. Reverberation as such enhances choral tone, and a reverberation not too long and not too short can give ideal choral conditions. And to-day the veritable renaissance in music must find some expression in church requirements. One might say that neither the extreme of pulpit conditions on the one hand, nor of choral or organ tone on the other, are now quite logical. The Free Churches are concerned to get good music, and Anglican and Roman churches with their musical services also want the sermon to be heard.

Here again let us pick up the intelligent acoustic traditions in order to see where we stand. First we must note that the very long reverberation of the lofty Gothic church, with its tonality or "note," produced in medieval times beautiful unaccompanied "plainsong" or modal music, which culminated in the services and masses of Palestrina and Byrd. There is no finer art than choral music of this kind, but its performance is difficult: it cannot be said to be a central requirement of to-day, yet must always attract, and exert a strong influence. And where it exists it must be respected. Any uninformed alteration to a large church where unaccompanied singing is a tradition may destroy that tradition. The reason is that the long reverberation with its allied phenomenon of a tonality or "note" enables the choir to keep in tune when singing unaccompanied, but if the reverberation be shortened the sustaining of pitch may be made very difficult or impossible. Conversely a very "dead" church can be improved for modal music by removing absorbents, distempering walls, or by adding a barrel vault, and thus increasing reverberation. Recent scholarship seems to show that there were many pre-Reformation organs in parish churches and that they were used for little more than "doubling the voices" in the plain chant. This looks as if their chief function was to keep priest, clerk and congregation in tune in the smaller churches which, unlike the cathedrals, had not a marked tonality able to give an easy reciting note and keep the pitch.

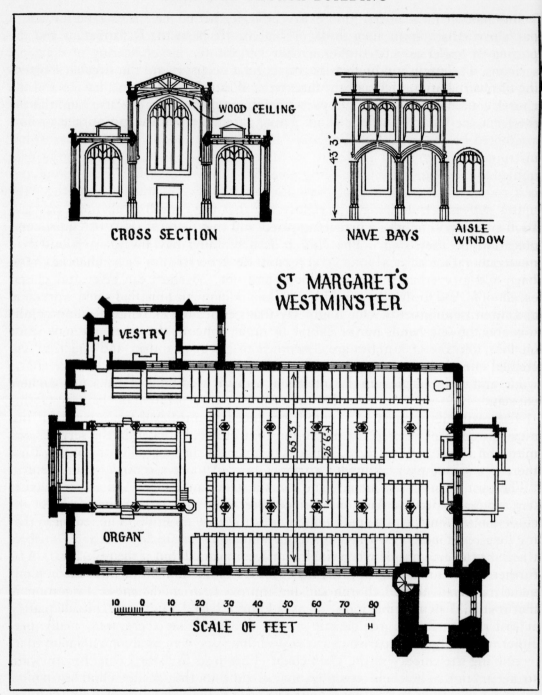

CROSS SECTION   WOOD CEILING

NAVE BAYS   AISLE WINDOW

ST MARGARET'S WESTMINSTER

VESTRY

ORGAN

SCALE OF FEET

FIG. 3. A GOOD ACOUSTIC PLAN TYPE.

84

But another musical tradition exists, namely, that of the "west gallery," and it has a particular significance to-day. This goes back to the Reformation and the putting of galleries into Lutheran churches for the larger hearing of doctrinal sermons. The result was an increase in sound absorption and a noticeable shortening of reverberation. This meant that stringed instruments when they entered the church could be well heard, and part-writing for strings was effective; and this set the scene for Bach. His cantatas, his great Latin mass and the two Passions—now attempted by choirs all over England—have not instrumental *accompaniments* but instrumental *parts*, and these are as important as the voices. The works gain immensely in their setting by being performed in a church rather than in a concert room, but if instrumental parts are lost owing to "cathedral acoustics" the music suffers seriously. The reverberation of the Thomaskirche at Leipzig—Bach's church (Fig. 4)—when I measured and calculated it was, with a full congregation, between two and a half and three seconds. This again points to a moderate rather than a long reverberation as desirable for large churches. The Bach Cantata Club in London found that St. Margaret's, Westminster, was excellent for the performance of the B Minor Mass with a choir of thirty-six voices and twenty-two instruments. The reverberation with an audience factor of 1,000 was about two seconds by the Sabine formula. A healthy national music depends on local centres and nothing is more hopeful to-day than the practice, increased during the war, by which several local choirs learn parts of a large choral work and combine together later in a festival performance in some suitable church.

The planning of choir and organ has a bearing on the problem connected with music in smaller churches. In the Report of the Archbishop of Canterbury's Committee on Music in Worship a number of very valuable suggestions are made. First there is a strong plea for unison singing *in order to improve congregational music.* "The term 'unison' is intended to include the simultaneous singing in octaves (*e.g.* women or boys singing the melody together with men) while it does not exclude the alternate singing in two different octaves, men and boys (or women) taking turns, and indeed this last is in many ways more musically effective. The choir when it is leading the congregational worship may then sing in unison also." And further, "when good unison singing is recovered some instrumental accompaniment may well be added without spoiling the singing." Another suggestion is that it should be possible in the smaller churches to "select and train adequately at least a quartet or double quartet of mixed voices. These 'chanters' could sing, either with the main body of unison singing, forming a vocal accompaniment to it, or else in alternation with it. They could either lead the rest; or, if the rest were strong enough to go their own way, they could then sing descants and settings in the tenor as well as the ordinary settings. Great variety and richness could thus be secured, but all on the basis of unison and congregational singing. To attain this

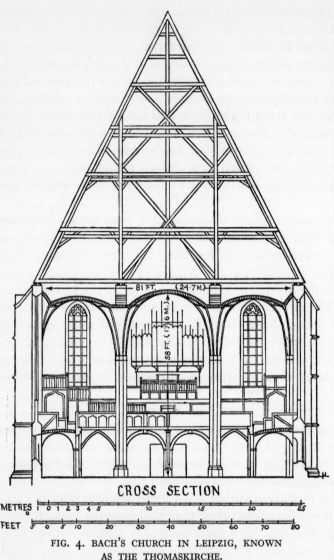

CROSS SECTION

FIG. 4. BACH'S CHURCH IN LEIPZIG, KNOWN
AS THE THOMASKIRCHE.

it would be often well worth while to transform a good deal of the inefficient part singing that now goes on in the crowded chancels of many small churches of this type. To the chanters would also naturally fall the task of supplementing the congregational singing by special pieces of their own, additional to the general service."

Part singing is not of course ruled out: "wherever an aptitude for part singing is found among members of a congregation, it should be encouraged . . . then the various alternations of unison and part singing should be carefully cultivated." The object is to "bring about an alliance of the choir and the musical portion of the congregation."

The Archbishop's report also recognises that "the chancel in most of our small medieval parish churches is too narrow to be convenient for a choir and too separate to be a place of worship." Clearly the relative position of the "chanters," of choir and organ, and of congregation, can help or hinder this movement towards better congregational music and more corporate worship. The tunnel chancel is now commonly superseded by a wider and less deep Sanctuary. Also a good method is to have a relatively small choir in the nave on the same level as the congregation with seats behind them for members of the congregation, who will lead the unison singing. A choir having stalls planned in this way is seen at the Keble Church, Mill Hill (Fig. 5), and it will be noted that a fairly wide nave is required. A suitable position for a choir without surplices is on a very slightly

86

raised dais at the west end behind the congregation, but this should be confined to naves fairly short in length.

It should be noted that the Archbishop's report gives official approval to the west position. "Although it is obviously impossible to lay down a hard and fast rule, experience shows that in most small churches the most satisfactory position for the choir and organ is behind the congregation. Support is best given to the congregation in this way." And it is added that "the Committee would like to think that, given the proper balance of harmony, the old village orchestra could be reinstated in the west gallery to accompany the hymns, the remainder of the singing to be unaccompanied. This west-end choir should be regarded as leaders of the congregation, but where there are 'chanters' also they may well occupy seats in the chancel."

Architects will note that all this points in planning to a demand for a shorter, broader, type of church; and such a plan type will help rather than hinder good hearing from the pulpit.

Position of the Organ

In the larger churches "unison singing," says the Archbishop's report, "ought to be steadier and more solid. Therefore, more can be attempted in the way of descants." It will be noted that the emphasis is still laid on the value of unison singing. "Also there should be more alternation or antiphony between the choir and congregation. And in both psalms and hymns there should be many verses sung in unison while the organ provides varied harmonies. . . . And endeavours should be made to bring about an alliance with the choir and the musical portion of the congregation."

In larger churches the principle could be adopted of having the nave more sound-absorbing and the choir portion more reverberant. A large church all in one cell tends to be dull, but if chancel and transepts are too long and narrow they will tend to have each a marked tonality which may not be the same as the nave, and this will not make for an alliance between choir and congregation. Yet on occasions of festival remote positions for the choir can be useful. "In many ways," says the report, "it would be a gain if more of the music appointed for the choir alone were sung without accompaniment. In some large

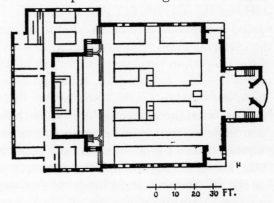

FIG. 5. PLAN OF THE JOHN KEBLE CHURCH, MILL HILL. (Architect: *D. F. Martin Smith*).

churches, on special occasions, the choir with its conductor could be stationed behind the altar, or in a chapel, or at the west end, when some great service of the polyphonic school might be executed. The effect of the delicate and distant sounds thus produced, by contrast with the sonorous tones of the organ and the voices of the congregation in singing the hymns, might be extraordinarily beautiful."

Organs from an acoustic point of view are well placed when they are in the main cell of the church and under the same ceiling as choir and congregation. This is specially important if they are to lead congregational singing. Thus neither a deep transept nor a bay of the choir aisle is a good position. But a shallow transept formed by carrying up a bay of the nave aisle the full height of the church gives a good organ position suitable for a choir in a forward position and is good also for leading congregational singing. A tall tribune gallery in the first bay of the choir allowing some projection of the choir organ can be satisfactory for a trained choir in a forward position, but often causes complaints for congregational singing. Choir and organ together on a west gallery are acoustically right, but the gallery must be large. In cases where consoles are detached the instrument itself ought not to be farther away than twenty or thirty feet.

The Presbyterian Church

Presbyterian churches to-day both in Scotland and in Northern Ireland are designed with the pulpit moved to the side and frequently with transepts. But this has altered the Presbyterian service which depended for its character and beauty on Knox's careful balance between the two sacraments of baptism and communion on the one hand and the teaching of the Word on the other. The true sacramental character of his church has been lost sight of in the attempt to imitate Anglican forms. The pulpit occupied a centre position, but as interpreting and teaching the sacraments when occasion required. Thus a sermon always accompanied a baptism, and in Presbyterian churches the font should be liturgically at the east end. Also when communion was celebrated the table was placed in front of the pulpit, on the axis of the church, and the minister then faced the congregation across the communion table, as occurred in many early Christian basilican churches in Italy. The æsthetic of the Scottish communion table is difficult because often the centre pulpit has been exaggerated into a large rostrum, and the open table in front then becomes inconspicuous. But, on the other hand, when the pulpit is placed to the side, and transepts are added, the acoustics of the preaching voice are often spoilt and the intimacy between preacher and congregation—a feature of Scottish preaching—is reduced. Deep transepts should certainly be avoided. A re-interpretation of the theology could order the instruments of the service in a more significant way as well as give the sense of worship which is now sought in Presbyterian as in Anglican churches.

It is the office of the architect to apprehend the delicate rationale of Protestant worship underlying the forms we know so well and so blindly. We must work for Christian unity but recognise a polarity of the spirit, given by God Himself; and in Protestant countries it is not likely that men will be satisfied with a uniformity of rite. To hope for a finer perception of these things is to believe in a better world, and in the harmonising of the varied religious activities of men.

Loudspeakers

Owing to the long reverberation common in large churches loudspeaker systems present difficult problems. There are roughly two classes of installation, the class having relatively few loudspeakers of the directional or semi-directional type at a high level above the floor speaking loudly, and the class having a large number of distributed loudspeakers of the cone or box type at relatively low level and speaking softly. The first class is simpler and cheaper and can easily be experimented with. But it is not suitable for cathedrals where the reverberation figure is known to be longer than five or six seconds. The system has given satisfaction in cases where reverberation is not more than that figure and where the loudspeakers give down at as sharp an angle as possible upon an area of well-filled seats, and owing to their directional effect cover approximately that area only. The second class, namely, the distributed loudspeakers at low level, is the more satisfactory for all large churches and the system could be improved by further experiment and by careful design. By limiting the output of the loudspeakers this method has the advantage of not "waking the echoes." Its disadvantage is that the sound source is liable to be fairly obviously on a listener's left or right rather than from the direction of the pulpit.

For the "distributed" method the cone loudspeakers should have a diameter of 6 in. or 7 in.; they have to reproduce speech only and not music. They should be spaced down the nave, a pair to a bay, at a height of from 6 ft. to 7 ft. above the floor. Their output need be no more than 1 or $1\frac{1}{4}$ watts and each unit should not, in fact, reach to a greater radius than 16 to 20 ft. They should speak in a direction either laterally across, or diagonally down, the nave. The arrangement of loud-speaker units in transepts, chancel and generally behind the preacher's back needs careful planning, more especially because in a large church it is for such seats on crowded occasions that an amplification system is valuable.

In regard to mounting, if piers are of a suitable shape the cones fitted in boxes can be placed upon them, or can be fitted with movable arms so that direction can be adjusted. If aisles are seated and habitually used it is better to have a separate set of loudspeakers for the aisles, but the cone type of loudspeaker if suitably mounted speaks backwards as well as forwards, and though this has certain acoustic disadvantages it has been successfully employed for partial aisle seating. The loudspeakers are improved if a small hat or sound-board is placed over each which helps to keep the sound, at high pitch, down at the seating level where it is wanted. But some piers—such as clustered Early English—are unsuited to take loudspeaker units, and experiments should be made with a standing fitting six feet high which could be placed centrally under nave arches. These also should include a shade or sound board just above the unit and about three feet in diameter. These shades would be seen edgeways and would not be noticeable. Another method is to employ pendants : these can be up to sixteen feet above floor level and can include light fittings also. Intelligent design and experiment are required both for stand and for pendant fittings. Pendant fittings have recently proved highly successful in a very large canteen hall, but one in which some means have been taken to reduce extreme reverberation.

A difficulty occurs in the neighbourhood of pulpit and lectern because of the interaction between loudspeaker and microphone when in proximity which may cause what is known as "feed back" resulting in "howling." The danger is reduced when speakers of low output are employed, and they can be brought as near as fifteen feet if the right type of microphone is used having a sharply directional effect. A moving-coil type of microphone is less liable to "feed back" than the carbon type, but some screening of the nearest pair of loudspeakers may prove desirable.

This raises the problem also of the loudness of the preacher's voice. He should aim, with a distributed system, at using the system as a substitute for, not a reinforcement of, his own voice : he himself has only to "carry" to the nearer rows of seats. He should also try to keep at an even distance from the microphone and within its directional range, and not alter that distance nor move from side to side. This means a restraint, and it must be recognised that the technique of good amplified speech in a large church is much more a reading than a free delivery. This is really more of a disadvantage than that of the listener hearing the sound from his right or left. Many people in their homes have become accustomed to listening to a mechanical source and will not take amiss the loudspeaker in church ; but the restriction to a good preacher of the microphone pick-up can become irksome, or he may presently forget all about it, and cause rapid variations of amplification.

Next in importance is the control board. This should be placed in a good position for "monitoring"; that is, in a position where the attendant can form a judgment easily of the loudness and quality of the sound and adjust it accordingly. It is useless, for instance, to have it in the organ loft. The attendant should be able to walk freely here and there and return easily to the control board to make the adjustments. The control board must have the switches for the various groups of loudspeakers, and these should provide for the switching off of the remoter loudspeakers when the congregation is concentrated at the front of the nave. Also it is

CARLISLE CATHEDRAL—PUBLIC ADDRESS SYSTEM

Installed by The Magneta Time Company Ltd.
Head Office and Works : Goblin Works, Leatherhead, Surrey

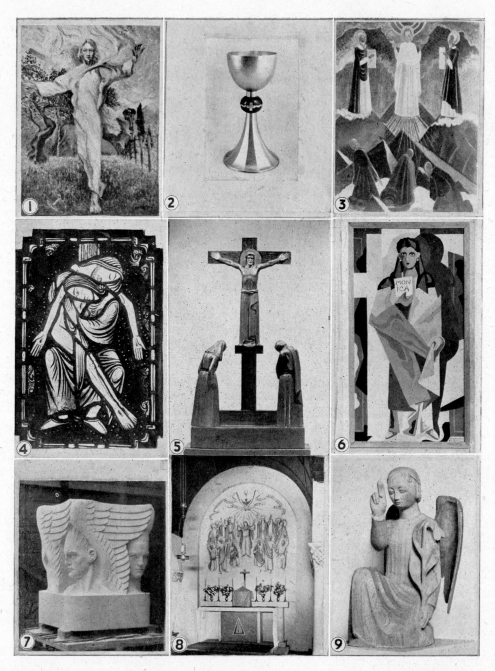

(1) Oil Painting. G. N. Burnand. (2) Chalice. Dunstan Pruden. (3) Tempera. Teresa Fuller.
(4) Stained Glass. C. Blakeman. (5) Bronze. J. A. Vasconcellos. (6) Panel. G. Houghton Brown.
(7) Stone Carving. D. Rawlins. (8) Altar and Mural. Joan Morris. (9) Wood Carving. Alan Durst.

Works by Members of the Church Artists' Agency,
25 Ebury Street, London, S.W.1.   Sloane 7051.

desirable that a master switch be provided for turning off the whole system when the organ begins, and for turning it on again when required. Intelligent use of the control board may make the whole difference between the success or failure of an installation, and special attention should be given to visiting preachers' voices. The volume level controls (*i.e.* loudness) should act without creating noises. The wiring radiates from the control board and it is, therefore, the focus of the scheme.

Control of quality is much more difficult than control of loudness. This is owing to the marked variation between the character of one male speaking voice and another, specially noticeable in church conditions. This variation may occur in the relative strength of the low-frequency components which give fundamental tone ; or in that of normal vowel tone over a wide middle pitch band ; or in that of the high-frequency components which give most of the consonants and the sibilants. Now the low-frequency components give, very roughly, *naturalness;* the middle give good *body of tone* to vowels ; the upper give *intelligibility.* In any given voice the disabling lack is a lack of consonants but at the same time the disabling blemish is a hiss or over emphasis of sibilants. Each of these are fairly common and the hiss may be increased by amplification. Therefore the upper frequency band (known as "tops") is the most important of the three and its adjustability is a necessity. An ideal control board would have then the three frequency bands with a control knob for adjusting the relative strengths. These bands should correspond roughly to:- bass 100 to 500 cycles, middle 500 to 2,000 cycles, tops 2,000 to 9,000 or 10,000. This is a very rough minimum. Pitch components exist both above and below these limits but are not easily transmitted through ordinary commercial equipment. It is at least necessary to have what is known as a tops lift and a tops cut and these are very frequently provided by commercial equipment, but in all cases they should be specified and some attention generally given to tone control.

The amplifier must have sufficient power to supply all the loudspeakers ; and it is desirable also to allow at least another twenty watts for possible additions. The amplifier and control board are better located together in order to save wiring. If they are far apart extra expense can be incurred. Also both amplifier and controls must be in a dry spot : a suitable amplifier cupboard should be about five feet square to give access all round it. Besides wiring for microphones and loudspeakers it is necessary to consider the possible employment of monitor equipment, signals, broadcasting and deaf-aids. The planning of the different wiring circuits needs care because good planning can mean economies, and also because wires to microphones if laid in existing ducts may suffer from interference due to induction if they run parallel to electric light wires or signal wires. Defence against damp is necessary throughout. Wiring should be in steel conduits.

Finally, maintenance is as important an item as any. It is well worth while paying an annual maintenance fee in order to have the equipment under constant surveillance. If it is not inspected and maintained it is liable to get out of order and give dissatisfaction.

If in a large church broadcasting requirements are to be considered, some special provisions should be made. A small "reception room" well lighted and with some sound absorption to prevent "ring" is required; also a mains point to take ten amperes, and good earthing for the B.B.C. equipment. The B.B.C. engineers should be consulted at an early stage.

Church Windows: ∽ ∽ ∽
Modern Stained Glass

By JUDITH D. GUILLUM SCOTT

TOO OFTEN THESE important items are regarded as outside the province of the architect to whom the design of a new church is entrusted. The choice of artists, and the subject treatment of glass, is left to the whim of some future donor who may offer the gift of a window, as the choice of plate and textiles is arrogated by the clergyman and his band of church workers. If the church, when it is completed, is to illustrate fully the impulse in the mind of the architect, he should be encouraged to express his idea in all the mediums involved, and to work it out to a logical conclusion in all the furniture needed to phrase the Church's offering of worship. Textiles and plate are an essential part of that furniture, and the glass should be considered as part of the architectural concept and decoration of the building.

It is not suggested that the architect, whose experience of handling materials is probably confined to bricks and mortar, concrete and steel, should produce the actual designs for stained glass, metal work, or textiles, unless, as in a few exceptional cases, he has specialised in these directions and has the necessary experience of the actual processes of manufacture. But the craftsmen in these materials should prepare their designs in consultation with the architect.

It is often the case that reasons of economy prevent the provision of any stained glass in the church when it is first built, and only a minimum of furniture, or in extreme cases furniture has to be borrowed from another church for the first few years. Even so, plans for future development should be made while the architect has the inspiration governing the design of that particular church still fresh in his mind. This is especially important in the case of stained glass.

The arbitrary selection by donors of a window "near where the person commemorated always sat," or for the like reason, may seriously affect the architect's carefully planned balance of daytime lighting: it may even appear to distort the proportions of the building. Similarly the colouring and design of those textiles which form part of the arrangement of the altar and sanctuary of chancel or chapels—frontals, curtains, hangings or carpets, should be part of the artistic climax of the whole building, and if they are discordant can unconsciously distract even the most insensitive worshipper.

These preliminary considerations passed, we may come to a more detailed treatment of the subject.

The Victorian era was so prolific in the production of stained glass, designed most frequently in a loose adaptation of the 13th or 14th century styles, that many people have come to think of stained glass only in these terms. Without a more widespread understanding of the technique of stained glass, it will be difficult to break this prejudice down. It is on this prejudice that "commercial art" flourishes, *i.e.* art which caters for the public taste at its lowest levels, at the expense of the artist's integrity, and does nothing to stimulate the patron's latent capacity for the appreciation of something better.

One of the misconceptions which must be dispelled is that there is any significance in the creation of a "dim, religious light" in every church or chapel building. The idea owes nothing to valid tradition, and was only one of the products of the romantic revivalists of the last century, which received strange support from a line chosen at random from Milton. Before that date, from early times, the ambition of the church builder, and his constant aim in evolving new styles of architecture in the West, was to admit more and still more light.

The architect in England and France throughout the middle ages was struggling to evolve a style of building suited to the climate, and to the needs of his clients. If we start from the Romanesque, we see a steady advance from a style imposed by limited knowledge of structural methods and possibilities, and based on the needs of a climate with extremes of heat and cold unknown farther west, to something almost ideal for its purpose, namely, the Gothic style of the 14th to 16th centuries. As the architect mastered his problems, of spanning a wider area, fining down his supporting pillars, and piercing his walls with more and larger windows, so the lightness of the building increased. The glass artist was in full sympathy with these developments and adapted his technique accordingly, taking full advantage of the changes in the form of the windows provided for him, and of the improvement in his own materials. Throughout the period from about A.D. 1200 to about 1500 the quality of the glass itself was continually changing in character.

Retrospect

The period of Perpendicular architecture saw the maximum achievement in window space, but when the Renaissance brought its revolutionary change in style, it did not break the established tradition of the large window, although it changed its form. It was not until the early years of the present century that the tradition was seriously questioned. To-day the stained-glass artist is often faced with a church in the modern style whose windows are as small as those of an Italian basilica designed to keep a building cool under a burning sun. How is he

NAVE AND CHANCEL SHOWING ARRANGEMENTS "AS IN TIMES PAST"

18. STANFORD-ON-AVON, NORTHANTS. THE CHANCEL
FROM THE EAST

Photo by C. H. Leighton, Harrogate

17. ST. JOHN, LEEDS. TYPICAL OF THE EARLY RENAISSANCE PERIOD

19. RANWORTH, NORFOLK, SHOWING A COMMON MEDIEVAL ARRANGEMENT OF SIDE ALTARS

Photo by O. G. Harvey, Harpenden

20. ST. JOHN THE BAPTIST, HARPENDEN, HERTS. THE SANCTUARY IN LENT

to treat such windows, and what treatment of them should the architect and the patron expect? There is as much dispute on this point as in any other part of the arts to-day, and, to be impartial, it is necessary to understand a little of the technical side of the development of stained glass. The first coloured glass that was available to the artist was very thick and uneven in texture, and it could be made only in small pieces. This meant that the proportion of leading to glass was much higher than it became later. Each piece of glass used was of one colour only, and the picture had to be built up like a mosaic, using the leading and a very little drawing in black line, to add details to the design. The 14th-century discovery of the method of painting with silverstain on white glass opened up possibilities, gradually exploited, of lightening design in many directions. For example, the head of a crowned and bearded king had no longer to be made up of two or more pieces of different coloured glass, leaded together, but could be painted in full detail on white. Soon after, the discovery of the process of sandwiching a piece of coloured glass with a piece of white, aciding out the parts of the coloured slab, and painting in silverstain on the white part, increased the possible proportion of glass to the leading. By the 15th century it had become "common form" to fill the upper part of a big window with canopy work, painted partly with silverstain, and admitting a great deal of light. Another formula was that of placing figures in full colour against a background of clear glass "quarries" only slightly decorated with a flower, emblem, or geometrical design, in silverstain in the centre of each or of some.

With the Renaissance, the technique of glass painting began to change: the practice was gradually developed of painting, not with pigment on coloured glass as in the past, but with enamels on clear glass. This brought a completely new outlook and fresh values. Formerly the artist used his medium quite as much as his painting to express the design he wanted. The leading lines were his emphasis, and the choice of the glass gave the picture texture and "interest." With enamel painting, on the other hand, the white glass was chosen only for its evenness and lack of "quality," the picture depended wholly for expression on the painter's capacity to paint, and the leading became a mere matter of utility, to break the window into conveniently sized panels, and give it strength.

In England during the late 18th century, and at the beginning of the 19th century, very little stained glass was produced, this craft suffering almost more than any other from the neglect of certain of the ecclesiastical arts during the earlier Hanoverian reigns.* Thus, when the Gothic revival, which came with the Oxford Movement, gave its impetus to church building and restoration, glass painting had become almost a forgotten form of expression. When the demand

* This country did, however, continue to make both true and enamel paint stained glass for longer than any other: some of the latest pre-revival English glass, of the end of the 18th and beginning of the 19th century being of the greatest interest.

arose those artists who strove to meet it had the difficult task of re-discovering the technical processes, as well as that of adapting their more pictorial form of art to the limitations of glass design.

The result of their efforts may be seen in nearly all the churches built or restored from about the year 1840 onwards. The earlier examples of this period have for that reason some considerable historic interest and should be tolerated, if possible, despite their crudity.

It must be realised to-day that in their method of reviving the Gothic styles and re-identifying them with all the arts ecclesiastical, the Victorians were attempting to put the clock back in a way which it is difficult to justify from a practical point of view. They were attempting with little or no practice to express themselves fluently in a dead language, the grammar of which they had not yet properly mastered. They could have either resumed the yoke of the Gothic style where it had been laid down at the dawn of the Renaissance, and continued the development of the style logically, or have evolved something original from the technique of the Renaissance. Instead, they plunged headlong back into the period which they thought to be the artistic climax of the arts, the 13th and 14th centuries, slavishly copying the mechanical imperfections which the original limitations of materials and craftsmanship imposed, and the medieval artists' misconceptions and conventions regarding anatomy and perspective.

As a result of this phase, many of our churches are now darkened and disfigured by what one can only describe as the equivalent in glass of the architects' restorations. In their efforts to throw themselves back into the past and with all their care over mechanical details, the men of the 19th century failed to catch the real animating spirit which lay behind the older work and gave it the vigour and vitality that so readily transcended all its imperfections of workmanship and gave it the intense beauty of form and colour which makes it what it is.

Prospect

So much for technique. What are we to expect from the artist to-day? The modern desire for sincerity, which has found typical expression in extreme functionalism, is unlikely to express itself in the medium of enamel painted glass. There is, however, a quite flourishing though small school of traditionalists who work in the Gothic or Renaissance idioms, but who are by no means copyists. The experimental period of the 19th century being passed, they have at their command a full knowledge of the old technique, and are free from the tendency to cover deficiencies in the quality of the glass, by over-painting, or to make the common 19th-century mistake of subordinating the leading to the drawing, and failing to give it its proper place as one of the primary elements in defining the composition of the subject. There is really little doubt that in most buildings, *i.e.*

those older than the third quarter of the 18th century, a traditional treatment, more or less modified, is suitable. In such churches the artist is bound to remember that the glass must be subsidiary, or complementary, to the architectural whole; that he must be guided primarily by the form of the tracery, by the existing balance of light and by the general style of existing stained glass. An extreme individualistic and brilliant window, however beautiful it may be when isolated in the artist's studio, after it is fixed in a church can be as vulgar and incongruous as an exotic plant in a herb garden.

In a new church of modern style the artist has, of course, much more freedom for originality. The chief difficulty he is likely to meet is one which may have been imposed by the architect: the English tradition is one for light, bright churches, but many modern architects have been so much attracted by the simplicity of the early churches of Italy, South France and Spain, that they have adopted the formula without considering the original reason for the small window openings. These give little scope for the stained-glass man, and, if he is to give the building the maximum of light these little openings will allow, give him little chance to develop his full technique. Small figures on a background of clear glass seem the only possibility, and even then he must use thin, smooth glass, with little texture to break up the light rays. Where the modern architect has provided large window openings, unbroken by tracery, the artist has his best chance to show his powers, and some very interesting pioneer work has been done towards developing a new school of design. But even here, lack of practical knowledge of the craft has too often led the architect to design windows so long and narrow that they give little scope to the artist for composition. In the new technique much use is made of the texture of the glass as well as of the leading, and the window is conceived as a pattern in colour and form, as well as a set composition. The minimum of over-painting is used. The French and Irish schools have been particularly bold, and there are some very promising young designers in this country. It would perhaps not be too much to say that this is one of the most interesting modern schools of art, and one with the greatest promise of developing on lines comprehensible to the "ordinary man," because in it merit is dependent on mastery of materials which in themselves are simple enough—glass, lead and elementary colours.

Planning

Ideally, then, the architect in consultation with the parish priest (or some specially competent theologian) and the artist, should together evolve a series of subjects for the stained windows of a new church—or for an aisle or chapel added to an old church. The architect must decide first how many of the windows can be filled with stained glass, and in what order they should be taken when donors can be found. Ideally, again, the architect will have had some hand in the choice of the artist, one whose style will be sympathetic to his architecture. If this policy were adopted, the scheme for the windows would present a planned whole, with a coherence of subject matter, colour schemes and design which the more usual piecemeal methods can never achieve. Such a scheme if it is roughed out, and put up in some prominent position, can be the focus for memorial gifts and bequests to the church over a number of years.

In many churches, those in towns where daylight is precious, and in town or country where the building is small, the architect will very likely decide that only one or two, or half a dozen, of the windows should have stained glass at any time. Even if the preparation of a full scheme is rejected, during his life time no windows should be put into a new building (or into a new section of an old building) without consultation with the architect.

The architect or donor should always make a careful study of several examples of finished work by the artist he favours. In order to facilitate this, firms of glass painters or of church furnishers should always be careful to give the name of the artist who will execute a particular piece of work on their behalf. Stock designs from a catalogue should never be offered or accepted.

Donors should always be warned not to commit themselves to any artist or firm beyond obtaining a design and estimate, until the necessary permission of any higher ecclesiastical authority has been obtained for its execution. If a donor pledges himself to an incompetent artist, the architect or the Diocesan Advisory Committee are almost powerless to help him, as no amount of criticism or advice can improve a really poor and uninspired project: they can only advise rejection, thereby causing the donor vain expense, and distress.

When any design is commissioned a sketch is generally made in water colour on board, but as the arts of painting in water colour and of staining glass are entirely distinct, it is not from a sketch that the artist's ability must be judged. There are plenty of so-called artists whose talent is sufficient to produce a pretty sketch, but whose work in glass would certainly not conform to the high standard required by the Church authorities to-day. To the eye of the experienced these sketches yield a good deal of information, but the layman should not trust his own judgment of a water-colour sketch to reveal an artist's ability as a draughtsman or colourist in his proper sphere.

A sketch has, however, its unquestionable place in settling the general format of the composition, with the details of figures and background, and as a medium through which the artist and his client can exchange their views.

Subject

Choice of subjects for the main windows of a church, at the east end of the chancel, or chapels, will probably be limited to the principal events of Christian

STAINED-GLASS WINDOW IN THE CHURCH OF THE DOMINICAN CONVENT,
HARROW-ON-THE-HILL

Designed and executed at the John Hardman's Studios, Birmingham and London

"The Deposition from the Cross"

DESIGN FOR ONE OF THE SERIES OF NEW WINDOWS IN
ST. CHARLES, GOSFORTH, NEWCASTLE-ON-TYNE

Executed by the Harry Clarke Studios, Dublin, Eire

history. During the past century a certain rigidity of convention has led to the Crucifixion being the almost invariable choice for the east window in Anglican and Roman Catholic churches. This subject was, of course, constantly portrayed in the middle ages, but generally in its proper setting, as part of a series of scenes (often oddly chosen, it is true) showing selections from the whole life of our Lord, and often other subjects linked to the incarnation. The recent custom of isolating this one subject is often an object lesson in the haphazard planning already referred to, the same subject being repeated in the reredos and echoed by the altar cross or crucifix, and perhaps also by a frontal with the same sign. The nativity, the baptism, the presentation, the transfiguration, the entry into Jerusalem, the trial, the betrayal, the resurrection appearances, the ascension, the coming of the Holy Spirit, might all be considered, besides other scenes of equal teaching value. The pictorial arts of the Church owe their birth and development in part to the need for a means of teaching the many varied facts of the Christian faith to congregations largely illiterate, and therefore dependent on sermons and pictures. That is largely a thing of the past, but we must not forget the possibilities open to us still of bringing home more forcibly the Christian doctrines by the latter means. Only if it is to be done effectively, the artist must have reasonable freedom to express the familiar scenes as they strike him—within the bounds of theological accuracy, of course.

In choosing the subjects for side windows, recourse might well be had to the more edifying parts of the Old Testament including the Apocrypha. Much use of both was made by the enamel glass painters of the 16th and 17th centuries, and of the Old Testament by the medieval stained-glass workers, but the Victorian revival largely neglected both sources. Something has been said already about the impossibility of dealing with naturalistic subjects successfully, and one of these, the Good Shepherd, is much too often attempted. It should be remembered, too, that the Last Supper is a difficult subject to compose effectively in glass.

Donors often try to impose inscriptions which are too long in proportion to the size of the windows.* An inscription relating to the gift should be painted on the glass rather than placed on a tablet on the wall below. Any description of the subject-matter of the window should generally be incorporated in the design itself, with a scroll or similar label, rather than added to the inscription at the base.

Plain Glass

Perhaps a few words should be said about plain glazing, and about glazing bars in old churches. The arrangement of the leads in a window glazed with clear

---

* The advantage of black letter is, of course, that it allows of considerable compression without loss of beauty, where a long inscription has to be fitted into a small space, but few people now can read it with ease.

99

glass is important: ill-proportioned diamonds or squares can break up the symmetry of a Gothic window. Special care should be taken to pick out and emphasise in the spacing of the leads the predominating lines in a Renaissance window. For the latter square quarries are, of course, in keeping, but for the former it is not always realised that diamond quarries are not essentially "correct": square or oblong quarries are less fussy and are often preferable. Where the glazing bars or ferramenta are still in position they will indicate the size of the quarries; where they are missing it is worth while to look for a window of similar design retaining its bars and its old plain glazing from which to copy the spacing. Old glazing bars should never be removed: they are generally contemporary with the window and have a functional purpose in strengthening the tracery, as well as helping to lessen wind pressure on the glass.

In both old and new churches plain glass is sometimes intended to be a permanent feature, but if so, except in the rare cases where adjoining buildings press closely and are really ugly, clear colourless handmade glass should be used. It may be slightly textured, with a reamy, bubbly, or uneven quality, but the use of machine-made green, pink, or yellow, so called "cathedral" sheet glass or machine textured colourless "bathroom" glass should never be used—though they often are. They give a glaring, unnatural aqueous light inside the building, and destroy the true colour values of any gold or polychrome textiles or carvings. Where the art of the glass painter has not been employed to try to capture and interpret the shadow of the Divine, why should we, by the use of this cheap tinted glass, shut out the natural beauty of trees, sky and hills?

NOTE ON ILLUSTRATIONS

These have been chosen to exemplify the stages by which modern glass painting styles have evolved. No illustrations of old glass are included, but it is only on a close study of ancient examples that an understanding of modern developments can be based.

The examples illustrated have been chosen from two groups:

1. Modern essays in traditionalism.
2. The new styles which are being evolved out of the roots of traditional craftsmanship and design.

The designs should be judged on three counts: craftsmanship (the artist's use of his medium—glass textures, leading and colour); design (arrangement of the subject in relation to the stonework of the window, and the effect of the design as a whole at a distance too great for study of the subject); and subject matter (drawing and interpretation).

DESCRIPTIONS

1. MODERN ESSAYS IN TRADITIONALISM

Exford, Somerset, by Reginald Bell

Window in the south aisle of the nave. The figures are rather larger than they would have been in a 15th-century window, but the layout, drawing and borders follow tradition fairly closely.

CHURCH WINDOWS: MODERN STAINED GLASS

Tenterden, Kent, by Christopher Webb

East window of north aisle. In this case money was scarce and light much needed. The design of the glass blends very skilfully with that of the tracery, and the natural background is not excluded by tinted glass.

Christ Church, Alert Bay, British Columbia, by J. E. Nuttgens

East window. For use where the natural sunlight is very strong and needs to be toned by the use of brilliant colours and some over-painting of the glass. This window compares very favourably with much of the glass this country exports to the Empire, the standard of which is commonly very low.

Strand Unitarian Chapel, Manchester, by Martin Travers

Side window (since destroyed by enemy action). A simple and inexpensive treatment where full stained glass is not desirable, and where the view of disfiguring neighbouring buildings must be excluded. Compare this with the crude kaleidoscopic coloured patterns usually employed for the purpose.

2. WORK IN THE NEW STYLES

Liverpool Cathedral, by James H. Hogan

South window of the central space. This scene is only a small part of one of these vast windows. The sill of the window is 51 ft. above floor level, and this scene begins about 75 ft. from the ground. The panel shown is 24 ft. high by 12½ ft. wide. Its subject, the Baptism of our Lord, is treated as design rather than for pictorial values. The great weight of the leading is needed to resist wind pressure and to emphasise the lines of the picture. Without such thick leading, from the ground the picture would be lost in a glow of colour and light. Note that there is practically no shading or over-painting, and that the essential drawing (of faces, hands, etc.), has been reduced to the minimum.

The Good Samaritan, by Barillet-le-Chevalier-Haussen

The Good Samaritan is the subject of these three scenes, treated by one of the leaders of the modern French school. It demonstrates the most extreme functional handling of materials: the drawing is almost entirely rendered with the leading, the modelling of figures and objects by the choice of very highly textured glass. What over-painting there is, is carried out in light tone to indicate masses rather than detail.

Bells and Bell Towers ᔍ ᔍ ᔍ

By ALBERT A. HUGHES

BELLS COME UNDER the heading of ornaments of the church and as such must take their proper perspective in the planning of new churches or in the restoration of those which have suffered damage.

It must be remembered that according to Canon Law a church service must be preceded by the chiming or ringing of a bell. Bells are, therefore, amongst the oldest, if not the very oldest, of the ornaments of the church, for in the earliest days of Christianity in these islands a handbell was used to summon the very scanty and scattered congregations to worship.

As the churches developed so their bells grew in size and number, and we all are now familiar with the fine rings pealing from the towers of our cathedrals, abbeys and parish churches, many of them of great age. Every parish looks upon its bells with pride as a great possession, and apart from their use for church services, they have for centuries been the means of public rejoicing.

This country has for long been known as "the ringing isle," and there surely is a joyousness in the traditional ringing of English church bells unknown in any other country in the world, except in those few instances within the Empire and in one or two cases in the United States of America where English change-ringing is practised.

It was not until after the ban had been imposed in June 1940 that we realised our loss. Efforts were made, but without success, to have the ban relaxed for Sunday morning service, and we all remember with what joy we listened once again to the ringing of bells when the ban was temporarily lifted to announce the great victory of the Allies in North Africa. Nor was our joy solely because of the victory, but in just hearing their cheerful sound after so long a silence. Our bells do really mean much to us. On the occasion to which I have just referred I overheard three separate groups of people in a street close by an old East London parish church (St. Dunstan's, Stepney) surrounded by bomb ruins exclaim: "Isn't it grand to hear them again?" On a later occasion after the ban had been completely lifted, I had attended service at my church in the City of London. Our City congregations are necessarily small on Sundays, but on this occasion we had two visitors from New Zealand. In conversation afterwards I asked: "What drew you here in particular?" "Well," was the answer, "I heard your bells." Here then is the proof of their voice.

102

The problem before us, however, is what are we going to do about bells for new churches to be built, and those to be restored? In the majority of churches damaged by enemy action the towers remain intact even though the bells may have been destroyed, and in these cases the problem is relatively easy; it is mainly a question of the necessary funds for replacement. There are, however, several important points to consider in the case of such replacements and these points apply also to new towers in which it is hoped to install bells. They are:

1. *The belfry.* In towers in which bells are to be hung in the traditional manner for change ringing, they should be so placed that they are well below the sound openings in order that the sound may rise before escaping. By far the best method is to have the window openings completely blocked up inside and for the sound to escape through a low louvred lantern in the roof. A good example of this arrangement is at St. David's Cathedral, where a ring of eight tenor 25 cwt. is hung in the old gateway tower. The belfry floor is only about twenty-five feet above ground level. The eight louvred openings are completely bricked up inside and all sound emerges from the lantern in the roof. The result is that the bells are not aggressive in the immediate vicinity and yet they are heard to good advantage in the distance. Similar examples occur at Bradford Cathedral, St. Martin's, Epsom, and at the Church of the Annunciation, Chislehurst, Kent. This sound effect is of the greatest importance and must be considered at all cost.

It is at the same time necessary that daylight should be admitted to the belfry and this can be arranged by fitting thick armoured glass in the upper part of the window openings in place of the blocking-up material. I am of course now referring to existing towers which generally have either louvred or traceried windows.

This matter of sound control ought also to receive attention in those towers where bells and structure are undamaged, more particularly in built-up areas. In the majority of such cases the bells have, following ancient custom, been placed on a level with the sound openings, and where these openings have been fitted with louvres they have the effect of driving the sound directly down in the immediate vicinity. This arrangement has frequently been the cause of justifiable complaint by people living nearby. In many such cases the trouble has been overcome by almost completely blocking up the windows, but there are many more where such attention is very necessary. The cost need not be high, but it will vary according to the size of the windows. A pre-war average in normal cases was from £50 to £60. A method often employed, and quite effective, is to cover the windows inside almost to the top with one and a half inch tongued and grooved boards, well painted, and then to cover the woodwork with a good sound absorbent material, such as Cabot quilting.

In towers yet to be built the problem is easy because we are, so to speak, starting from scratch. Whether, however, a new tower should have dummy belfry windows or plain surfaces to the walls is not in my province; it would, however, seem that dummy windows for the sake of an architectural feature would be "false."

2. *The ringing chamber*. This should, where possible, be not less than twelve feet high, and also where possible, a deadening or sound diffusion chamber should be arranged between bells and ringers. If this is not possible it will be necessary to have a deadening ceiling immediately below the belfry floor with sound absorbing material packed between. It is, however, important that the belfry floor and deadening ceiling should be independent of each other, *i.e.* floor and ceiling should not be fixed to the same set of joists. It will also be necessary to have skeleton trunks for the passage of the ropes. The windows in the ringing chamber should, where possible, have their sills not less than six feet above the floor. This will prevent sun glare interfering with rope sight for the ringers. Good ventilation is also important.

3. *Floors*. In a new tower or in those which will have to be completely re-floored, the belfry floor at least will probably be of reinforced concrete, which will serve two purposes, (*a*) considerably strengthening the tower and (*b*) making the tower fire-proof. We have seen the effect of fires in towers floored throughout with timber. I am of opinion that brick concrete would be preferable to ballast, being less resonant.

If in the ringing chamber or in the intermediate space there should be an entrance to the roof of the church, it is important that the door should be fire-proof.

The use of concrete brings us to a rather difficult problem in the construction of new towers, *viz.* the conductivity of sound. New towers under modern methods of construction conduct sound through the walls to a greater extent than is the case in old ones where the core is chiefly rubble, and this is further aggravated by concrete floors. Unless an effective method of insulation is incorporated in the construction the volume of sound and echo in the ringing chamber will create a serious difficulty to ringers in the execution of their art. It is most important for good and accurate ringing that the ringers should hear each bell clearly and distinctly. This is essentially a matter for the architect. The use of lime or lias mortar instead of cement in the construction of the walls would reduce transmission of sound, but treatment of concrete floors is also of first importance. If concrete floors can be effectively insulated from the walls without causing loss of strength a great improvement will have been made. Even then, I still feel that an independent timber floor will be necessary about three feet below the ringing chamber ceiling. It would probably also be necessary to line the walls of the bell-chamber with acoustic plaster or some other sound absorbent material. I know of one tower containing a fairly heavy ring, where the bell-chamber walls are covered with Cabot quilt with good effect. The high degree of sound conductivity was strikingly brought to my notice a few years ago in a new tower. The bell frame was of teak and rested directly on a ten inch concrete floor. The middle chamber floor (ten feet below) was also of concrete about nine inches thick. When the bells were first rung the sound in the ringing chamber was deafening. The middle chamber floor was then covered with bags of sawdust, but with only slight improvement. Further, the tonal quality of the bells suffered in the ringing chamber. My experience has been that wherever concrete has been extensively used the bells suffer in tonal value.

A ring of bells is a costly musical instrument which with ordinary care and attention will live for centuries. It is, therefore, of the greatest importance that every step should be taken to obtain the best result both inside and out.

This then is the problem for the architect in the planning of his tower. It is, of course, customary for the architect to discuss with the bell-founder the question of bells and the method of their installation in a proposed tower.

Other points which arise are:

(a) Trapways. Central trapways should be formed in all floors of sufficient size to allow the passage of the largest bell. That in the belfry floor should be of loose sections laid on a rebate, and those in the lower floors should be hinged. They should also be made of non-inflammable material.

(b) If access to the belfry is by a turret staircase it seems hardly necessary to add that it should be of sufficient height to allow a tall man to ascend without bending; and of sufficient width.

(c) Artificial lighting. It is often necessary for the tower keeper to enter the tower during hours of darkness and as he will often have to climb about over the bell-frame, it is important to have efficient lighting as such work is not without risk. I would suggest a light in each corner of the tower, but I do not consider a loose lead as being necessary, in fact it is often a nuisance, and a much better proposition where the above-mentioned lighting exists, is for the tower keeper to have a good torch for close inspection work. In the ringing chamber the artificial lighting should be placed well above the heads of the ringers. It is also important to have the turret staircase lighted.

(d) Number and weight of bells. This will naturally depend on the tower. It is desirable that all bells in a ringing peal should be hung on one level. This is not always possible, but there have been cases where two tiers have been adopted merely in order to have heavier bells and a greater number. This is overcrowding and should be avoided.

I have dealt so far with towers which are obviously built to carry a "ring" of bells, but many new churches will be built, where funds or other means prevent the addition of such a tower. Many will have a small open turret at the east or west end capable of accommodating a single small bell. Such cases are already familiar and comments are unnecessary. Others may have a small west end belfry capable of holding a few small bells hung for "chiming," *i.e.* for swinging just sufficiently to operate the clappers. Here again the bells should be in keeping with the structure. Either have one good bell or a small chime which can be operated from a bracket or a keyboard. The use in such belfries, or in fact in any tower, of amplified gramophone records of any particular "ring" of bells should be strongly deprecated.

It may be that a tower will be built which will not be of sufficient strength to carry a "ringing" peal, but which at the same time is of ample size to carry a set of six, eight or more bells. In this case the bells should be hung stationary on the carillon principle for operation from a keyboard.

In such cases the question of sound effect presents an entirely different proposition. The sound waves are projected downwards and outwards, and the clappers having a very short stroke (not more than two to three inches) the volume of sound is feeble as compared with ringing bells which swing through a complete revolution. It is therefore necessary to adhere to the traditional sound openings and to so place the bells that their mouths are well above the sills of the windows. Further, the belfry floor should be level with or only just slightly below the window sills. There is also no objection to arranging the bells in more than one tier. Traceried windows will be better than louvres.

Cost of bells

It is impossible to give close details on this point in a short article more especially as the range is so vast, say, from about £20 for a small turret bell to £5,000 for a great "ringing" peal of twelve. The following approximate figures will, however, give a slight indication :

£650 to £750 would provide a light chime of eight in the key of B♭ or A for operation from a keyboard. £1,450 would provide a light "ring" of eight tenor weighing, say, from 10 to 11 cwt. in the key of G, and about £2,000 would cover a ring of eight tenor weighing about 20 cwt. in the key of E, whilst about £3,200 would provide a ring of ten tenor weighing about 30 cwt. in the key of C♯. £4,000 would cover a ring of twelve tenor weighing about 40 cwt. in the key of C.

I have refrained from going into close technical details in connection with the bells themselves or their fittings and supports. Such details would be for discussion with the parties concerned and would to some extent be governed by prevailing circumstances. The chief point at this stage is the planning and provision of correct conditions, in short, a correct start.

CHURCH OF OUR LADY OF WILLESDEN AT THE CANONICAL VISITATION
OF HIS EMINENCE CARDINAL GRIFFIN, JULY 1946

This new Sanctuary was designed and executed by Fenning & Co., of London, W.6

RESERVE ALTAR

DESIGN FOR HIGH ALTAR AND RESERVE ALTAR IN REAR
CHURCH OF THE SACRED HEART, GOLDTHORPE, NR. ROTHERHAM

Burns Oates & Washbourne Ltd., London

Building and Furnishing an Altar, according to the Roman Rite

By GEOFFREY WEBB

IN THE ROMAN CATHOLIC liturgy the term "altar" means a consecrated stone structure upon which the Holy Sacrifice of the Mass is offered. This Holy Sacrifice, which is the very centre of the liturgy, may in exceptional circumstances be celebrated elsewhere than in a church, provided that it be on a duly appointed altar. It follows, therefore, that the church is built for the altar, without which the central act of the liturgy may not be celebrated, and not the altar for the church which shelters it.

Recognition of this fact at once introduces considerations essential to its architectural treatment. Since the altar is the very *raison d'être* of the church, it should be made unmistakably to appear so to all inside; it should be quite evidently the focal point of the building; and all possible emphasis should be given to it by architectural skill in its setting: uninterrupted floor space, sufficiently ample for the due performance of ceremonial, should provide dignity, and colour which in itself is a medium of emphasis should be concentrated on the altar before being applied to its surroundings.

But the significance of the altar extends far beyond the scope of being the chief architectural focus of any building: it is regarded in the liturgy as a figure expressly deputed to represent Christ Himself *—the first and most important of all representations of Him in any church with a pre-eminence attained by no sculpture or painted figure. This is so because our real Altar—the Altar of the Catholic Church—*is* Christ Himself, and all material altars are identified with Him. Among several passages from the liturgy which state this it may be well to quote one which refers to the first Christian altar to receive solemn ritual consecration—the high altar of the Lateran Church given by Constantine in the year 311. It occurs in the Divine Office for the feast of the Dedication of the Lateran Church, Nov. 9, first lesson of the second nocturn. "Although, even from Apostolic times, places were dedicated to God ... where ... the Christian people were wont to partake of the Eucharist, yet these places used not to receive such solemn ritual consecration. nor had it yet become a custom to erect in them an altar *in titulum* which, anointed with chrism, would be an express figure of our Lord Jesus Christ, our

---

* Cf. *The Mystery of Faith*, by Maurice de la Taille, S.J., Vol. I, Ch. v, § 2. "Christ as Eternal Altar," p. 232.

Altar, Victim and Priest." This passage may indeed be taken as supplying the one main principle governing the visual presentation and the furnishing of the altar from the time of Constantine to the present day; and although this chapter deals with the altar from its architectural rather than its theological aspect, still it is of the utmost importance to the architect that the theological foundation be briefly stated, in order that he may use the greater freedom in designing the details without violating the main principle, or obscuring the significance which those details should enhance. That is only another way of saying that any architect should study the functional requirements of his subject before the æsthetic. And the functional requirements of the altar are that it be an express figure of our Lord Jesus Christ, our Altar, Victim and Priest.

Here then is the problem for the architect's solution, to be borne in mind in planning and designing the details of the whole building; and reference back to this main principle needs to be made by him again and again. This principle should govern his planning of seating space, that all may have a clear view of the altar; and at the same time reverence dictates its withdrawal to some extent from too close a contact with the laity who share in the sacrifice, lest the awe of the Holy of Holies be diminished. The same principle governs the interior elevations which should lead the eye to the high altar without conscious effort. It governs the employment of colour, whether on roof, wall, or in coloured glass of the windows. And above all it governs the design of the altar itself, so that prominence is bestowed on the rectangular block of the altar, instead of on its accessories. The design fails in its functional purpose when the essential features of the altar's rectangular elevations and upper surface are made a mere support for a more elaborate altar-piece above it; or when the altar itself is deprived of colour which is profusely displayed around it; or when it is broken by the shadows of recessed panels and surfaces, so that it becomes a shelf for the support of an extravagant display, like a bench at a flower show or a counter in a church furniture shop. The few simple rules now laid down by rubrics and decrees, and the age-long practice of the Church's tradition when allowed to function without transient interference, are the architect's best friends and the surest help in achieving the effect of a truly functional design. With the rules and tradition as guides, the amount of thought and skill expended on the altar may be limited only by the means available; and whether the means are great or small, the high altar should be the first and chief consideration and the last object of compulsory economy.

Form of Altar

Altars may be of two kinds, "fixed" or "portable," with a third alternative of a "quasi-fixed" which includes points from both. Architectural considerations are not concerned with the portable altar, which is a solid piece of natural stone, small enough to be carried about; it is consecrated, but does not receive the title of a saint. It is square or oblong and must be of a minimum size sufficient to hold the host and the base of the chalice, or most of it. In general its dimensions vary from twelve by twelve inches to fourteen by sixteen inches and about two inches in thickness. A quasi-fixed altar is one which supports a portable altar on a structure corresponding to the shape and dimensions of a fixed altar. The supporting structure may be of any suitable material such as wood, stone, brick, cement, concrete or metal. The portable altar-stone is sunk into the upper surface of the support, or table, about one inch back from the central point of the table's front edge, with enough projection above the level of the table top for its position to be felt under the linen cloths; one sixteenth of an inch is enough for this. Unlike a strictly portable altar, the quasi-fixed altar may bear the title of a saint and the advantage of a "privileged" altar. Architecturally its furnishing and ornamentation follow the rules of a fixed altar, an examination of which will cover both types.

Construction

The Code of Canon Law, in Canon 1197, defines a "fixed" altar as "a table with its supports consecrated as one whole." Those in charge of designing and erecting a fixed altar are responsible for the correct provision of four features:

A. The Table (*mensa*).
B. The Support (*stipes*).
C. The Sepulchre for the relics (*sepulcrum*).
D. The substructure or flooring.

A. *The Table*

This must consist of a single slab of natural stone which must be durable and not easily broken: artificial stone, however hard and durable, is forbidden. On its upper surface, which should be smooth, five crosses are incised, one on the centre and one at each corner above the centre of the support below it—if the altar has four supports.

B. *The Support*

This must be of natural stone also, but not necessarily of one piece from table to floor. It may be a single column, or several columns—four being the most usual— or it may consist of a solid block of built up stones or of four stone walls. If four stone columns are used, the four spaces between them may be filled in with material other than stone, such as brick or concrete, so long as the table rests directly on the top of the columns of natural stone with only the cement fixing between; these junctions of table and supports are anointed at the altar's consecration which must be made before Mass can be celebrated. Walls of stone or brick, etc., need air vents to allow them to dry out after the *mensa* has been laid above them. A sixth cross is marked on stone, by incision or other permanent method, on the front elevation, preferably in the middle. When the filling between the supports is of brick or material other than stone, a stone may be inserted in the brick to receive this cross; or it may be incised on the centre of the front edge of the *mensa*.

A possible but rare variation of a fixed altar is one consisting of a single solid block of stone or marble as in the case of the high altar of St. Peter's in Rome, and that of Westminster Cathedral.

For the validity of its consecration, which requires the anointing of the junction of the table with its support, shallow stones under each end or corner would form these supports,* or, according to Dom Nicholas Bliley in *Altars according to the Code of Canon Law*: "In order that the altar may be morally united with the pavement the unctions would have to be made at the four corners where the altar-stone is connected with a stone foundation or they would be omitted, the consecrator having first obtained an indult from the Holy See."

C. *The Sepulchre*

The cavity for the relics is a square or oblong sinking made in the table top towards the front edge of its centre, or in the centre of the front or the back elevation, where either is of natural stone; or it may be sunk in the centre of the top surface of the supporting structure where this is a solid mass of built up stones. The difficulty in this case arises during the altar's consecration, since the solid stone *mensa* becomes the lid of the Sepulchre, and must be anointed on its under side before being lowered on to its *stipes*. Its dimensions vary to suit the size of the reliquary to be enclosed in it. It must be closed by a lid of natural stone which is cemented on during the act of consecration; for this purpose the lid should fit with some ease to allow for the cementing and should rest upon a rebate which supports the top of the lid flush with the table top; it should be engraved with a cross upon both its upper and under side. The reliquary is usually of silver or gold and has a cross engraved in a shallow round sinking in the outer side of its lid. This sinking serves to receive the round seal on the knot tied in the ribbon with which the lid is secured after the insertion of the relics. These must be authenticated ones of at least two saints, one of whom must be a martyr (Fig. 1).

D. *The Substructure*

This must be a foundation sufficiently solid to render the altar immovable in practice. Other points mentioned by Dom Nicholas Bliley in his *Altars according to*

* Rev. J. O'Connell in *Directions for Altar Societies and Architects*, p. 2.

21. SEDILIA AT MONYASH, DERBYSHIRE

22. ANCIENT AUMBRY AT KINTORE, ABERDEENSHIRE

23. MODERN AUMBRY AT ST. BARTHOLOMEW THE LESS, LONDON

EAST ENDS SHOWING VARIETY OF TREATMENT

25. ST. LUKE, COWLEY. REREDOS IN TWO
STAGES BENEATH EAST WINDOW

24. ST. MICHAEL AT THE NORTH GATE, OXFORD. ALTAR WITH
15TH-CENTURY LOW REREDOS AND MODERN FIGURES

the Code of Canon Law are: stone, brick, concrete, clay-tiles or terra-cotta will answer the purpose; where the floor is of wood, rubber tiling or other than stone or earth substance, the flooring must be cut away below all the stone forming the altar supports and be replaced by a stone, concrete, brick or other permanent surface.

No church may be consecrated unless at least one

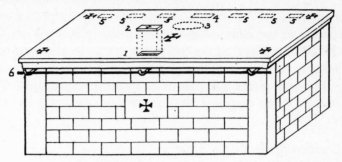

FIG. I. DIAGRAM SHOWING CONSTRUCTION OF ALTAR WITH ITS SEPULCHRE AND INCISED CROSSES: ALSO POSITION OF ROD FOR HANGING THE FRONTAL. I AND 2, SEPULCHRE AND LID; 3, SITE OF TABERNACLE; 4 AND 5, CRUCIFIX AND CANDLE-STICKS; 6, FRONTAL ROD AND PEGS.

fixed altar—and that the high altar—is consecrated in it: the consecration of the altar-stone in a quasi-fixed altar is insufficient for this purpose. This confirms the point that the church exists for the altar, rather than the altar for the church, since an unconsecrated church must have at least a consecrated altar-stone on every altar where Mass is celebrated.

Dimensions of Fixed and Quasi-fixed Altars

The height of an altar, though not prescribed, is determined by practical convenience. For a high altar 3 ft. 4 in. is a useful average and 3 ft. 6 in. a maximum. For side altars 3 ft. 3 in. is convenient. The length may vary according to the size of the building, and the altar's position in it. High altars from the 4th to the 12th centuries were less in length than those of the later middle ages, being from $3\frac{1}{2}$ to 4 ft. long. Some of those remaining in England from the later Middle Ages exceed 12 ft. in length, *e.g.* our Lady's altar, Ely Cathedral Church, 16 ft. $4\frac{1}{2}$ in., Tewkesbury Abbey Church 13 ft. 8 in., Arundel, FitzAlan Chapel, 12 ft. 6 in. In smaller parish churches they are naturally shorter, *e.g.* 9 ft. at Bishop's Cleeve. Side altars are governed by the width of the aisle or chapel; to give one instance, in the north aisle of Winthorpe Church, Lincs., an altar 5 ft. $6\frac{1}{2}$ in. remains against an east wall of 11 ft. from side to side.

The depth of an altar, front to back, depends on whether it supports a tabernacle. In general practice the value of this depth is underestimated; a high altar with a tabernacle requires from 21 to 24 in. between its front edge to the tabernacle, 18 in. for the tabernacle itself and about 9 in. or more for the base of the crucifix behind it, giving a minimum of 4 ft. 3 in. to 4 ft. 6 in. Incidentally the medieval high altar at Bishop's Cleeve, the length of which has been already given as 9 ft., has a depth from front to back of 4 ft., although it never supported

9

a tabernacle. An ample depth has an æsthetic as well as a functional value, since it adds to the altar's dignity and prominence—a dignity which is diminished when the altar is elevated on too many steps to allow its upper surface to be visible, as became the practice during a transient period towards the end of the 19th century.

For side altars a depth of 24 in. is a minimum for convenience in allowing free space for the corporal, and an average nearer 3 ft. is preferable.

Position of the High Altar

The only rubric which bears on this point is that which directs the bishop consecrating the altar to pass round it seven times. The high altar, therefore, needs to be set at a minimum of $2\frac{1}{2}$ ft. from the wall behind it. More of course is advisable, since the consecrator makes these seven encirclements, and other later ones, in cope and mitre and with a thurible: the ceremony is long and exhausting, and unnecessary obstacles hardly add relief or dignity to the proceedings. Beyond that requirement an architect is free to plan the altar's position to meet the needs of priest and people and to satisfy the claim of the altar as focal point of the architectural interior. Among these problems is the need of the people to see the altar clearly. That requires the absence of obstruction and the presence of light. Unlike many late medieval churches in England, many recent ones have more light given to the nave than to the sanctuary enshrining the high altar; and this is no doubt due to intention rather than oversight, because it is asserted that an east window behind an altar produces glare, which is true enough when the east window is isolated from its context. But if the altar cannot be seen clearly in the glare, it can hardly be seen more clearly in the dark. Very many late medieval churches, especially in East Anglia, developed the principle of setting the high altar in a lantern, with the light playing all round it, by making north and south windows together occupy more wall space than the single east window. Even without the stained glass which originally made the altar's setting a rainbow rather than a lantern, the result is to flood the altar with daylight of a clarity and softness that no artificial flood lighting can match for beauty, and yet with the same absence of glare which the artificial method provides. And while all the original jewelled and silver glass still remained in place, the altar's setting must have mirrored the glow of the fields and flowered hedgerows outside, which could be seen through the glass as if through the mist of sunrise. This rainbow setting of the high altar has its dawn from the first examples, back in Constantine's century, when the altar stood well forward on the cord of the apse, or even farther forward on the intersection of the side transepts with chancel and nave, with the great arch of the apse above or behind it, and the glowing jewellery of mosaics encircling it. The very origin of our English glass, with its tendency to admit more and more light as its design developed through the middle ages, arose from the challenge of these mosaics of the Mediterranean and the Bosphorus. What else can explain the remarkably sudden appearance of a new art in the 12th and 13th centuries fully endowed with a perfection of technique? The effort and concentration needed to bring it to birth came from the realisation that our northern light was too pearly and not fierce enough for the glass mosaic reflecting the southern sunlight, and consequently the new method of passing our daylight *through* the glass, instead of reflecting it, was conceived and born in all its splendour. It is small wonder that no masterpiece of mosaic has been acclaimed in this country, when our ancestors were long since convinced that the attempt would be still-born.

In rare medieval cases in Spain the high altar was set even farther forward, well into the nave, which would give the greatest opportunity of being clearly seen by all the congregation.

This plan recalls that of some of the early Greek churches, such as Sancta Sophia at Constantinople in the 6th century when the altar was set below the middle of the great central dome. The revival of this plan has been suggested in recent years and also carried out. Should it be further developed, it seems important that the balance between prominence and reverent seclusion should not be hastily upset. There is all the difference between the excess of mystery resulting from the withdrawal of the altar behind the impenetrable screen of the Eastern Orthodox rite, and the opposite extreme of defenceless proximity of an altar to a congregation pressing all round it. The rules and decrees of the Church, however, have provided a protection against any danger of this excess by requiring the altar to be housed within a civory—a canopy on columns (*ciborium magnum*), or under a suspended canopy in cases where the altar is set back against the wall. This requirement, which has been constant through the centuries and renewed in decrees of the Congregation of Sacred Rites, is considered in the next section—The High Altar Canopy.

But first it may be asked how medieval tradition, not only in England but in most of Europe outside central Italy, ever came to set high altars back against the east wall, as they undoubtedly did, to the neglect of all convenience for the altar's consecration. One explanation is given in Edmund Bishop's "On the History of the Christian Altar" in the *Downside Review* for July 1905. He traces the innovation to the influence of the increasing cult of veneration of relics between the 8th and 14th centuries; by the end of that period the reliquaries had become too large for a place on the altar, and a shrine had been built to hold them, close to the back of the altar. Then pilgrims gathered round the shrine and obstructed the altar; that led to the erection in greater churches of a stone wall, or screen, being built between altar and shrine as at St. Albans, and the shrine being moved farther eastwards. But by now the altar was standing against a stone wall, and the smaller parish churches, which had no shrine, imitated the practice of the greater, and set their altars back against the east wall of the chancel.

Another important feature of the setting of a high altar is the spacing of the steps and of the pavement. Plain uninterrupted spaces contribute much to the architectural dignity of the building's focal point and they are rarely provided with generosity sufficient to effect this dignity, due no doubt to the lack of means. A high altar, where high Mass is celebrated, normally requires three steps: the uppermost, the footpace, should extend in width to the two sides of the altar and may be wider if desired; its depth from the altar front to its western edge should not be less than three feet nine inches to permit genuflection without the foot projecting over its edges. The second and third steps may be returned on the north and south sides of the footpace, or they may be carried across the sanctuary as in most medieval churches. They should be wide enough for deacon and subdeacon to stand on comfortably, thirty inches being a reasonable average and twenty inches a minimum. The pavement to the west of them should be a plain surface proportionate to the size of the building.

The High Altar Canopy

The tradition of surmounting the altar by a canopy has been constant from the earth 4th century when Constantine had one placed over the high altar in the Lateran Church in Rome. The rubrics require it over all altars, but especially over the high altar and the altar where the Blessed Sacrament is habitually reserved. In pagan basilicas it marked the magistrate's royal authority derived from the emperor, and was adopted in the Christian basilicas as a symbol of the altar's royal dignity. It serves to complete the "express figure of our Lord Jesus Christ, our Altar, Victim and Priest" by uniting these three offices under one symbol, and by crowning the altar, the Holy Sacrifice and the priest, who represents Christ's priesthood, with a single crown. For this reason it is essential that the canopy covers not only the altar, but also the footpace upon which the celebrant stands; and a shallow canopy projecting only over the altar does not fulfil its primary function.

Its most constant form down to the present day has been that of the Civory (*ciborium magnum*). It consists of a covering, or roof, supported on four columns, and it persisted as the only type from the 4th to the 12th centuries. During all that period curtains, or ridels, were hung on rods between all four columns, as may be seen to-day by the rods still remaining in place on the civories of some of the older churches in Rome such as St. Clement's and St. Paul's outside the Walls. When altars were set back against a wall, as described in the preceding section, the canopy was detached from its columns to form a tester and moved up higher— in England, above the east window—while the ridels, and often the columns in the form of ridel-posts as well, remained behind (Fig. 2). This was the arrangement generally found in paintings of the later middle ages, and familiar in the revival of the last fifty years or more (9).

Photo by F. Goldring, Haslemere

26. WISBOROUGH GREEN, SUSSEX

27. CHURCH OF THE ASCENSION, HANGER
HILL, EALING

28. SIDE ALTAR AT ST. COLUMBA, ANFIELD, LIVERPOOL

29. LAWTON MOOR, WYTHENSHAWE, MANCHESTER

TWO FORMS OF ALTAR FRONTAL

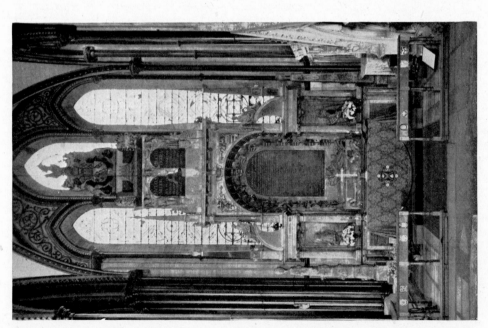

31. ALTAR IN SIDE CHAPEL AT ST. CUTHBERT, BRISLINGTON, SHOWING FLAT FRONTAL.

30. ALTAR IN ST. STEPHEN'S CHAPEL, SALISBURY CATHEDRAL, SHOWING FULL FRONTAL.

The use of canopies on four columns in England—at least in the greater churches —is wider than is generally recognised, for it lasted into the 12th century and possibly later.* Daniel Rock, in Vol. I of his *Church of Our Fathers* gives a line illustration from a contemporary painting in a Benedictional and mentions the references to them to be found in Anglo-Saxon Pontificals, quoting the prayer for their blessing. He also quotes the rubric for the drawing of the curtains from the Order of the Dedication of a Church in the Ecgbert Pontifical. His line illustra-

tion is taken from St. Ethelwold's Benedictional (between 963 and 984) which was painted by a monk of Winchester. A reconstructed perspective is reproduced in 10. It shows a dome pierced by four arches, and supported on four columns which was the usual type, Byzantine in origin, extending from the 4th to the 12th centuries. It has been recently revived, for example, over the high altar of St. Thomas More's Church at Seaford (11), and in the United States of America in Nazareth Hall, St. Paul, Minnesota.

The type which succeeded the civory in the later middle ages was the elevated tester mentioned above, set above the east window owing to the altar being set back against the wall. Only two original testers remain in position in this country, both of them in Shrop-

FIG. 2. DESIGN SUGGESTED FOR THE HIGH ALTAR IN THE CHURCH OF ST. PHILIP, ARUNDEL, SHOWING THE CANOPY RAISED AS A SUSPENDED TESTER ABOVE, AND THE FOUR POSTS AND CURTAINS BELOW, VEILING THE ALTAR.

shire, the one over the high altar at Clun,† and the other over the altar in the north aisle at Ludlow. Their revival has made them familiar during the last fifty years. A recent example in the Church of the Holy Family at Manchester is shown in 12, and in that of St. George, Polegate, Sussex, in 13, as well as the beautiful and well-known example at Downside Abbey in 9.

* For a French example see (Plate 1) in *Fifty Pictures of Gothic Altars, Alcuin Club Collections, X,* showing a contemporary painting of the early 14th century, where the altar is surmounted by a domed canopy, the arches of which are cusped and supported on thin columns.

† Illustrated in the Author's *Liturgical Altar*, 2nd edition, p. 74.

A variant of the wooden tester is the Baldaquin which is made of textile material instead of wood. The dimensions of both forms are governed by the prescription requiring them to cover both altar and footpace. Either form may be connected with the altar by a dossal, in the absence of a window, like the canopy of a bishop's throne (12); and in this connection it is worth recalling that the *Cærimoniale Episcoporum* directs that a canopy be erected over the Bishop's throne in his cathedral church, with this qualifying condition: "provided that there be a similar, or more splendid one, over the altar."

One of the last contemporary drawings to be made of a medieval tester must be that drawn in the obituary roll of Abbot John Islip in 1532. It shows the tester then existing over the high altar at Westminster Abbey Church, apparently of 15th-century design. The last canopy to be set up in that church, before the expulsion of the Benedictine community, was completed in 1526 over the altar of our Lady in Henry VII's Chapel. It is remarkable in that it shows a return to the earlier type of four-posted civory, but with Renaissance detail, designed by Torrigiano. It remained in position until demolished by the Puritans in 1643. In 1935 a conjectural copy of it was erected incorporating a few original fragments. It would be interesting to speculate whether this return to the earlier principle of the civory would have further developed in this country, if Benedictine life had continued without interruption.

The Civory, with its four posts and sometimes with its accompanying ridels, is also among the revivals of recent years. One is shown (14) over the high altar of the Church of the Sacred Heart of Jesus and St. Joseph at Ware, in Hertfordshire, and over the altar in the Church of St. Mary, Holly Place, Hampstead (15).

The Clothing and Furnishing of the Altar

The rules governing the altar's clothing and furniture are found in the General Rubrics of the Missal.

Number 18 lays down: "The clothing of the Altar, of the Celebrant and of the Ministers is to be of the colour conforming to the Office and Mass of the day, according to the use of the Roman Church: which has the custom of using five colours, White, Red, Green, Purple and Black."

Number 20 adds: "This altar is to be covered with three cloths, or clean linens, blessed by a Bishop or another having authority, the upper being long enough at least to reach the ground (*i.e.* at the two sides) the other two shorter, or consisting of one cloth folded double. It is to be adorned with a frontal of the colour conforming, so far as is possible, to the Feast or Office of the day. On the Altar is to be placed a Cross, in the centre, and at least two candlesticks with lighted candles on either side. At the foot of the cross is placed the Altar-card. On the Epistle corner a cushion for supporting the Missal, and at the same Epistle side is set the wax taper to be lighted at the elevation of the Sacrament, a small bell, glass cruets for wine and water, with a small dish and clean towel, in a niche or on a small table prepared for them. On the Altar nothing whatever is to be placed which does not pertain to the Sacrifice of the Mass or to the ornamentation of the Altar itself."

The first of these two prescriptions reveals that the vesting of the altar is of sufficient importance to be named before that of the celebrant, and the second shows that all elevations of the altar are to be clothed—the front by its frontal, and the sides by the linen cloth which reaches to the ground. A rather later direction in the *Cær. Episc.* adds that where the back elevation is free of the wall, it too must have an *antependium*. It also adds gold to the scheme of five colours, as an alternative to red, green or white.*

This clothing of the altar with colour is of such vital importance to the architectural interior of any church that a brief examination of its historical background is necessary, to establish the continuity both of its doctrinal intention and of its use in practice.

In the first three centuries the clothing of altars, which were often of wood, was in white cloths only.

In the early 4th century, from the time of Constantine, the clothing was a close-fitting coloured vesture, like a box-cloth, with a white cloth laid above it—an arrangement which has persisted with little change ever since in the Eastern Orthodox rite (Fig. 3). Of this pattern was the clothing of the high altar of Constantine's church of the Lateran.

In the West, and with evidence of English practice from the 7th century, altars were covered with a full-draped coloured robe, surmounted by

FIG. 3. SIXTH-CENTURY MOSAIC IN THE CHURCH OF ST. VITALE, RAVENNA, SHOWING AN ALTAR BETWEEN ABEL OFFERING A LAMB, AND MELCHISEDECH OFFERING BREAD AND WINE. THE REFERENCE TO CHRIST, ALTAR, VICTIM AND PRIEST, IS UNMISTAKABLE.

* For further references, see *The Celebration of Mass*, by Rev. J. O'Connell, Vol. I, p. 241, and footnote referring to his statement on p. 242: "Liturgical tradition and the rubrics demand the use of the frontal."

a full white cloth on the table top. These robes were frequently bequeathed by donors from the richest in their wardrobe. Thus, in the life of St. Wilfred (634–709) it is stated: "The altar also with its bases they dedicated to the Lord and vested it in purple woven with gold; the people shared in the work, and thus all was completed in a canonical manner." * An altar of this type is that illustrated (10) from St. Ethelwold's Benedictional.

In the same century, by the time of the Venerable Bede (672–735), the doctrinal significance of this clothing is already recognised and stated. Amalarius, who died in 859, writes: "The altar signifies Christ, as Bede narrates. . . . The robes (*vestimenta*) of the altar are the Saints of Christ." This statement at once recognises the altar as an express figure, not only of Christ, but of *Christ clothed with the members of His Mystical Body*. This is the accepted interpretation of the altar's clothing which became more and more explicit with the development of time.

By the 9th century, in the greater churches altars were sometimes being clothed with gold and silver plates screening the whole of the front elevation, and sometimes with separate ones for each of the other elevations. Contemporary references to them in England are frequent, and English goldsmiths were recognised as so supreme in their craft that their work was in much demand on the Continent. Such was probably Walwin who in the 9th century made the four metal hangings—one of gold for the front, and three of silver for the sides and back—which still remain in use in the Church of St. Ambrogio, Milan. These metal hangings are usually true *antependia* since they are removable in conformity with the stripping of the altar on Holy Thursday. These 9th-century examples also emphasise their function of representing the members of Christ's Mystical Body by their design; a central figure of Christ in glory is flanked by apostles or other saints, as shown in the example from Komburg in Fig. 4. Detachable frontals of painted wood were also employed. Examples from the 15th century remain in the Church of the Holy Spirit, in Florence, and one in Westminster Abbey.

In the 12th and 13th centuries the coloured and full-draped robes were superseded by flat rectangular hangings of silk, velvet or other textile material. In their embroidery the English craftsman was again supreme, and *Opus Anglicanum* was in great demand abroad. The change from folded robes to flat textile hangings may have been suggested by the experience of the greater prominence rendered to the altar by the flat metal screens, in contrast to the broken lights and shadows of the folded drapery. The same symbolism appears to have persisted universally, for of the ten examples in *Der Christliche Altar* selected by Fr. Joseph Braun, S.J., to illustrate the frontals of the 12th and 13th centuries, each one represents a central Christus "girded with the multitude of saints." Since these flat textile hangings were usually limited to the front and back elevations, the top white cloth was pro-

* By Eddius Stephanus: translated by Bertram Colgrave.

FIG. 4. DETACHABLE FRONTAL OF GILDED COPPER FROM THE ABBEY CHURCH OF KOMBURG.

longed to reach the ground at the two sides in order to complete the altar's clothing.

In the Office of Ordination of Subdeacons, which was authorised in the later Middle Ages, the doctrinal purpose of this clothing became officially recognised. The bishop, in addressing the Ordinands on the care of the altar, uses words which may be translated as follows: "For the Altar of Holy Church is Christ Himself, as John bears witness, who in his Apocalypse tells us that he beheld a golden Altar standing before the throne in and through whom the oblations of the faithful are made acceptable to God the Father. The cloths and corporals of this altar are the members of Christ, God's faithful people, with whom the Lord is girded as with precious robes, as the Psalmist says: The Lord is enthroned; He hath clothed Himself with beauty." (Psalm 92, 1.) Here the cloths refer to the white linen, the cleansing of which is the immediate subject of the bishop's address. But later he adds, "St. John in the Apocalypse saw the Son of Man girded with a *golden* cincture, that is the Multitude of Saints," thereby including the coloured clothing also in the symbolism.

With the full recognition of this doctrinal interpretation, the symbolism of the altar clothing should have become the legitimate heritage of small and poor churches as well as of large and wealthy ones; but in practice only the greater churches could afford frontals elaborately embroidered with figures. This was one problem requiring solution. Another was how to check the decline from the high standard of doctrinal symbolism which began to appear in frontals of the 14th and later centuries when miscellaneous subjects, other than that of Christ's Mystical Body, became the general theme. Both these problems were met by a single solution. Instead of pictorial figures to represent the members of our Lord's Mystical Body, a sequence of colours was designed to do so. At one stroke the handicap of expensive elaboration is lifted from smaller churches, and at the same time the doctrinal symbolism not only remains undimmed, but is considerably increased and rendered more intelligible. The "express figure of our Lord" is girded with the golden or white robes of Christmas and Easter and thereby clothed with His faithful people who share in His Birth and Victory. It is clothed in the red robe of the martyr in whom His own victory is realised afresh, and in the white of a Confessor or Virgin crowned with His own faith and purity. It assumes the purple robe of His people's penance, as He Himself once wore it in Herod's Court, and is clad in the green of common foliage, uniting to Himself the multitude from whom spring the more chosen flowers of canonisation.

This device of the colour sequence was first practised to a limited and local extent by Pope Innocent III who died in 1216. It appears in print in Burckard's *Ordo Missæ* of 1502 and becomes finally crystallised in 1570 in the General Rubrics of the Missal, as described above. It has remained in force ever since.

When this principle of the sequence of coloured clothing for the altar is recognised and accepted, architectural and other advantages inevitably follow.

1. The Church is provided with a representation of her Lord clothed with the members of His Mystical Body in a manner which no sculpture or painting can achieve.

2. The focal point of the building is emphasised by concentrating colour where it is most wanted.

3. The solid rectangle of the altar gains prominence from the flat surface of its frontal and from the elimination of the broken lights and shadows caused by recessed panels. A series of alternating shadows and high lights is the basis of camouflage, which is the art of rendering a surface inconspicuous.

4. By changing the colour of the frontal the central accent of the whole building's colour scheme is changed, and the variety thus introduced becomes a constant stimulus.

5. Colour when sufficiently provided on the chief feature of the building, can be made to radiate out from that centre by a less concentrated application to the roof and walls of the sanctuary.

English wall and roof painting was once a great art, taking its place beside the craft of stained glass, screen painting and embroidery, and all of them so harmonised that the united effect exceeded the sum of the individual parts. When stained glass is freed from the advertisement pages of church catalogues, and more of our painters' output removed from easel and frame and restored to roof and walls, both arts may derive benefit for themselves as well as render service to God's House.

In practice the frontal is best hung, as its name, *antependium*, implies. The most convenient way is to furnish it with rings, spaced about two inches apart along its upper edge, each ring being large enough for a rod of about half inch diameter to pass through it freely. The rod is supported on metal pins with crooked ends to receive the rod, one at either end and preferably a third in the centre, fitted into the joint of the underside of the *mensa* (Fig. 1). The pins then protrude between the rings without interrupting the hang of the frontal and causing a ruck. The frontal should be backed with sail-cloth, and interlined, to ensure a flat surface—an effect recommended in the *Cær. Episc.*,* which requires the absence of any ruck or fold. A pleated frontal diminishes the prominence of the altar's front elevation, which a flat frontal enhances. The rod and the rings are then concealed from sight by a narrow orphrey, or strip of damask, from five inches to seven or nine inches deep, called a frontlet (the *frontellum* of the medieval inventories). It is best attached to a stout cloth of linen or hemp covering the table top, laid below the three linen cloths. If it is sewn to one of these three, it needs to be unsewn each time the cloth is washed. This cloth should have a rectangular space cut out of its eastern end in order to clear the tabernacle. The flaps left on either side of the cut-out may be extended to hang down six inches or so over the table's back edge. Each flap may terminate in a two inch slot, and a single rod passed through the two slots and extending the full length of the altar will keep the cloth and its frontlet in position.

The Altar Furniture

The directions for the altar's furniture, quoted above from the General Rubrics of the Missal, have been further qualified in minor points since 1570. Six candlesticks are required by the *Cærimoniale* on every high altar instead of the earlier two; on other altars four or two are placed. A seventh candlestick is set in the centre in line with the other six on a high altar at a Pontifical Mass sung by the bishop, the cross being moved forward for the purpose.

The six candlesticks may rise in height, stepping up in echelon from the outside to the two in the centre,† or they may be all of the same height.‡ They are to be set on the plain surface of the altar (*in planitie altaris*).† A subsequent decree of the S.R.C. permits this surface to include also that of a gradine, if there already exists a custom to that effect.

Of the high altar candles all six are lighted for solemn Offices on greater feasts; four on lesser; two on simple feasts and ferias. Real candles should be used in the candlesticks: as Fr. J. O'Connell points out in *Directions for Altar Societies and Architects*,§ it is an abuse to burn candles of proper size at Benediction and other lesser functions and use up candle ends in dummies for the Adorable Sacrifice.

* Lib. i., cap. xii., § 11.
† *Cær. Episc.* I, XII, 11.
‡ S.R.C. 30357 (1855).
§ Burns, Oates and Washbourne, Ltd., 1936 edition, p. 27, footnote.

On every altar on which Mass is celebrated a crucifix is to be placed in the centre between the candlesticks, *super altare*,* *i.e.* normally on the *mensa* (14). The concession granted later to local custom in the case of the candlesticks would operate also in this case. Where there is a tabernacle the crucifix stands behind it. It must be clearly visible to the congregation as well as to the Celebrant. Alternatively, it may be hung above the altar (12), or it may be incorporated in a reredos or altar-piece, provided it forms the chief figure and is clearly visible to all.

The Altar-card mentioned in the Missal Rubric is now replaced by a set of three; they are usually framed and glazed, and a strut at the back is a convenience for enabling them to stand at any distance convenient for reading; or they may rest against the edge of a reredos or shelf, should there be one. Well-spaced, clear type can be more beautiful, as well as more practical, than elaborated borders or other "decoration." The cards should be removed from the altar after Mass.

The cushion for supporting the Missal is to-day more usually replaced by a stand of wood or metal. In churches enjoying a sufficient staff the cushion, or the cloth for the Missal-stand, will be of the colour of the day.

This, then, completes the list of furniture, stated in the Missal to "pertain to the Sacrifice of the Mass or to the ornamentation of the Altar itself." The perfect altar, writes Fr. J. O'Connell in *Directions*, "Consists of the consecrated table without additions of any kind. Such, for example, is the high altar of the chief basilicas of Rome and of Westminster Cathedral." In parish churches, or any church where the Divine Office is not publicly recited, the Blessed Sacrament is reserved on the high altar. A tabernacle is therefore a *necessary* addition.

The Tabernacle

Canon Law † requires the reservation of the Most Holy Eucharist in an immovable tabernacle, placed in the centre of the altar (*in media parte altaris positum*), of high-class workmanship, securely closed on all sides, and adorned in accordance with the liturgical laws. It should therefore be firmly fixed to the table of the altar and be allowed to appear clearly as what in fact it is—a feature distinct from the altar itself. A convenient position is for its front edge to be from twenty-one inches to twenty-four inches back from the front edge of the table. It may be of any material consistant with its security, and of any shape, *e.g.* round (14), square (13), or octagonal on plan, and preferably domed or bluntly spired for the convenience of the conopæum which must completely envelop it. The dome, or pyramid, may terminate in an ornament which can be removed when changing the conopæum. The tabernacle may not be used as a base for reliquaries, flowers, or indeed for any object—"not even for the cross" adds the note in *Directions*, p. 24, in reference to some am-

* General Rubrics of the Missal, 20.
† C.J.C., c. 1269, 1.

32. FONT IN ST. ALBANS CATHEDRAL
By W. H. Randoll Blacking, F.R.I.B.A.

ALTAR PLATE SHOWING VARIED TREATMENTS OF THE CHALICE YET FOLLOWING TRADITION

33. A SIMPLE BUT WORTHY DESIGN FOR A POOR PARISH

34. CIBORIUM IN BEATEN SILVER WITH A PIERCED KNOP

By Dunstan Pruden

35. SILVER CHALICE WITH A DULLED FINISH

By W. F. Knight

36. A VERY SIMPLE DESIGN IN SILVER GILT

By W. F. Knight

biguity in the law. It is convenient for it to be raised on a base two inches or more above the table of the altar, so that the door, or doors, open freely above the corporal; and two narrow doors, rather than a single wider one, obviate the danger of obstruction from the chalice. The interior of the tabernacle must be damp-proof and, if made of marble, lined with cedar wood or other protection. The interior walls should be lined with silk or with gold or silver plates, or they may be gilded with gold leaf. A pair of curtains hung inside the door are not ordered and are not desirable, since they have no function.

The Conopæum

The conopæum is a covering, like a tent, enveloping the whole tabernacle above and all round. It is not a matter of choice, but of obligation, being prescribed by the Roman Ritual (IV, 1, 6) and confirmed by replies of the Congregation of Sacred Rites. It cannot be too strongly emphasised that no circumstances excuse the omission of the conopæum; a pair of curtains hung before the door are not enough and are no substitute for the full conopæum; and no wealth of precious material or eleboration of craftsmanship on the tabernacle itself may be exposed for admiration at the cost of omitting the conopæum. A designer may well be grateful for the Congregation's insistence on this principle; for no display of metal work or other casing, undraped or partly draped, can equal the dignity and beauty of the fully draped tabernacle set on a duly clothed altar. The colour of the conopæum corresponds with that of the frontal, or, less suitably, it may always be white.

Other additions, not required by law, but permitted, are a temporary throne for exposition, reredos or altar-piece, reliquaries, flowers and gradine.

Throne for Exposition

The rules governing this throne were clarified by a reply from the Congregation of Sacred Rites in 1912 to a question from Westminster. They are given in detail in *Directions for Altar Societies and Architects*, 1936, and in the present author's *The Liturgical Altar*, 2nd edition, 1939, and may, therefore, be briefly summarised here.

No tabernacle should ever be surmounted by a permanent or fixed throne; but a movable one should be set above and behind the tabernacle for exposition, and afterwards removed: this accords with the practice of removing the chalice, missal and stand, and the cards, after the celebration of Mass. The most practical form is a light stand of gilded wood, or of more precious material; it requires no dossal or canopy, unless the altar canopy itself should have been omitted, in which case a small canopy is required covering the monstrance. The altar cross may in no circumstances be placed on any stand or in any throne for the Blessed Sacrament.

In a chapel where Perpetual Adoration is observed, a small permanent throne, such as a bracket or a niche, may be constructed at the back in the wall or reredos away from the altar, but near enough to form a unit with it. Such an arrangement may be seen in the chapel of Tyburn Convent. For simple Benediction no throne is required when the altar is duly surmounted by its canopy, the monstrance being placed on the altar-table as it is at the end of the Corpus Christi procession.

Reredos or Altar-piece

The altar, in order to fulfil the requirements of the Liturgy, does not require any backing; painting or sculpture, where desired, can be above the back of the altar and be supported on the floor, so long as it is not too large to stand by itself away from any wall to allow the consecrating Bishop to pass round the altar. If a larger structure is desired, it can be attached to the wall behind the altar and the necessary free space left between it and the altar. In the later Middle Ages a favourite device was to use an upper frontal, harmonising with that on the altar-front, hung on a rod between two ridel-posts, so that it rose above the back of the altar. Two other ridel-posts completed the approximate square (on plan) by standing in line with the west edge of the footpace, or in line with the altar-table's west edge, or on some line between these two. Several such upper frontals have been preserved; but the only complete pair of upper and nether frontals now remaining is that at Campden Church, in Gloucestershire. Together with the two ridels and the four posts, they are easily recognisable as the descendants of the posts and veils of the primitive civory, and they are now familiar from their revival in the 19th century.

Reliquaries

Where the altar is large enough as, for example, in greater churches, reliquaries and images of saints may be used for adorning the altar, but only on the greater feast days, and never when the Blessed Sacrament is exposed. They are to be set on the altar between the candlesticks which normally limits their number to four. They may not be placed on the tabernacle, nor before it.

Flowers

The rubrics of the Missal make no mention of flowers as pertaining to the ornamentation of the altar, nor are they used on the high altars of the chief basilicas of Rome. The *Cærimoniale Episcoporum* * recognises them as an ornament for the altar and civory on great feasts; and their use on the altar on the feast of the Puri-

* C.E. I, XII, 12, 14.

fication, on Maundy Thursday, and on Holy Saturday is permitted by the *Memoriale Rituum*, in places where there is a custom to that effect. Great restraint is needed in their use, to avoid their detracting from the effect of the altar's permanent furniture of cross and candlesticks. They should be confined to the clear space between the candlesticks without being allowed to confuse them with their sprays. This danger of confusion was well guarded against by the primitive custom of limiting flowers to garlands hung between the columns of the civory. The altar itself still riveted the attention of the people who would be conscious of some festive enhancement of its appearance. But a bank of flowers on, or just above, the altar in itself claims priority from admiring eyes; and the altar itself becomes a secondary, though possibly beautiful, base. It is quite otherwise when the beauty of the altar is so contrived as to display this greater festivity by the added splendour of the most precious of its frontals, strictly pertaining to its ornamentation.

Gradines

The gradine, or altar-shelf, is not ordered anywhere, nor is it forbidden. If one is used the two candlesticks for Low Mass may stand upon it. Minor inconveniences attend its presence; it is apt to interfere with the complete veiling of the tabernacle by the conopæum; and it causes difficulty in allowing the altar cross to be moved forward in order that the seventh candlestick required for a Pontifical High Mass may take its place in line with the other six candlesticks. Its convenience begins when candles are used exceeding in number the twelve required for exposition and for solemn Benediction, all of which may stand on the altar-table. But where additional lights are required a shelf can be erected behind the altar on the back wall, or formed in the reredos, on the same level as the surface of the *mensa*. Such a shelf, like a detached gradine, would provide a stand for the extra candles without encumbering the altar itself or interfering with the position of the crucifix or the other candlesticks upon it. The chief loss in using a gradine is to contribute, however slightly, to the tendency of obscuring the altar's true symbolism.

Summary

The purpose of *expressing a figure of our Lord Jesus Christ* is a major principle of the altar, and not a by-product. Hence any tendency to obscure this principle by the addition of non-essentials has constantly to be kept in abeyance. Throughout the Church's life and growth its rubrics for the form and furnishing of the altar have been meticulously selected and regulated with the aim of establishing this principle; and it may well seem remarkable in how slight a degree the details have been modified since the Church emerged from the catacombs. For the altar, with no additions beyond the furniture required by the liturgy, does in fact satisfy ; it wins the attention, and the affection, of learned and unlearned alike ; and those familiar with it express no desire to change it.

But once unessential features begin to be added, equilibrium is upset, and then there is no end to the suggestions for an altar's further "decoration" : ornaments, flowers and lights are increased, steps and shelves are added. As a result there is a sacrifice of plain spaces—one great source of architectural distinction—and the altar loses that valuable detachment which was so wisely ensured by the rubric requiring for its consecration a clear space all round it. Further experiments follow in an unsatisfied attempt to achieve some effect of dignity which always seems to elude its devotees. And by the time they have all had their way, it becomes very hard to recognise in the altar a figure expressly deputed to represent Him who is our Altar, as well as Victim and Priest.

RECENT ENGLISH AND CONTINENTAL WORK CONTRASTED

38. CHALICE IN SILVER AND ENGRAVED IVORY
From the School of Beato Angelico, Milan

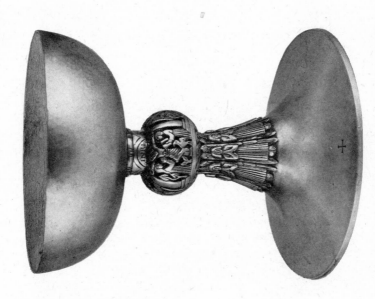

37. SILVER CHALICE WITH DEEPLY CHASED AND
MODELLED ORNAMENT ON KNOP AND STEM
By Dunstan Pruden

39. PRISMATICALLY CUT ROCK CRYSTAL MOUNTED IN SILVER
By Edward Hines

40 (*a*). GILT OR SILVERED
WOODEN ORNAMENTS, PRE-
FERABLE TO CHEAP BRASS
By W. H. R. Blacking,
F.R.I.B.A.

40 (*b*). CROSS AND CANDLESTICK IN SILVER,
WITH SYMBOLS OF THE EVANGELISTS
By the late Cuthbert Atchley

41. STANDARD CANDLESTICK
FOR A MODERN CHURCH
By Bernard A. Miller,
F.R.I.B.A.

The Anglican Tradition: Ornaments and Fittings

By FRANCIS C. EELES, O.B.E., D.Litt.

FORMS OF SERVICE for the consecration of churches usually specify that the Archdeacon must certify to the bishop that the arrangements of the building and its fittings are in accordance with the use of the Church of England. This means that all existing rules must be observed, the chief of which are included in what is known as the Ornaments Rubric, printed at the beginning of the Book of Common Prayer, opposite the first service contained in it. That rubric runs as follows:

"The Morning and Evening Prayer shall be used in the accustomed Place of the Church, Chapel or Chancel; . . . And the Chancels shall remain as they have done in times past.

"And here is to be noted, that such Ornaments of the Church, and of the Ministers thereof, at all Times of their Ministration, shall be retained, and be in use, as were in this Church of *England*, by the Authority of Parliament, in the Second Year of the Reign of King *Edward* the Sixth."

Accurately interpreted this is very comprehensive.

The reference is in three parts. The first governs the form and arrangement of the church building, the second the ornaments or movable fittings of the church, the third the vestments of the clergy. This last section does not concern us here.

The canons, the articles of visitation issued by bishops, and decisions by their courts also contain rules relating to the fittings of churches which are contained in this summary.

We begin by explaining exactly what existing law requires before dealing with what is merely tolerated, or discussed in regard to exceptions, or changes of an experimental nature.

Here are pictures illustrating chancels which "remain as they have done in times past."

The first (16, 17) look from the nave of the church towards the east end and show the screen with its gates separating the chancel from the nave. Above the screen there used to be a rood loft, a gallery provided in the later medieval period for those who sang the more modern type of music not provided by the liturgical books, and above which the rood, or great crucifixion scene, was arranged, with angels or other figures around it, often set against a boarded background in the upper part of the chancel arch. The wave of puritanism which overspread the

country at the beginning of Elizabeth's reign caused the removal of the figures *
and of the loft below, but the screens were ordered to remain. On either side of the
east end of the nave altars were sometimes placed, particularly in churches without
aisles, as at Ranworth in Norfolk, shown here (19), where there was no other
space for additional chapels.

Then we see (18) the chancel from the east, looking westwards towards the back
of the screen, showing the stalls for clergy and choir. Those for the clergy are
against the screen facing east. Those for the choir face north and south. These
stalls are at Stanford-on-Avon in the diocese of Leicester; they belong to the 15th
century. Other illustrations show the altar and its arrangements (20, 24–29).
Rails for the communicants to kneel at were introduced in the first part of the
17th century when they are insisted on in episcopal visitation articles, and stand on
the step between the choir and the sanctuary: sometimes they have gates, sometimes not. In some places a movable bench is used instead of fixed rails, in which
case a step is not necessary.

There may or may not be one, or two, steps across the floor of the sanctuary, but
there is usually one for the holy table to stand on. Against or sunk in the south
wall, and sometimes adjusted to combine with the steps, or contrived by the
lowering of a window sill, are the sedilia; three seats for the three ministers of the
altar, celebrant, gospeller and epistoler (sometimes spoken of as the priest, deacon
and subdeacon) arranged either on one level or rising, step by step, from west to
east. The highest in dignity sits in the eastmost seat according to English use.
East of the sedilia a piscina, or water basin and drain, are provided in a niche in the
wall, with a shelf above, which in practice is generally supplemented by a small
table called a credence for the sacred elements to stand on before they are placed
on the altar, with the alms dish and anything else required for use in the service.

In the wall on the opposite, or north, or left side of the altar, may be an aumbry
or locker, one use of which would be for the reservation of the consecrated elements for the sick: this may be enriched to a greater or lesser degree: a modern
one is shown here from St. Bartholomew the Less, London, and a richer ancient
one from Kintore in Aberdeenshire. The use of aumbries in the wall for this purpose became common in England after 13th-century legislation.

All that has been described so far must be reckoned as required by the rubric to
be provided to-day.

The Altar or Holy Table

The central place in the sanctuary, of course, is occupied by the altar, which
may be of wood or stone, constructed of a large thick slab, or *mensa* as the table of
the altar is sometimes called, set upon pillars or an ashlar-faced construction, or

* In recent years the courts have again been granting faculties for roods.

made like a wooden chest or table. The *mensa* must project beyond any lower part of the structure and have a plain right-angled upper edge, though it may be chamfered or moulded on the under side. In many cases wood will definitely be required; this may be a survival of an old controversy regarding the material, which began at the time of the Reformation. In the 17th and 18th centuries a good many stone altars were set up, but the controversy was revived in the 19th century, and there was a decision against stone in a case at St. Sepulchre's, Cambridge. In view of the older precedents, this ruling is now increasingly regarded as becoming obsolete.

The top of the altar should be normally three feet three inches from the ground: in a small church it may be an inch less or in a large church an inch or two inches more. The altar should be at least two feet six inches from back to front; this allows about two feet in front of a cross if one stands in the centre. The high altar of a fairly large church should be at least three feet from back to front. The length of the altar must vary according to architectural requirements. In the traditional Gothic chancel the altar should be as long as the glass of the east window, but in the case of a very narrow window it may well have to be longer or, if the window is extremely large, it may have to be shorter. The idea that it must be a third the width of the chancel is inaccurate and misleading: it may be well to remind the reader that most of the altars of the 19th-century tradition were too short.

The top step or footpace should never be less than two feet six inches deep in front of the altar, or in the case of the high altar two feet nine inches. It may well be more if space permits.

The second and third steps should be alike: never less than one foot eight inches deep, better one foot ten inches as a minimum, and if space permits two feet. The risers of these steps should not exceed five inches in a large church, four inches in a small one.

Between the lowest step and the altar rails there must always be space for the ministers to pass and repass each other when administering communion: this means at least five feet six inches or better six feet as a minimum.

The rails may be narrow, only occupying three or four inches, or they may be like benches with flat tops about nine inches or more in width. A good average height is two feet. The space on the step in front of the rails should be at least one foot (clear of the top of the rail). Under no circumstances may there be two steps at the altar rails, and for the sake of infirm communicants more than a single step further west at the entrance to the chancel is undesirable.

Between the rails and the choir stalls there must be room for communicants to pass and repass each other; five feet six inches or six feet or more should be allowed for this.

If there be an aisle or aisles to the chancel, easy access should be provided so that the communicants on returning can reach them without difficulty.

The altar is covered with a textile frontal which may take more than one form, and the top must be covered when the altar is in use with a linen cloth, which normally reaches down each end nearly to the ground.

The covering of the altar is dealt with in Canon 82 of 1603 which runs: "the same Tables shall from time to time be kept and repaired in sufficient and seemly manner, and covered in time of Divine Service with a carpet of silk or other decent stuff (*i.e.* handsome material, in modern words), thought meet by the Ordinary of the place, if any question be made of it, and with a fair linen cloth at the time of the administration."

The frontal may be flat (31) of rich material with panels or stripes of contrasting colours and trimmed with a fringe or braid, or it may hang more or less full, like a curtain (30). In either case along the edge of the table should hang a narrow band of material not more than five inches deep which hides the attachment of the frontal, and is itself attached to one of the linen cloths. In the case of a very short altar the frontal may be of a type associated with the Renaissance period when it took the form of a large cloth thrown over the altar and drawn out at the two front corners. This form of frontal continued in use through the 18th and early 19th centuries until almost abolished by the Gothic revivalists who tried to make the flat type universal.

There is something to be said for the use of a movable frontal of material other than textile: stamped leather for example, as at York in the 17th century, or even painted or decorated wood, so long as it is really a covering that can readily be detached.

The absence of a frontal and the decoration of the altar itself was not unknown of old; it was common in France and became widespread after the Counter Reformation abroad, notwithstanding the rubric in the Roman missal. In this country there is evidence that the Puritans liked to display the bare table. But the fact of a 17th-century altar table being richly carved is no proof that it was left uncovered in service time. We recollect that the canon already quoted orders the table to be covered *in time of Divine Service*. Medieval altars were no doubt often left uncovered (and devoid of other ornaments) out of service time. Artistically the contrast between the altar frontal and the reredos is valuable as it serves to emphasise the altar in contrast with its surroundings.

The Reredos

Behind the altar rises a series of decorative panels, in sculpture or painting, called the reredos, usually the same length as the altar, and according to the more general English tradition not very high, so as not to cover the great east window which is characteristic of the architectural lay-out of Gothic east ends in this country (24). If the east window be exceptionally high, a second stage of somewhat different character will provide the necessary extension of the reredos as in (25). On either side of the reredos, rods at right-angles to the east wall very generally were provided to carry curtains called ridels, close to each end of the altar. In some cases a textile hanging or "upper frontal" may take the place of a wood or stone reredos, and in some large chancels, pillars can be introduced to support the rods for the ridel curtains.

As a rule the architect should avoid any very large or high curtain behind the altar. The use of such an arrangement tends to encourage a demand for over large altar ornaments, which improperly dwarf the altar, and large curtains are apt to fade, difficult to clean and costly to renew. In any such case the immediate background to the altar, where textiles are needed, should be a rich hanging in place of the reredos properly so called, with, if necessary, another hanging above that (19, 20, 26).

What have been here described are historical adaptations to Gothic and later east ends of the earlier arrangement in which the altar stood beneath a massive canopy on four pillars between which hung curtains. In course of time the canopy became severed from the pillars, and was raised, or even transmuted into the form of a decorated ceiling, while the pillars, only having to support curtain rods, were made much lighter or disappeared. The reredos developed when the altar was no longer accessible from behind, and had been made to stand against a wall or a screen or against the elevated shrine for the relics of a saint.

It is necessary to emphasise the need of colour on the reredos whether it is of painted wood or stone or merely a textile hanging. The Victorian type of reredos one often sees carried out in uncoloured stone or wood, and with nothing more than a cross, a monogram, or the like, upon panels with cusped heads in poor imitation Gothic, is an artistic abomination.

This is only a very rough outline of the history of the change from the altar of the earlier period, such as still survives in the older basilicas in southern Europe (and having existed of old is still legitimate in the Church of England), to that which became common in the later middle ages in northern Europe. This lasted till it was changed in consequence of new Renaissance methods which spread from Italy with the Counter-Reformation and became combined with other extravagances of very late origin. These latter, having developed outside the Church of England after the Reformation, are not legitimate as interpretations of the Ornaments Rubric.

It is possible in some cases to design a modern altar of the early basilican type with the massive pillars supporting a canopy or ciborium. Such an altar was actually provided in Henry VII's chapel in Westminster Abbey early in the 16th century and has lately been restored there. Peterborough Cathedral has a modern one; so has Carlisle.

Where a triptych or similar lofty or multi-sectioned reredos is provided, it must be so designed that the part immediately above the altar is richly decorated and is not merely an architectural base for the rich upper part: it is indeed this part of the structure which is really the reredos.

In constructing a triptych care should be taken that the leaves actually close, as this is required throughout Lent. The backs of the leaves should be painted white or grey, or in such a manner as to combine with the Lenten array, as it is called, when imagery and pictures are veiled and the altar itself vested in unbleached linen.*

The numerous and large candlesticks, etc., and shelves or "gradines" to carry them, familiar in so many Continental altars of the Renaissance, and subsequently adopted for use during the Gothic revival, found no place on the English altar,† nor for that matter on the other altars of the older type in western Europe. Only two candlesticks stood, or may stand, on or immediately behind the altar, though candles were, and can be, added on the curtain rods or in hanging candelabra or in standards on the floor of the sanctuary.

Flower vases are not ornaments of the liturgical altar, and are borrowed from continental practice of late date. Flowers, if required, should be placed on ledges, window sills, or stools in the sanctuary and elsewhere in the church. There should be nothing of the nature of a shelf on or behind an altar. The two altar lights should stand directly upon the table.

The arrangements here described are those of the normal English Gothic church. But they have been carried out in other architectural styles and can be adapted to modern formulæ and materials also. The great classical church of All Saints, Derby, by James Gibbs, 1725, now the Cathedral, is a striking instance of the persistence of the old traditional arrangement carried out in Renaissance detail. Here we have the great east window and the chancel enclosed by rich screen work, in this case of iron. A more recent instance of strict interpretation of the traditional arrangement in Renaissance terms was (until recently destroyed by enemy action) at St. Matthew's, Bethnal Green, London, where the church was of the 18th century and the fittings were designed by Mr. F. C. Eden. There are still

---

* According to English use, the veiling of pictures and closing of reredoses takes place from the beginning of Lent instead of only from the fifth Sunday as in the Roman rite. (*See* 20). Moreover, the colour is unbleached linen, as may be seen in many English cathedrals. The dark red colour corresponding to the Roman "purple" is without English authority for the veils, and is not used for other things save in the last fortnight of Lent. Blue was occasionally used for the veils, and is now often used for the altar hangings, though with less dramatic effect than the old unbleached white with red or blue stencilled or applied designs.

† The term "English altar" has often been rather misleadingly used for an altar surrounded by curtains on rods supported by two or four posts. Such altars were not exclusively English or particularly common. The term grew up before the last war to describe an altar of this kind when contrasted with the Victorian type which had been so largely influenced by Continental practice. As a rule the four posts belong to a very big chancel or to a situation where for some reason the altar must stand a little distance from the east wall.

a large number of Renaissance screens in all parts of the country, for example at St. John's, Leeds (18).

The accompanying picture of a side chapel at St. Columba, Anfield, Liverpool, shows how the same thing can be done in modern style and with a new use of materials (28).

In most of our later medieval churches there hung above the altar the vessel called the pyx which contained the sacrament reserved for the sick. This was suspended within a textile canopy and was covered with a veil. Both pyx and canopy were sometimes themselves suspended from a flat tester. Where the pyx was not suspended in this manner it was placed in an aumbry in the north wall as already described, and this is the method ordered by Anglican authorities at the present day. The tabernacle set upon the altar or built into the reredos behind it, so familiar in the Roman rite, was scarcely ever used in England, and English church authorities regard it as illegal in the Anglican church. The aumbry for the Reserved Sacrament should have an inner, well ventilated, metal safe. A decorated outer door or grille set within an architectural structure is desirable in addition to the silk curtain so often provided to-day.

We now have to consider exceptions to the rules given above.

First of all there is a long tradition, originating with the puritan element in London after the Great Fire, and begun under Sir Christopher Wren himself, of a type of church like a large auditorium without a screen, and in which there is no chancel. There were often galleries at the sides as well as at the west end. The actual arrangements of the altar, even when much money and skill were available, differed in their proportions from the older traditions. The space within the altar rails was very limited: this definitely would never be permitted now. The altar itself had become much shorter, the reredos much higher. A later development of this type of church, due to what is known as the evangelical revival of the 18th century, placed the pulpit in the centre, and sometimes, with flagrant illegality, the font beside it; here again this would not be allowed now. But the omission of the screen and the elimination of the separate chancel and its choir stalls, though contrary to the strict letter of the law set out above are, and have been, widely tolerated by competent authority all over England, though not now to the extent of omitting ample provision for the clergy stalls to the west of the altar rails.

To recapitulate briefly: three main types of arrangement of the altar are legitimate in the Church of England to-day. First, the basilican, with an altar only a little longer than its height and breadth, standing under a canopy supported on four pillars. The pillars may or may not be joined back and sides by curtains, and the frontal to harmonise may be of the gathered type with a flat frontlet.

Second, the Gothic type of altar, which usually accompanied the large east window, generally in length at least one and a half times its depth and often much more, with behind it either a reredos or triptych, richly coloured or gilded; or for economy, a good textile hanging. The whole may or may not be surrounded by four posts or have ridel curtains without posts at right-angles to either side. The posts or rods may or may not have additional candles upon them. The frontal may be of the flat Gothic type or gathered. A tester, or decorated ceiling panels, may take the place of the canopy of the earlier type.

Thirdly, the Renaissance form as it developed in the Church of England, with an altar square, or a little longer, often with a full frontal like a table cloth thrown over it, and falling in stiff folds at each corner, the reredos taking any of the forms familiar in our Renaissance churches or in the architectural arrangement of monuments of the period, but without shelves or gradines and with the reredos immediately over the altar. In all three types of the altar the ornaments remain the same, two candlesticks, and probably a cross, with or without a cushion (or two cushions) for the book.

The provision of a special throne or seat for the bishop is unnecessary in a parish church, where a visit from the bishop is very infrequent. Should one be provided, however, in a church of special importance, it should be movable, to allow of its use at a confirmation and should normally stand on the north side of the sanctuary.

Side Chapels

A side chapel is arranged like a miniature chancel. The most strict reading of law and tradition requires such a chapel to be screened. Of old the larger ones were furnished with stalls behind the screen and with sedilia on the right side of the altar. The provision and position of the piscina is, of course, invariable. At the present day it is more common to find the aumbry for the reserved sacrament in the wall of the left side of a side chapel than in the high chancel. Anciently, an altar cross was not required on a side altar. Otherwise a side altar is arranged exactly like the high altar, the arrangements varying only artistically according to its position and surroundings. No additional altars are now permitted unless they are properly constructed and furnished, and provided with sufficient space within and outside the communion rail. This means that structures having a superficial resemblance to altars, but which do not fulfil canonical requirements, are inadmissible as adjuncts to memorials or "Children's corners." The English tradition has been and is very firm in requiring all altars to be orientated.

In a side chapel or a small church where no choir is provided for, or where the choir is placed in a gallery or in the nave, the officiant must be provided with a convenient desk outside the sanctuary, on the south side. This should, properly, face east in the same position as the stalls of a larger choir.

The Nave

The nave requires seating in such a manner that both congregation and processions can move easily. There should be no passage-ways where two robed clergymen cannot easily walk abreast. The pulpit and lectern should not be so erected as to interfere with a procession. The litany desk should be either readily movable or surrounded with sufficient space for the procession to divide on either side of it. The needs of weddings and funerals which require ample space in front of the chancel should be borne in mind.

The series of pictures or sculpture known as the Stations of the Cross has no ancient English precedent or authority: they are not covered by the Ornaments Rubric quoted above: but modern authority has occasionally allowed them to be placed in position merely for seasonal use, and to be removed again, so that they cannot be regarded as forming a part of the permanent decoration of an English church. This is parallel to what is now sometimes practised in the Roman church where only the small crosses beneath which the Stations of the Cross are hung are treated as permanent fixtures. From the artistic and architectural point of view, these fourteen pictures usually either look trivial if small, or they overpower other decorations if large.

The Font

According to the English law, the font must be of stone, fixed, provided with a cover and a drain, and set up within the church near a west door. Canon 81 of 1603 provides that "there shall be a font of stone in every Church and Chapel where Baptism is to be ministered; the same to be set in the ancient usual place." This excludes the use of a separate building or baptistry. The bowl of the font must be undivided and lined with lead; there is English precedent for placing it on one or more steps, but not for sinking the floor round it as in the Roman rite. There is post-Reformation precedent for surrounding it with a rail. The cover should be provided with gear for raising and lowering, unless very light and easily lifted, or arranged to open out at the sides as is sometimes found in late medieval examples.

Care must be taken to make it possible for the officiant to stand at the font facing east, for a procession to pass the font without difficulty, and for the christening party to be comfortably accommodated near the font.

In the ancient churches of East Anglia the tradition was, latterly at any rate, to place the font on steps as at Stoke by Nayland, Suffolk, at the west end of the nave, but never actually under the tower, a position to which some fonts have been moved by ignorant restorers. Although Canon 81, following a general practice, orders stone for the material of the font, there are exceptional cases of metal ones, which may be regarded as tolerated, provided that the font is of normal size and immovable.* A ewer must be provided for water, and there must be a source of pure water in the church, churchyard or vestry.

Finally, if an incumbent asks for the *omission* of imagery or candlesticks the architect may accede to this, and he need not appeal to any higher authority. But if he wishes to *add* to the ornaments specified here, or to alter their character the architect must personally, or through the incumbent, obtain the direction of the Archdeacon. The Diocesan Advisory Committee for the Care of Churches will always help in any difficulty.

Many are now looking forward to new building methods and new materials. The architect should explore the possibilities of everything of the kind, but he must respect the framework of the liturgical use of the Church and its fittings as outlined.

It is important for the architect or artist to remember that while a new church does not require a faculty for its erection, as soon as it is consecrated a faculty becomes necessary for any addition, whether structural or decorative.

ILLUSTRATIONS OF THE ENGLISH TRADITIONAL ARRANGEMENT OF A CHURCH

Sefton, Lancashire. Showing ample space in nave, medieval screen, Jacobean pulpit, 18th-century chandeliers.

St. John, Leeds. Built and furnished in 1631–4; original screen, pulpit and seating, an example of the old methods used in the early Renaissance period of the 17th century.

St. Luke, Cowley, Oxford. Built and furnished just before the war. The same arrangement carried out to-day. Architect: Alderman H. S. Rogers.

Ranworth, Norfolk. A fine example of a common medieval arrangement, showing nave altars and an ancient desk.

Stanford-on-Avon, Northants. The chancel "as in times past" with the strictly rubrical arrangement of stalls.

Monyash, Derbyshire. Sedilia of c. 1200 graduated in height.

Aumbry or Sacrament House, at St. Bartholomew the Less, London. Modern. Architect: LL. E. Williams, A.R.I.B.A.

Kintore, Aberdeenshire. A rich Sacrament House, early 16th century.

Font, St. Albans Cathedral. Architect: W. H. Randoll Blacking.

* The use of small portable vessels of metal or other material has been repeatedly prohibited.

SOME ENGLISH ALTARS SHOWING LEGITIMATE VARIETY OF TREATMENT

St. Cuthbert, Brislington, Bristol. Side chapel. The simplest form, altar, picture reredos and window. Architect: P. Hartland Thomas.

St. Stephen's Chapel, Salisbury Cathedral. Altar showing full frontal.

Wisborough Green, Sussex. A 13th-century chancel refurnished. Here the altar has curtains at each end. Note absence of unnecessary steps.

St. Michael-at-the-North Gate, Oxford. Fifteenth-century reredos, niches decorated and filled with sculpture. Architect: Harold S. Rogers. Sculptor: Harold Youngman.

St. John the Baptist, Harpenden, Herts. An altar in "Lenten Array" unbleached linen marked with simple devices covering or substituted for rich coloured work.

St. Columba, Anfield, Liverpool. Side altar. Small altar and reredos of the traditional form in a modern style. Architect: Bernard Miller.

Ascension, Hanger Hill, Ealing, Middlesex. A modern altar. Architects: Seeley and Paget.

SOME MODERN INTERIORS

These are without screens or the ancient arrangement of the stalls in choir, but otherwise conform to modern requirements.

St. Andrew, Hornchurch, Essex. Chancel added to a hall, so that the rest of the building can be used as a hall or as a church. Architect: N. F. Cachemaille-Day.

St. Cuthbert, Brislington, Bristol. An original design with a suggestion of the traditional West of England waggon roof. Architect: P. Hartland Thomas.

Lawton Moor, Wythenshawe, Manchester. A complete breakaway from architectural tradition, but the liturgical arrangements conform to requirements. Architect: N. F. Cachemaille-Day.

Church Plate ⌇ By JUDITH D. GUILLUM SCOTT

THIS COMPREHENSIVE TITLE may cover a very wide selection of ornaments: chalice, paten, ciborium or pyx, and cruets; altar cross or crucifix, and candlesticks; censer and incense boat; portable lights, processional cross and verger's mace; alms dish; font ewer, ablutions ewer and basin. All these are required both for the Latin rites and for the full interpretation of the English Prayer Book by the Ornaments Rubric of 1662, with the exception of the font ewer which is only a convenient means of supplying one of the essential requirements of any rite. The requirements of the Presbyterians and of the Free Churches are simpler and for them chalice and paten, font ewer and alms dish, will probably be all that the architect and the building committee will have to concern themselves with.

The Chalice

When considering the design of the chalice and paten, the first items on this list, it must be remembered that although a wide range of materials was used in early times, such as rock crystal, glass, sardonyx, jasper, and even wood and earthenware; silver or gold are required for the cup of the chalice to-day by the Roman authorities, and if silver is used, the cup must be gold plated within. Other materials such as ivory or crystal may form the stem. English tradition indicates gold or silver, but other metals, particularly pewter, were sometimes used in the 17th and 18th centuries: their use in pre-Reformation times was strongly reprobated, but apparently went on in some places.

At the beginning of the Christian era we may assume that, whether the chalice preserved at Valencia is or is not the original cup used by our Lord at the Last Supper, the chalice, like most other liturgical furniture, was derived from the ordinary domestic practice of the time of its first use. No one set out to design the first chalices: their form is a development and enrichment of a simple functional object. There have been three stages in this development: the first chalices which have survived are of the Greek Kalyx type, a wide low bowl usually with two handles, supported on a short stem springing from a flattish base, whose diameter is usually about half that of the bowl. These belong to the period when the early Church was strongest in the east; and we have few examples in the west, though the lovely chalice of Ardagh, now at Dublin, probably of the 8th century, should be known to all modern craftsmen. This type was gradually modified, though it

138

THE ROYAL VICTORIAN ORDER
ALTAR PLATE
IN THE KING'S CHAPEL OF THE SAVOY,
LONDON.

AN OUTSTANDING EXAMPLE OF
MODERN CHURCH SILVER CRAFTSMANSHIP

*Designed by the late Professor R. M. Y. Gleadowe.
Executed by Blunt & Wray Ltd., London.*

The design was selected in Open Competition
organised through Goldsmiths' Hall.

*Illustration reproduced by kind permission of the
Chaplain of the Order.*

CHALICE IN HAMMERED SILVER WITH PIERCED ORNAMENTS
IN THE BASE, KNOP, AND STEM

Designed and made by Osborne of Gower St., London, W.C.1

probably lived on for administration,* being accompanied by the newer style of chalice for consecration. The first known English chalice is an example of the new style, the Trewhiddle chalice of about 875, now in the British Museum. The change was very gradual, and was not really complete until the 13th century. The stem of the chalice had gradually become elongated, and a knop or bulb developed in the centre for convenience in handling, the cup had grown deeper and narrower and the base larger, the stem gradually increasing in size from the knop downwards, to meet the base, which was often octagonal or hexagonal. The whole was very convenient to handle, unlikely to be knocked over or to spill if shaken, and easy to administer from. This was the type which persisted through the Middle Ages with only one further modification. After the Council of Constance in 1415, and gradually during the century preceding it, the right to be communicated from the chalice was withdrawn from the laity, and consequently the size of the chalice bowl diminished. Chalices of this style continued in use on the Continent under the Roman rite with little alteration to modern times.

At the time of the Reformation in England vast quantities of plate were confiscated and melted down for the benefit of the Royal Treasury and that of lesser despoilers.†

From 1548 onwards there was a return to a larger form of chalice, introducing the third modification of the basic design.‡ This brought a deeper cup (usually half to two-thirds of the total height of the vessel), generally with the lip slightly splayed outwards, the base generally circular and of about the same diameter as the base of the cup. A knop was a general, but not an invariable feature of the stem. The decoration departed altogether from the traditional medieval goldsmith's and silversmith's work with its use of enamel and filigree, canopied niches and figurines modelled in the round. Instead, as the 17th century went on, the sole ornaments were the austere mouldings forming an integral part of the design, and often an inscription in freehand italic lettering, an incised coat of arms, or a band of lightly incised floral or arabesque ornament. The whole treatment was severe, dignified, and rather architectural in conception. Late in the 17th century increased richness sometimes returned in the form of embossed work. Some interesting plate of pre-Reformation type was made in England under Laudian influence in the 17th century, and specimens may be seen at Fulham Palace, at Lambeth, at many of the Oxford and Cambridge college chapels, at Rochester Cathedral, and in some forty parish churches. The later plain work was sometimes

---

* A chalice of this type is listed in an inventory of Westminster Abbey in 1388.

† A few medieval chalices survive, e.g. at Nettlecombe, Somerset.

‡ There are also two types of chalice found in Scotland, but little known in England. The one has a much wider and rather shallower bowl than usual, on a moulded and knopped stem, and the other has no stem at all, but is in the form of a beaker. The latter type, once common in the Aberdeen area, both in Episcopal and Presbyterian churches may be regarded as limited to that area, but the former has possibilities for some places.

engraved with an Agnus or an IHS in a "glory of rays." After this, however, the style was not used again until the Gothic revival, since when almost all the chalices made in England have been of the Gothic or pre-Reformation type.

Although some 19th and 20th century designs have been successful, especially some of Pugin's vigorous, original work, and the delicate rather French designs of Mr. J. N. Comper, or the less conventional pieces by Mr. Bainbridge Reynolds and the late Mr. Omar Ramsden, nothing really contemporary has emerged. Probably the simpler treatment of the English Renaissance chalices would provide a better background than the late medieval type, which still seems to be the most popular model—at least, with the ecclesiastical patron, but any of the three traditional forms of the chalice would be legitimate, for adaptation by the craftsmen of to-day. The 1920's and early '30's produced some unpleasant angular designs which were so awkward to handle that they were certainly not the products of direct functionalism that they purported to be. Since then nothing in a modern idiom, worthy of comment, has emerged.

The principal points for the guidance of design are: that the chalice must be safe and convenient to handle; it must be easy to clean, particularly as to the inside and outside of the cup; for the Roman rite the cup may be small, but for the Anglican and Free Churches it must be sufficient to communicate whatever number usually attend the communion services.* There must be no engraving or decoration of the interior or near the lip outside; the lip, if the cup does not slope outwards must be straight and must on no account turn inwards or sharply outwards; the cup must be wide enough for the celebrant's hand holding the purificator to wipe the bottom comfortably; none of the decorative work should be sharp enough to catch in linen or vestments.

The Paten

The early forms of paten varied both in size and shape. All sorts of materials were used, including glass, alabaster, and semi-precious stones, and examples of oval, oblong and multi-sided patens survive, often very richly embossed or engraved and decorated with precious stones in heavy settings. Many of these early patens were indeed large, and so heavy that it is doubtful if they were intended for use on the altar, and it is probable that they were used only to receive the people's offerings in kind. After the 9th century the form of the paten began to be standardised as a circular dish, generally of gold or silver, with a circular or multi-foil depression in the centre, the depression coming to be generally of a size to fit the top of the chalice when inverted. The decoration was generally confined to engraving in the

---

* It is useful to note that a cup six inches high will usually communicate sixty people, and that eight inches is the maximum height for convenient handling. Beyond this number two or more chalices will be needed.

centre or in the spandrels of the lobed depression, and certain subjects were almost invariably selected: the *Manus Dei*, St. Veronica's napkin, the Trinity, the Agnus Dei, or, occasionally, the figure of a saint or the symbols of the Evangelists. About a hundred such pre-Reformation patens survive in English parish churches.

With the change in the form of the chalice that took place at the Reformation, in order to provide for others than the celebrant receiving communion from it, there was introduced a new form of paten. This had a small foot or base, and was made both to fit the chalice as a cover, and also to stand by itself so that it could be used for administering to the communicants. The medieval practice of consecrating the bread on the linen cloth * continued, as obviously these small chalice-cover patens would only hold a limited amount, just enough for each group of communicants. But this post-Reformation form of paten developed in a distinctive and interesting way, probably as a result of attempts to return to a more primitive method for the consecration. A stem was added to the paten, and when the 17th century brought contacts with Eastern Orthodox churchmen, the paten grew in size until it became like a salver on a stand, and the chalice was provided with a separate cover, often ornamented with a cross, and therefore not usable as a standing paten. Large standing patens of this type are still used throughout the Orthodox East, and by Uniate Catholic groups in communion with Rome. The post-Reformation paten was decorated with an engraved design round the rim, or with the arms of the donor, or an inscription in the centre, or on the rim. In the Anglican communion or for the Free Churches the paten to-day may be of either the stemmed or of the flat type, and any form of appropriate decoration that can be thoroughly cleaned may be used; both the central depression and the lip should be without mouldings; the metal should not be highly polished so as to reflect the face. The Roman rubrics require that, if the whole paten is not of gold, the depression at least should be gilded, and that the surface of the depression should be without decoration of any kind; they also require the provision of a second and larger paten, to be held beneath the first when communicating the people, in case any particles should be spilled. According to English tradition going back to medieval times, there should always be a device engraved in the centre of the paten.

The Ciborium and Cruets

The terms Standing Pyx and Ciborium are interchangeable; historically the vessel has served two purposes, that of holding spare bread at the altar before the

---

* In the earlier centuries in the West the bread was consecrated on the paten as it still is in the East. Later, in the middle ages the custom of consecrating on the corporal became general and the paten was only used for the fraction or breaking of the bread and for the administration. The form of blessing in the pontificals was changed from *ad conficiendum in ea* to *ad confringendum*.

consecration and of containing the consecrated Elements to be reserved in the sacrament house. There are no English pre-Reformation examples which can definitely be identified as having been designed for either of these purposes. Post-Reformation examples in Anglican use (until recent times) would be solely for containing spare bread for the altar; some of these were rather like stem patens with lids. Those used by Roman Catholic congregations in England were generally of foreign manufacture and type, like a chalice with a cover usually surmounted by a cross or sometimes a figure of a saint. Since the Gothic revival, and the resumption of reservation in the Church of England, most of these vessels, used by both communions, have been of the Gothic form, usually over-elaborately ornamented. Here, too, there is still room for the development of something more original without eccentricity.

The hanging pyx took more than one form: there were cases where it was made like a dove with a small receptacle for the eucharist concealed in the body. Sometimes it was in two parts, the vessel itself and a cup or container into which it fitted and which was attached to the suspension gear. Judging from inventories this seems to have been the most usual arrangement.

At the present time the vessel for reservation for Anglican use must be made in two parts, as both kinds of the sacred elements must be provided for. The most convenient form has a small circular glass vessel fitted into a cylindrical metal case, in the upper part of which is a separate container for the consecrated wafers. The vessel should be such as to be able to stand without risk of falling and at the same time to be small enough to be conveniently carried hanging round the neck, to the sick person. It should also be so constructed that it can be kept clean, and if necessary, sterilised. The Monstrance for holding the Host for exposition was not very common save in greater churches in England before the Reformation, and only one incomplete example survives, at St. Martin's, Ludgate. The form now required by the Roman rite is very strictly prescribed, and full description is given in the *Celebration of the Mass*, O'Connell, Burns Oates, 1941, Vol. I.

Only two ancient sets of English cruets remain. Both are pear shaped, the neck of the pear being considerably elongated, of silver gilt, standing on a broad foot, and with a thumb piece to the lids; one has an engraved inscription round the body. The post-Reformation cruet or flagon took two forms, a large pear shaped jug with an "S" handle, standing on a short stem or directly on a trumpet-mouth foot. The provision of a hinged cover was invariable. The second type was the straight sided or tankard shaped flagon. The most usual form of ornament was engraving, generally a coat of arms of the donor or an inscription, but sometimes bands of geometrical patterns. The post-Reformation flagon was of course much larger than its predecessor. To-day a glass cruet mounted with precious metal is popular, but if an opaque material is used the cruets should be distinguished by the engraving of A (qua) and V (inum) respectively. A common fault in the design

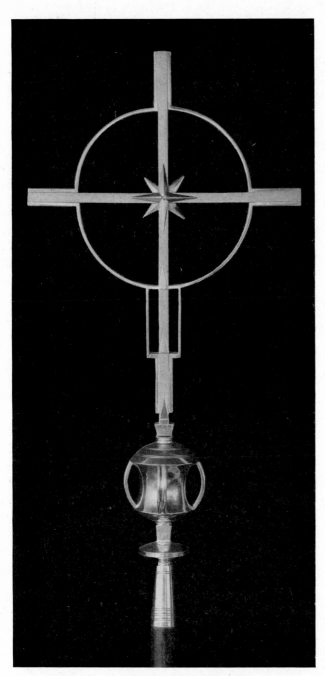

43. IN SILVER, IVORY AND CRYSTAL
By W. F. Knight

42. IN NICKEL AND BRASS, WITH AN EBONIZED SHAFT
By Bernard A. Miller, F.R.I.B.A.

44. INLAID WITH ENAMEL. DESIGNED
FOR ST. NINIAN'S CATHEDRAL, PERTH
By J. N. Comper, Archt.

EXAMPLES OF THE MORE ELABORATE WORK OF THE TWENTIETH CENTURY

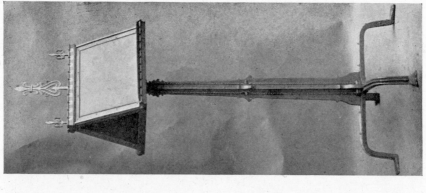

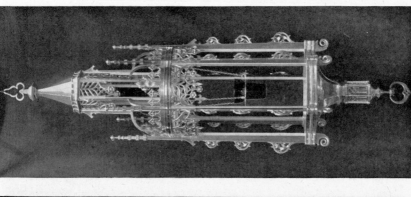

45. SUSPENDED PYX IN SILVER, TRA-
DITIONAL IN FORM BUT ORIGINAL
IN THE HANDLING OF DETAIL, DE-
SIGNED FOR THE CONVENT OF THE
HOLY NAME, MALVERN

By J. N. Comper, Archt.

46. SANCTUARY LAMP IN MODI-
FIED GOTHIC STYLE CARRIED
OUT IN ALUMINIUM BY THE
LATE BAINBRIDGE REYNOLDS
TO A DESIGN FOR ST.
PETER'S, LANCASTER

By Sir Giles Scott

47. CROZIER IN SILVER-GILT AND
COLOURED ENAMELS, DESIGNED
FOR THE BISHOP OF WINCHESTER

By J. N. Comper, Archt.

48. LECTERN IN A MATERIAL TOO
SELDOM USED, WROUGHT
IRON DECORATED IN BLUE
AND GOLD

By the late Bainbridge Reynolds

of cruets is to make them so narrow in the neck that they are hard to clean, and both wine and water leave a sediment which is often difficult to remove. Stoppers should be of glass to enable them to be kept perfectly clean. The base should be sufficiently large in proportion to the height to keep the cruet steady; they are usually rather easy to knock over. The lip should also be adequate; and the base of a kind to arrest any drips which by staining linen are a great trial to the sacristan; and if a metal lid takes the place of a stopper it must be dust proof. There is no reason why the jug or tankard type of cruet should not be revived.

Censer and Incense Boat

The censers in the Middle Ages fell into two categories: first, the plain sphere standing on a trumpet mouth base and with geometrical piercings (sometimes a dome or spire was added, but this was not treated architecturally, in this type), and the second a completely architectural treatment.

These "architectural" pieces are the most attractive, and it is surprising that so little of the kind has been done to-day. The supreme English example is the Ramsey censer, now in the Victoria and Albert Museum, but others of equal beauty are to be found depicted in wall paintings and in stained glass. Most surviving English examples are of the spherical type. Latten, copper and silver-gilt were the usual materials, but brass is commonly used to-day, though iti s not in any way preferable to white metal. If silver is used the inner part must be of a harder metal to withstand the heat. The overall length for censer and chains should not exceed forty-three inches. The incense boat or ship should have a lid that opens at both sides and a sensibly shaped spoon with little ornament.

The Altar Cross or Crucifix

A cross on the altar was not invariably used in England before the Reformation. Where the Crucifixion forms the subject of the reredos or east window, it is doubtful whether it is appropriate to use one to-day. The majority of illustrations in old service books show the altar with not more than two candlesticks, and only in some instances with a cross or crucifix. Certainly the earliest crosses are without figures; the older form of the crucifix in use throughout Europe from about 1000 to about 1300 most commonly bore a robed Christ often in an attitude of benediction. The traditional medieval place for the portrayal of the crucifixion scene was above the screen rather than the altar. The only cross which the churchwardens were required to provide before the Reformation was the processional cross, but during the Middle Ages the custom grew up of making this cross such that it could be detached from its staff and fitted into a base on the altar, at the end of the procession, during service times. The cross and candlesticks were commonly removed from the altar out of service times, as they often are in Spain to-day. No complete pre-Reformation English altar crosses survive,* and only one post-Reformation one is known to have existed, at Ely Cathedral, but this alas, disappeared more than a hundred and five years ago. ‡

There is room for much originality of treatment and material in the making of the altar cross or crucifix and candlesticks, but proportion in relation to the altar and its surroundings is of the greatest importance and it is often wise to make a rough wooden or clay model first to test the proportions *in situ*. Cross or candlesticks should never be accepted as gifts without trial in position first.

There is now no question but that the correct interpretation of the English Ornaments Rubric requires two candles only actually upon or behind the altar, and although other lights may, and in early times often did, stand about the altar, there is no pre- or post-Reformation precedent for more than this number actually upon or behind the altar. The Roman rubrics to-day require six lights on the High Altar, and two or four on the side altars: the material is not restricted. A seventh candle is required for a pontifical high Mass by the Bishop of the Diocese.

The forms of church candlesticks followed so closely the contemporary fashions for secular candlesticks that there would be no point in describing them here. Any good book on metal work, or a visit to any county museum should illustrate the development of their design. The modern designer can make the fullest use of modern durable materials, including aluminium, steel and unbreakable glass, as well as the older materials, bronze, copper, iron, gold and silver, or pewter, with insets of such contrasting things as ivory and rock crystal. Whether a pricket or socket is provided for the candle, the cup below it should be adequate to catch falling grease, and protect the altar linen.

Processional Cross and Lights

It is a common fault to make the head of a processional cross too heavy for comfortable carrying, and the staff rather too long; six feet eight inches is a convenient overall length. It is convenient for cleaning and repair if the top is removable, but if so, its fastening must be such as to inspire confidence in the cross bearer. A very usual form for the processional cross in England was that of a cross with a plaque attached to each of the four arms, bearing a figure, often the symbols of the Evangelists. Frequently brackets were attached on either side at the base of the cross on which stood figures of St. Mary and St. John. A fine example of the 15th century remains at St. Oswald's, Durham, in white metal gilt. There are no post-Reformation English examples. It is usual for a church to have

* But there are several processional crosses, and two bases for setting the cross upon, when placed on the altar.

‡ The Roman rite requires a crucifix on or above every altar. For this and the tabernacle see *The Celebration of the Mass, Vol. I*, already quoted.

in addition a plain cross of wood, often coloured red, or red and black, for use in Lent and at funerals. Here, too, there is room for experiment with new techniques of craftsmanship, and materials.

There is some ground for thinking that the two standard candlesticks, which the English Ornaments Rubric required, were originally portable lights placed here at the end of the procession. Processional candlesticks can be of any size, and may be either ordinary candlesticks of convenient shape, complete with their own bases, ready to be set down at will, or plain or moulded wooden staves, with drip pan and socket for the candle at the top, for which heavy bases are provided on the appropriate step of the chancel, in which they can be inserted. In either form they should be light in weight, and a wider drip pan is needed than for a stationary candlestick.

The Verge or Mace

It is customary to provide the churchwardens with wands of office, and the verger, if he has any ceremonial functions, with the verge or mace from which he takes his name. These can be the simplest white painted wands of wood, or the most elaborate and costly pieces of metal work. The most usual form, with ample precedent from the 17th century onwards, is the simple staff, four to six feet in length, topped by a wrought metal head, usually in the form of a figure of the patron saint of the church, but sometimes only the saint's emblem is displayed. The heavy short mace is still to be found in cathedrals and many important churches, in the City of London especially.

The Font Ewer, Ablutions Ewer and Basin

The font ewer should be of adequate size, but not too heavy to be easily lifted and carried when full of water: this mistake is not uncommon. Copper and bronze as well as the more usual brass are suitable metals: if silver is used the ewer will have to be kept under lock and key. There do not seem to be any old English examples, so the designer has complete freedom from any obligations to tradition.

An inventory of St. Peter Mancroft, Norwich, gives, for the ablutions, two pairs of basins, with a lion's head spout, the principal having figures of St. Peter and St. Paul in the bottom engraved on roses of pounced work. Presumably one basin served to hold the water, which was poured through the lion's head spout into the other, over the priest's hands. This form could be adopted by the modern designer, but a jug- or tankard-shaped ewer is easier to handle. Three-quarters of a pint to a pint is sufficient capacity for it. The basin should be adequate to hold this amount of water easily a few inches below the rim, to avoid spilling when carried.

The Alms Dish

The rubrics of the English communion service require the churchwardens to provide a "decent basin" for this purpose, and in any church, whether bags or plates are provided for the initial collection of the alms, something is needed to receive the whole with dignity, and carry it to the altar or to the vestry. The design of such a dish gives ample scope for the use of heraldry, whether personal arms of donors or the traditional heraldry of the Church, the emblems of the saints, or of the Passion. Here, also, new metals might be experimented with. The dish should not be too massive, remembering that it will be loaded with money offerings—all too often in heavy copper!

In whatever metal they are made, none of these pieces should be laquered: laquer is popular with church cleaners, but it gives a very unpleasant colour to the plate, and when it begins to deteriorate, its appearance is quite unfit for use in connection with the services of the Church.

SOME CHURCHWARDENS' STAVES AND VERGES

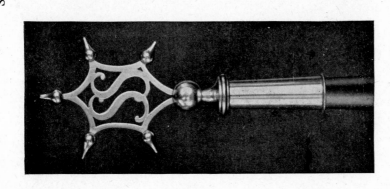

49. SIMPLE AND INEXPENSIVE
VERGER'S STAFF
By W. F. Knight

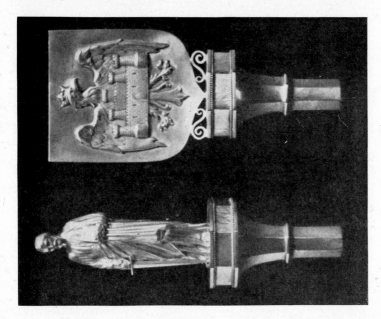

50. CHURCHWARDENS' STAVES IN SILVER: THE PATRON
SAINT OF THE CHURCH FOR THE VICAR'S WARDEN,
THE ARMS OF THE TOWN FOR THE PEOPLE'S WARDEN
Designed and executed by A. J. Wilkins

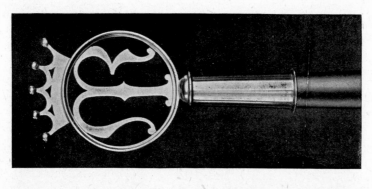

51. ANOTHER SIMPLE VERGE
IN BRONZE, SO PREFERABLE
TO BRASS
By W. F. Knight

52. PEWTER AND ENAMEL EWER
By the late Omar Ramsden

Heating and Ventilation

By BERTRAM SHORE

THE KEEN CHURCHWARDEN or church councillor, reading this book to fit himself better for the work of improving his ancient church or of building a new one perfectly, and arriving at the heading of this chapter, will, I think, suddenly feel flat: "Abandon hope, all ye who enter here," and join the uncreative, uninspiring ranks of those who acquiesce in old evils which we can now safely do without.

No, it is not really a dull or prosaic subject, and soon, with imagination and a keen mind, it may be seen, after all, to be bound up with everything worth struggling for.

General Considerations

The development of comfortable, non-injurious, and generally pleasing heating systems for churches, ancient and modern, in this relatively cold and damp country has lagged far behind the standard which could reasonably be demanded by a generation capable of assessing the effects on animate and inanimate matter produced by any type and quality of installation. The natural urge towards mental laziness goes hand-in-hand with dishonesty of thought: the great majority of our churches are ancient and very difficult to heat, and for new churches familiar, conventional practice has been followed with a mistaken assessment of "safety first" and economic principles. These rather constant factors have often been reinforced by the fact that people in this country have been brought up through the ages to expect to be, on many days in the year, a little uncomfortable in their homes and very uncomfortable in church (this has been the general view of the foreign, Dominion and Colonial troops I have had to do with) and that our climate is so uncertain that we can at all times put things off, hoping that all will be better than we have sufficient justification for believing.

No claims that the old churches have lasted a long time and are largely still there or that our fathers were not too soft to worship in them will do. Our national treasures are fewer and more important than they were, and they have become more delicate with increasing atmospheric pollution. We have condemned and swept away the largely draught-proof loose-boxes in which those who were able to do so, the leading families, protected themselves against mental and bodily ills. The average age of our total population has advanced very much and the average age of members of most congregations has advanced still more. Old and ageing human circulation systems cannot keep feet warm and heads lively for an hour and a half when the body is stationary in cold air, often over damp floors (the damp floor will be the coldest part of a building and the air immediately over it the heaviest, coldest air: even with a new building or a dry floor the cold air from outside, being relatively heavy, hangs about the floor surface, chilling the feet and ankles). As for children in the congregation, they are better off than the elderly people, but, looked at from the coldest and the least psychological standpoint, they are perhaps now overscarce for subjection to this doubtfully worthwhile test. These remarks apply both to ancient and modern buildings.

With the passing of some centuries of our history, the priceless fabrics of our ancient churches have slowly depreciated in soundness until many suddenly lost a great proportion of their æsthetic, historical and sentimental appeal through wholesale re-facing or reconstruction. We must do everything in our power to check this process of depreciation and to preserve the identity of the buildings. We must preserve the identity of the buildings because we love them and because we like the æsthetic, historical and sentimental appeal which they have. If any further argument is needed to move thinking people to preserve the visible character of our medieval buildings there is a very powerful one. We believe that our influence is necessary for the advancement of civilisation—I don't think that we need put it more diffidently than that—and this is a little island in a world where quantity tends to become more important than quality. We cannot hold our Empire together unless we do so by the spiritual hold of Britain on the people of the Dominions and Colonies. If we like we can translate "the spiritual hold" into the half-acknowledged consciousness that here, in England, are visible and audible signs of the history and cultivation and ideas which have received their character from our land and our race and which have contributed so much to the development of the associated and the younger members; the consciousness that here is a proper cradle of thought and leadership.

If, then, we want to do our utmost to preserve the more beautiful things our country has produced and to aid people in their spiritual life we should review all those methods which have been used in this climate of ours for heating buildings. Having considered the merits and defects of each we shall perhaps be able to choose the best which is practicable under any limiting circumstances.

Aims and Principles

First let us put down, very shortly, the qualities which we must look for and the things we must beware of in connection with the heating, lighting and ventilation of places of public worship.

1. Æsthetic

We do not want to clutter up any church, ancient or modern, with objects

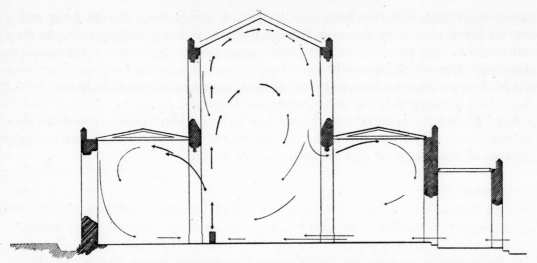

FIG. I. SECTION OF AISLED CHURCH SHOWING AIR FLOWS SET UP BY ISOLATED HEATING UNITS.

which catch the eye without contributing to the general design and thought of the building. We can hardly be too cautious when there is a suggestion of putting things on walls.

2. *Physical*

(*a*) We should maintain a comfortable, even temperature, without draughts.

(*b*) It is in every way better for the fabric and for the fittings if they can be kept at a fairly constant temperature, when this is financially practicable.

(*c*) It is undesirable to heat from widely separated hot spots because these will be bad for objects near them and the air immediately above and around them, being very much lighter than the bulk of the air in the church, will rush up to the roof or ceiling causing steady draughts of cold, heavy air to flow over the floor towards the heat sources to occupy the partial vacuums.

(*d*) Any hot spots, such as radiators, will with the upward draught drive dust and dirt particles, in time disfiguring any objects immediately above the heat source as though with smoke.

(*e*) Neither comfort nor convenience will be achieved unless the air pressures can be kept fairly evenly balanced. The weight and pressure of air depend upon its temperature and unequal pressures inevitably set up movements which will flow with great steadiness. It may be easier for some people to realise this subject if they remind themselves that the weight of the air in a large church will amount to several tons. I have known churches where the candles on the altars could not be kept alight when the heating was in operation. Any steady movement of air in a church will cause a cold flow over the foot-level: it is uncomfortable—and for the elder and delicate people injurious—to remain for long periods with the feet in a colder layer than that occupied by the head. I have drawn a section through a typical aisled church to show air flows set up by isolated heating units, heating units which, because they are too widely separated or for other reasons, cannot maintain balanced air pressures.

(*f*) It is undesirable that solid fuel should be carried into a church and stoking done there as the grit is bad for flooring and fabrics.

Before leaving this section of the subject I should like to make my usual plea, so rarely successful, for the fitting of casements to some of the windows of a church, so that sweet air and sunlight may be let in.

3. *Chemical*

(*a*) The products of the combustion of any fuel, whether solid, liquid or gaseous are chemically injurious to life and to a large proportion of our building stones.

No heating apparatus which burns any fuel, absolutely irrespective of what form that fuel takes or whether the products of combustion are visible or not visible, should ever be fitted or placed in any building without a carefully constructed flue. Those in charge of ancient buildings should look to this matter particularly urgently when the masonry of their fabric is liable to become damp in the interior during wet periods: very destructive to limestones under any circumstances, the acids from the consumption of fuel will penetrate deeper and more quickly into masonry when combined with carbonated water (rain water) which recedes outwards during drying periods. This is not just a theoretical or a small matter nor is it a matter about which there should be any doubt.

(*b*) If possible we should avoid forming a flue where smoke and soot will be ejected over valuable masonry. Sooty fumes are no worse, chemically, than others, but the accumulation of solid matter leads to a concentration of sulphur acids being washed into the stone by rain.

Historical Survey

The heating systems which have been used in our country group themselves into three major periods. Firstly, the Roman-British; secondly; the Medieval, which may be held to have lasted through the 17th and 18th centuries; and, thirdly, the Ironmongering period.

1. *Roman-British. The Hypocaust*

Those people in Roman Britain who were in a position to secure healthy and comfortable conditions—and they seem to have been very numerous—constructed buildings with floors and, to some extent, walls which could be warmed. The floors were constructed with shallow spaces under them and the hot gases from furnaces travelled through these spaces before going up the walls in flues. A great volume of hot gases was always necessary and as whole faggots would be thrown in the furnaces large areas of woodland and much cheap labour were necessary: the system would not work with small coal furnaces (53).

We could not adopt this method of heating now. If we could we should be able to make comfortable churches, though the discharge of the products of combustion would be injurious to masonry.

2. *Medieval. The Bonfire*

Throughout the Middle Ages rooms and halls were commonly heated by entirely open fires, built upon flat hearth-stones more or less in the middle of the floor-space, or by braziers. Churches were also heated by open braziers. In either case the products of combustion rose to the roof and found their way out through a louvre. The gases would be injurious to all life and to most masonry. The protection to woodwork by the discouragement of the death watch beetle would be very marked. Probably the braziers were about as efficient, as heaters, as modern oil stoves. Churches, great and small, were perpetually being burnt down by them. It was largely in order to create a fireproof ceiling that the medieval vaultings were developed. As with most of the glorious features of English medieval work, the glories arose from the urge to make beautiful a feature which was desirable for practical reasons. Obviously these methods of church heating would not be contemplated now.

3. *Modern Plumbing and Ironmongering*

Perhaps it will be most helpful to tabulate these systems in a concise way first and then to apply our aims and principles.

(1) Large gilled stoves, with flue-pipes, giving heat by direct radiation and fuelled with coke.

(2) Water pipes in open trenches covered by gratings. Large-bore low-pressure pipes operated by a boiler.

(3) Water radiators. Boilers operating low-pressure hot-water systems with radiators of various types placed in more or less convenient positions.

(4) Water radiators. High-pressure system.

(5) Hot air. Oven-heated air from furnaces, which thrust hot air into the building, usually over the heads of the people, and suck cold air along the floor level.

(6) Water under-floor heating. Boilers operating a system of low-pressure hot-water pipes placed under the whole of the flooring, so that the whole of the floor-surface is warmed, as in the Roman system.

(7) Gas heaters.

(8) Electrically-heated oil radiators.

(9) Electric radiant heaters, which are placed fairly high up and in their most efficient forms tend to look rather like the large light-projectors familiar in cinematograph studios.

(10) Electric convector heaters.

(11) Low-temperature electric tubular heaters.

(12) Low-temperature electric under-floor heating. Low-temperature electric heating elements placed under the whole of the floor, so that the whole floor surface is warmed, as in the Roman system and in number 6.

(13) Since number 12 was carried out a proposal has been put forward by a consultant scientist for achieving the same effect in a cheaper manner by laying a flexible plastic flooring surface, about the thickness of linoleum and stiffer and infinitely tougher than rubber in which low-temperature heating elements were woven. This system has not yet actually been carried out anywhere, though specimens of the material have been made.

I have myself been responsible for installing the first, third, sixth and eleventh of these systems in churches and I have made use of the ninth and tenth for special places; but I was always anxious to do something better, and for a number of years before the war I worked at the subject. I was encouraged by *The Protection of our English Churches*, the fourth report of the Central Council for the Care of Churches, which contains the following passage under the heading of "Disadvantages of Present Systems":

"Meanwhile it is well to recognise that each of our present systems has serious disadvantages, which are briefly as follows. . . ."

According to the Central Advisory Committee all existing systems were, then, more or less unsatisfactory and this view corresponded with the observations and the scientific arguments which troubled me.

The report went on to say, under the heading "Anticipating Electric Heating":

"As a general rule it is advisable to maintain existing systems as long as they will last, inasmuch as it may be hoped that in a few years electric heating will be so far developed as to be reasonably inexpensive and efficient."

Finally, the report says, under the heading of "Floor Heating":

"The heating of the floor itself, either by hot water or by heated air passing beneath its surface, is both the oldest and the most pleasant form of heating a building. . . ."

It has been agreed that the Roman method of heating had probably been the most comfortable and effective that had ever been used: and it was, also, æsthetically unobjectionable.

If the floor area is to be warmed by electricity it is obvious that there are various methods by which this could be done, securing the advantages of the Roman-British system without the liberation of sulphur acids over masonry and the wasteful or lavish expenditure of labour and fuel. I think that my original specification, crystallised, after unsuccessful contacts with other large manufacturers, in consultation with Mr. E. McA. Young of the Unity Heating and Mr. Evans of the Granwood Flooring Company is probably more generally useful than others we have since considered, and it has the additional advantage that it has been installed in buildings and in use for eight years. There is nothing strange about any of the parts of the installation and they could be put into production by any really good firms of electrical or flooring manufacturers. The re-laying of the floor, when the installation is used in an ancient church, may appear daunting—but because of damp and unhygienic conditions this is generally desirable in itself.

For some years I could not persuade any Church Council to adopt so novel a scheme and eventually, in 1939, I installed it throughout my own house, laying new floors. This installation was quickly followed by one in the chancel of North Lancing Church, Sussex. For this church an agreement was signed between the Church Council and the Shoreham Electricity Supply Company, a company which normally charges $2d.$ a unit for power, for the supply of electricity for under-floor heating, clock-controlled to avoid peak periods, at $\frac{1}{3}d.$ a unit (to be exact, $.35d.$ a unit).

The heat storage under the floor is so considerable that the temperature of the church does not fall during the peak periods, when the current cuts out. The whole community gains by this, the supply company because they are selling current during periods when their overhead charges are going on, though the demand does not justify them, and the consumer because he can take current at cheap rates without inconvenience.

The installation is carried out as follows:

The site is excavated about eighteen inches. The utilisation of the whole floor area is the ideal, though this need not be done where there are special difficulties. Four inches of waterproof concrete is laid over the site. Over this waterproof concrete is laid a layer of suitable imperishable insulating material, backed underneath with tinfoil. On the insulating material are placed pre-cast specially designed concrete sleepers. Between the sleepers are laid long rectangular boxes—the equivalent to the familiar tubes—containing low-temperature (black heat) heating elements, with a consumption of only sixty to one hundred watts a foot run. The boxes or cases are double, one set of elements being thermostatically controlled and the other hand-controlled, so that extra heat can be put on when this is necessary. Over the element cases (the equivalent of tubes) are placed strips of insulating board, and thin reinforced concrete slabs are laid over the whole, resting on the sleepers. Lastly the actual flooring material is laid down. This can be anything but it is better to have some material, such as Granwood blocks, which is a poor conductor of heat, than to have a material through which the warmth travels relatively quickly—(54, 55).

The radiation surfaces are so great that very low under-floor temperatures will suffice to give the required air-temperature. The floor surface is below blood-heat. Because of the great radiating surfaces and the correct position and distribution of heat, air temperatures soon rise to the controlled level after any air-changes.

When wiring any electrical installations in churches I have always used copper conduit, with capillary soldered or soft copper cone joints. If these are properly earthed they are lastingly safe as conductors in the event of a failure of the insulation of a wire.

This system, number 12, appears to me to fulfil our aims and to accord with our principles, but a church may be in a position unserved by electricity or the cost of current may be too high for electric heating: we cannot, therefore, tell what conditions will be everywhere so we will weigh the faults and merits of all the systems as shortly and well as we can, always remembering that the conditions of no two churches are exactly alike, and what may be possible in one may be impossible in another.

The first six of these systems operate with relatively large furnaces and from flues eject a concentration of soot and the other products of combustion directly upon the exterior masonry of the building. The seventh is gas and the last six are electric systems. The major objection to the first six, the destruction of valuable masonry, can largely be removed or mitigated by building a boiler-house at a considerable distance, several hundred feet from the church: it is seldon that it is practicable to do so (56, 57).

(1) *Large gilled stoves*

With their flue-pipes, giving heat by direct radiation. These are easily and cheaply fitted and are very efficient when driven hard and not expected to deal with too large a space and with excessive heat losses high up in the building, when it becomes impossible to balance the air-pressures reasonably. People stationed near them are apt to be tried, but it does not necessarily follow that those at a distance need be cold. They have the additional advantage that they will be easily and cheaply removed. The flue pipe should be supported vertically from the floor and not depend upon the balancing wall-attachments and the elbow.

They are fed with coke, which will be carted and distributed about the church, with resultant damage to floors and fabrics and the danger of general squalor. They are so remarkably ugly that even the average person will often resent them. Care in maintenance of the flue-pipe joints is necessary or any interior masonry near will suffer. Products of combustion are necessarily discharged over or against the exterior of the fabric (59).

ANCIENT METHOD : UNDER-FLOOR HEATING

53. ROMAN–BRITISH HYPOCAUST AT CHEDWORTH : THE HOT ROOM

54. SHOWING CONCRETE SUB-FLOOR AND DWARF WALLS ; PRE-CAST SLEEPERS; HEATING
ELEMENTS ; COPPER TUBE CONDUITS FOR WIRING

55. SHOWING SCREED BEING LAID OVER CONCRETE SLABS ; FLOORING BLOCKS BEING
LAID ON THE SCREED

(2) *Low-pressure hot-water pipes in grating-covered trenches*

This system can be fairly effective. The heat starts where it should start, as low down as possible, and the heat sources can be distributed better than with a relatively cheap and care-free radiator system. It has the advantage of simplicity: a boiler, set low down in an excavated boiler-house, supplies large bore flow and return pipes which are given, or should be given, such gradients that the water circulates naturally.

Examples of this system are quite common.

As economy would be a motive in the choice of this system the boiler-house would be constructed against the walls of the church. As it would be an excavation and one that would be likely to cause localised drying and shrinking of foundation soil, unequal settlement of the foundations and cracking of the walls is extremely probable.

Organic matter is brought into the church on the soles of the shoes of the congregation and deposited through the gratings on to the hot beds, which are not sufficiently hot to sterilise the germs, but are admirable for incubation. The brisk upflow of warm air wafts light-weight matter and germs into the lungs of the congregation.

Products of combustion are, inevitably, discharged immediately over or against the exterior of the fabric.

(3) *Low-pressure hot-water radiator system*

It is possible to heat any church comfortably by this method and, if the number of radiators is sufficient and the distribution correct, excessive cold draughts on the floor level can be avoided, though the air immediately over the floor will be the coldest in the whole area of the building. The system will not affect the purity of the interior atmosphere of the church.

Great care must be taken not to place any radiators near any expressional features or under anything which can quickly be ruined by the steady upflow of dust (58).

It is very difficult to distribute the radiators about the church in such a way as to secure a reasonable balance of air-pressures, but the utmost care must be taken to do this as well as possible. They can be placed at the ends of the pews, if they are not ancient and valuable pews, or on the backs or fronts of blocks of pews. They will have to be placed against the walls, especially below large windows, where cascades of chilled air will otherwise descend. They must never be set against piers.

An underground boiler-house against a wall or walls should be avoided.

Unless a boiler-house can be constructed at a considerable distance from the church, sulphur acids will be liberated in a concentrated form and in relatively great volume on to the exterior masonry (56).

This system reduces the hope of eliminating any normally redundant seating.

(4) *High-pressure hot-water radiator system*

This we need not waste thought on because responsible architects would not recommend it and no Diocesan Advisory Committee would allow it.

(5) *Oven-heated air*

Installations on this principle can be anything from the cheaply made, crude, short-lived arrangements which have been adopted in a number of churches to the highly developed and elaborate air-conditioning plants so much used in the large buildings and blocks of flats in America.

The cheap installations have not been generally popular. They tend to send hot air over people's heads and suck cold air along the floors.

Probably the elaborate air-conditioning plant would almost always be a ridiculously wasteful and economically unsound proposition for a church in this country, where air-cooling is never necessary.

Here, again, the furnace with its flue is a trouble.

(6) *Low-pressure hot-water under-floor heating*

This is by far the pleasantest and best form of water heating. The heat is started where it should be started, on the floor level. The heat is perfectly distributed and the balance of air pressures correct so that no draughts are set up and no down-draughts are possible. In old churches the floors will have been made dry and hygienic. The air inside the church is unpolluted. No damage can be caused to the interior of the building or to fittings. There is no apparatus or plumbing to disfigure the church.

It has the incidental advantage that with the removal, temporary or otherwise, of fixed seating, it is possible for people to see a fine building as it ought to be seen.

Owing to the floor renewal, this system is more expensive to install than number 3. It is the most expensive installation except for highly developed examples of number 5, air-conditioning.

An underground boiler-house against a wall should be avoided.

As in the other boiler-house installations, the flue will precipitate soot and sulphur acids directly on the exterior masonry unless the boiler-house can be erected at a considerable distance from the church (56, 57).

(7) *Gas heaters*

As these have to be distributed about the church in order to keep some balance of air-pressures, they are practically necessarily flueless gas heaters. These liberate the products of combustion upon the interior masonry of the building, except in so far as they are carried out of the church in the lungs and blood-streams of the worshippers.

We ought not to consider these.

(8) *Electrically heated oil radiators*

Electrically heated, oil-filled radiators are free from all dangers to health and to the fabric, except for discoloration of any objects over them, which will, in time, blacken as with smoke.

The idea behind this type of installation is that there will be very considerable heat-storage: oil cools so much more slowly than water.

This system retains the difficulty met with in all radiator installations; that it is almost impossible to distribute the heat sources scientifically without committing crimes against taste or against the building. Unless a comfortable level of temperature is maintained continuously the foot level is very noticeably the coldest level of air.

(9) *Electric radiant heaters*

With radiant heat, objects are warmed by the rays and not by warmed air. This quality will be familiar from experiences of sun warmth with steady frost in rarified air on mountain tops.

This system can do no harm to a church if it is properly wired and if the heaters are carefully placed and fixed, though we should generally rather do without their appearance, usually approximating to that of the large light-projectors familiar in film studios.

The heaters must be fixed high up or the rays will be monopolised by one or two immobile human bodies and many people will remain cold. Obviously by this system bald heads would get warm, but heat on the head and not to the feet is a basically unsound arrangement and cannot make for comfort or healthy conditions unless the air, too, is warmed: in which case we should probably economise by dispensing with the radiant heat.

(10) *Electric convector heaters*

These heat air in a box-shaped heater. The hot air flows out naturally at a high level, its place being taken by cold air which is drawn in from near the bottom.

This system, again, provided that the usual precautions about wiring and fitting are followed, can do no structural damage.

They have all the objections attendant on the use of radiators. It is very difficult to obtain a reasonable balance of air-pressure, especially in high churches, and the upflow of hot air is liable to leave much space poorly heated and most of the floor area cold.

(11) *Low-temperature electric tubular heaters*

Except that it is arguable that low-temperature electric heaters are better not placed under valuable ancient pews—and very few churches have these—there can be no physical or chemical objection to a properly installed system of this type and æsthetically they are very unobjectionable.

The heat is started low down and is well distributed so that the air pressures can be better balanced than in any of the other systems except numbers 6, 12 and 13.

The main forces of the tubular heaters would normally be placed under the pews. The feet of the congregation would be in a slightly warmer air than their heads. Subsidiary tubes must be set far back on the sills of windows where the air would be kept from becoming chilled against the relatively thin window glass.

A regrettable result of this installation is that it makes the removal of any fixed seating even more difficult.

This system can give very good results indeed and the capital cost of the installation is low.

The cost of running is higher than for number 12.

At present rates the cost of running any of the electric heating systems is greater than the cost of running solid fuel operated systems, though comparisons are difficult because of the labour factors and other matters. It is much to be hoped that charges for power will be reduced soon as a result of the use of our great tides or by other means.

(12) *Low-temperature electric under-floor heating*

This system avoids all the objections which we have tabulated and fulfils all the requirements. It will bring about no deterioration of the fabric or fittings; in common with number 6, water under-floor heating, perfectly comfortable and healthy conditions can be obtained with it even without continuous use through the week.

In time, as with all electric installations, new wires will have to be drawn through the conduits: otherwise, with copper conduit there is hardly anything to depreciate in the installation.

With an old church this system requires the re-laying of the floor, but I think this is by no means always a disadvantage: old floors are generally damp and cold and often we find them forming imperfect seals over still very unhygienic burials.

A number of competitions have shown that the cost of installation is always less than the cost of any efficient water-heating system. This is because the generating is done by the power company and the cost of the heat-generating plant, boiler-house and boiler is saved.

We must conclude by saying that every case must be considered individually, and if I appear to show bias towards my own child this does not blind me to the fact that in some cases one of the other methods should be used.

57. DAMAGE DONE TO EXTERIOR MASONRY BY SULPHUR ACIDS FROM THE BOILER HOUSE

56. BOILER HOUSE, SHOWING SOOT STAINS AT THE TOP OF THE CHIMNEY STACK FIVE DAYS AFTER THE FIRST FIRE WAS LIT

PRODUCTS OF COMBUSTION : EFFECT ON INTERIOR MASONRY

59. HEAT BY DIRECT RADIATION FROM STOVE. NOTE THE DAMAGE
TO ADJACENT WALL, ESPECIALLY AT THE FLUE-PIPE JOINT

58. DIRT AND SULPHUR ACIDS ABOVE RADIATOR HAVE EATEN INTO
THE MASONRY

Church Lighting ∽ By BERTRAM SHORE

CIRCUMSTANCES COMBINE to make the successful artificial lighting of medieval churches an enormously difficult problem. The lighting of Renaissance churches is less difficult, and it is to be hoped that the lighting of modern churches will be thought of as part of the idea of the original design, but if we deal with the difficulties of the medieval church we shall be in a position to consider the lighting of the others.

During the great church-building centuries in our country light, during hours of twilight and darkness, was obtained from candles, principally in the sanctuary and chancel : the congregation did not require to have light to read by. The effect produced by this form of lighting in a medieval church is very beautiful and very helpful to concentration, but it is not generally practicable nowadays. The qualities would be largely lost if the whole of the body of the church were similarly lighted and the expenditure would be very great. The oldest members of a congregation now expect to be able to read small print with bad eyesight in the most obscure corners of the church, and the Church Council must go a reasonable distance towards meeting their often rather unreasonable desires.

Light can be obtained by burning things, such as candles or gas, by heating things to white-heat, as we do with incandescent gas-mantles and with incandescent electric lamps, or by exciting the atoms of suitable vapours to give off light in vapour-discharge containers.

We know how beautiful a sanctuary and chancel can look when lighted by candles, but most of this beauty is killed when the nave is given stronger lighting. Apart from the expense, the lighting of a church nave with candles is not practicable.

Gas should never be used because the products of combustion are injurious to the fabric of most churches and to furnishings which may be used in any church.

We are, of course, left with electric incandescent and electric discharge systems of lighting and which of these two we use will depend upon individual circumstances. Eventually the more scientific discharge method is bound generally to displace the old incandescent system, which should have been considered obsolete years ago, but we need not worry over much about that because the general principles of lighting and the same wiring (with local transformers) will do if we eventually change over from the older to the more scientific method.

With electric lighting we are faced with two major bugbears—the ease with which an all-overish, flat effect is achieved and the fact that whilst a candle flame is a pleasant thing, the concentration of perhaps sixty times the intensity of light from a source only a little larger becomes an extremely tiresome thing to look past for any length of time and it must be injurious to the eyes.

There is another, a minor, point worth mentioning. The beauty of a church is often greatly helped by the brightness of some colour or of gold and silver work or well-polished brass, but all this bright, sparkling work will lose its life if we look past strong light-sources—spots of light more intense than the brightness from glass or silver; as any thoughtful person who has considered the lighting of a dinner table furnished with fine glass and silver will know.

Plotting the Sources of Light

These considerations, creating a problem that is indeed formidable, would seem to point to the placing of the light-sources, or shading the light-sources, so that the eye does not normally see any naked light. They would also point to the fact that we must place the light-sources in positions from which they will give enough light where the light is wanted and from which, whatever else they do, they will not give a flat even light over the building. The selection of positions at very high levels should be avoided whenever we can do so. This entails the use of ladders for maintenance that are so long as to be clumsy to handle and may be powerfully destructive. A very high position may also mean an unwarranted expenditure of current, in order to provide the necessary intensity of light at floor level.

Fairly high-powered projectors are often used in sanctuaries and chancels for the lighting of the altar, but if this is done very great care must be exercised as it so easily leads to a very offensive theatrical suggestion. It would not be putting the matter too strongly to insist that anything that gives the suggestion of a theatrical striving—and especially anything that reveals, to some extent, the mechanism of a theatrical effect—should be avoided at all costs. It is often possible to light the sanctuary and the choir of parish churches by placing projectors quite simply and vertically on tie beams, or, if the roof is low, on the roof. The same effect can be achieved by pendant lights, but suitable shades or reflectors for this type of pendant lighting generally require to be made specially for any particular place, if they are to be at the same time pleasant and efficient. Every church, Medieval, Renaissance or Modern, must be considered as an individual case. By lighting solely from the aisles I have often found it possible to light a nave efficiently, without glare in any one's eyes, without breaking up the flow of the architectural lines with suspension chains and tubes to pendant lights, and without flatness of effect. A good method is to place the lighting units on the aisle side of the wall over the pier arcade, just above the highest point of the arch opening. On this principle, if the arcade be of suitable proportions and the placing be done carefully, it is possible to overlap the zones of lighting sufficiently to give a good intensity of light at about five feet from the ground, namely, at book level, near the centre-aisle ends of all the pews. It will not matter that the good light level is found much lower towards the middle of the centre aisle. When this method is adopted very pleasing alternations of light intensity can be obtained without making reading difficult anywhere, and the points of light are generally screened. The effect of scale and the light and shade, modelling and depth, sought for in the architecture are obtained by this means.

I believe that this effect has been aimed at during the last few years with pendants, and, if shades could be obtained which effectually cut out the effect of bright spots of light, the strong vertical lines of conduit and suspension falling from behind the centre of the soffit of each arch would remain the only objection to this modification of the aisle-lighting scheme. It must be remembered that it is not permissible to hang the pendants in a church by the electric wiring.

Wiring the Church

If the church is ancient it is an heirloom which is irreplaceable; if it is modern it is, presumably, the result of the best effort that can be made. In either case no risk of fire must be run through the use of inferior materials. Electric current is not always treated with the respect which its potential danger demands.

Every one will realise that the current is carried by wires which have insulating material over them so that the electricity shall be kept from breaking out anywhere except where it is carried through some apparatus, such as a lighting unit. These wires must be of capacity and strength to give a large margin of safety and it is best to say that they must be specified for the particular job they have to do, by an architect who specialises in church work. In a church the type technically described as 3/·029 is the smallest size that may be used. Everywhere, but especially in churches, buildings generally under less close observation than houses, these wires should be carried in tubes, "conduit" as these tubes are called. The tubes must be made of a material which is a good electrical conductor and must be reasonably stout; there must be perfect contact at each junction and between apparatus and tube, and the tube must be "earthed" by connecting it with a water-pipe which goes underground or by bringing the end of it (non-ferrous) five or six feet in the dampest practicable piece of ground against the church—not just one of those places where the gutter has been overflowing; we hope that will be mended. If all this is done the insulation will not be rubbed through, broken, or gnawed through, or have drawing-pins or nails driven through it. I have known, personally, all these things to happen to lead or hard-rubber covered wiring, and I have known an electrical installation earthed through the fabric of a building by the driving of a nail through a floor-board. The nail went right through a flimsy lapped sheet-iron tube and the insulated wire. The slight bending of the tube broke a joint, and, with that, the electrical continuity; after the current had been switched on to that circuit for a time the fact that some one had blundered was not in doubt.

With a suitable conduit not only will these damages not occur, but any breakdown of the insulation of the wires or of any apparatus will be rendered harmless to people and to the building because the current will flow unobtrusively to earth in the materials of the tube.

Any loose fit at the jointings would be liable to make a jumping-place for the current, a sparking place. For this reason a heavy-gauge, solid-drawn, screwed, galvanised-steel conduit is generally recommended. The parts that have had threads cut in them must be kept painted or they will rust; but a copper conduit, with capillary soldered or bronze soft-copper-cone compression-joints, is much better. It looks far nicer, always, and it doesn't get squalid-looking with age, as galvanised steel pipes do after a few years, and there is absolutely no danger of it corroding away with damp settling in the inside or on the outside, from condensation or other causes.

An architect must remember that for the wiring of a church the customary coating for secular wiring is insufficient. He should study the regulations of the Central Advisory Committee or the Diocesan Advisory Committee and so draw up his specification that it will conform with these regulations.

Bringing the Current into the Church from the Mains

The current can be brought to a building from the mains either overhead or in relatively expensive, heavily insulated cable underground. Whenever possible the mains current should be brought across the churchyard and into the church underground: overhead wires, with their brackets attached to the building, are very harmful to the appearance of a beautiful church and the extra cost should somehow be faced.

This cable is led into some convenient part of the church where the supply company's immediate responsibility for the current ends with a mainswitch, a meter or meters, and safety fuses.

It is well, if possible, to choose a place for this mainswitch installation which will be near a convenient spot for the distribution board, from which all the sub-circuits, each of which has a fuse, branch off.

It is very convenient for the control of lighting by the verger during a service if the lighting switchboard can be situated somewhere in the west end of the church.

Great care should be taken that the instrument boards and switches are arranged in a neat and tidy manner: a mass of instruments is a revolting sight, whereas a well-arranged instrument board can be very pleasing to look upon, if the materials are good.

The individual light switches can be arranged on a teak or slate board, mounted

61. AN UGLY ARRANGEMENT OF CONDUIT, DISFIGURING AN EXPRESSIONAL FEATURE

60. A NEAT AND EFFECTIVE ARRANGEMENT OF INSTRUMENT BOARDS AND SWITCHES

62. AT THE FRANZISKANER HOFKAPELLE,
INNSBRUCK, *circa* 1569

63. AT ST. NICHOLAS, HARDWICKE, GLOS. A
DESIGN BASED ON THE INNSBRUCK CASE
By S. E. Dykes Bower

64. AT LEIGHTON BUZZARD. CHANCEL CASE
By G. F. Bodley

65. AT GREAT BARDFIELD, ESSEX, *circa*
1870, WHERE THE DESIGNER RE-
CAPTURED THE SPIRIT OF A BY-
GONE AGE

clear of the wall in the pattern the lights would make on a plan of the church. Here is a simple example (60). The lettering can be on ivorine labels fastened on the board.

If this is done, the switching on and off of the lights during a service is made easier and mistakes need not occur.

An oak switchboard should be painted at the back with solignum and then backed with a sheet of copper before fixing to the wall, from which it should be held away with distance-pieces of some material not subject to rot or the attack of beetles.

Leading the wiring to the lighting points

From the switchboard the circuits have to be led in a neat and orderly way to the points which have been decided upon for the lighting system. No lighting sub-circuit may carry more than 600 watts. It is best to have all the wiring (in its conduits) on the surface and accessible. The conduit, or tubes, should be kept clear of the wall or other surfaces over which it is led by mounting it on a pillar type of clip

Brass screws only should be used and lead wall plugs.

No beams should ever be drilled unless this is absolutely unavoidable. Practically, we may say they should not be drilled.

No expressional features, such as shafts, should ever be drilled.

Naturally, we shall wish that the circuits should be led in such a way that they are as inconspicuous as possible, but it is even more necessary to insist that neat, straight runs should always be aimed at: they will look much better than awkward-looking bent ones in rather more obscure positions. It is also necessary to insist that lines should never be run up or against moulded or expressional features, such as piers, responds, shafts or pilasters. I have known Church Councils and individuals, whose business should have made them know much better, who thought that where there are many lines one line more or less would hardly matter—but the awful example which I illustrate will show how great a difference one more line may make. A straight vertical or horizontal run on a plain wall surface need not catch the eye disagreeably and matters very little: very little indeed compared with an addition to and ruination of the expressional features of the church (61).

Every foot of every run of conduit must be carefully planned and gone over by eye on the spot and the runs must be clearly and minutely described on the specification so that the contractor shall not have to use his judgment in the matter, however good that judgment may be expected to be.

The customary procedure in arranging the lighting of a church is as follows:

1. An architect or engineer who has the confidence of the Diocesan Advisory Committee is appointed and the subject is discussed with him.

2. The architect prepares full and careful specifications, with a plan and a section or sections of the church.

3. The architect meets the Parochial Church Council and explains the scheme which can then be criticised by the Church Councillors and any amendments made.

4. The architect obtains estimates from reputable firms of electricians, enclosing, with his specifications and drawings a copy of the *Regulations to be Observed by Contractors* drawn up by the Central Advisory Committee, obtainable from the Press and Publications board of the Church Assembly.

5. The architect submits the estimates to the Parochial Church Council.

6. The architect writes to the Insurance Company with which the church is insured, attaching copies of the plan and specifications and asking for their approval.

7. The architect submits the drawings and specifications, with the letter of approval from the Insurance Company, the estimate and the name and address of the contractor to the Diocesan Advisory Committee.

8. The Diocesan Advisory Committee advises the Chancellor of the Diocese to grant a faculty.

9. The work is carried out.

The Organ in the Post-War Church

By ANDREW FREEMAN, B.Mus.

ALTHOUGH THE SCOPE of this essay is limited by its title, it is hoped that parts of it will be found applicable to new or renovated organs in existing churches. The problem is as complicated as it is important: it is here dealt with—by no means exhaustively—under three heads, and in the order stated:

(1) The position of the instrument.
(2) Its outward appearance.
(3) Its contents and cost.

Those who disagree with the writer in placing the appearance of the organ second instead of third (which really means nowhere) are asked to scrutinise the organs in the next twenty churches they may chance to enter, and then to compile a list of those few that add to the beauty of the building and those many by whose removal the church would be enabled to recapture its erstwhile charm. The figures would be revealing.

In an ancient church the problem is to cure the disfigurement: in a new one it is to prevent ugliness from getting a foothold. To ensure this there must be prevision.

Position of the Organ

Amongst the questions that have to be discussed and settled before the plans for a new church can be accepted is the position to be occupied by the organ, and the first thing to be noted in this connection is that there is no "correct" position for it other than that dictated by the purpose it will have to serve and by its architectural fitness. Both choir and organ can be placed in any suitable part of the church for which the architect has made provision: they should, of course, be in fairly close proximity to each other.

It is probable that those responsible for the arrangement of post-war churches will, in many instances, decide that their organ shall be placed in or near the chancel. There can be no insuperable objection to this so long as the site is spacious enough to take an adequate instrument without overcrowding its pipes or muffling its sound, but a few points, for and against, should be taken into consideration. Thus, in those places where it is desired that the congregation shall take its full part in the services, the chancel position cannot be described as entirely satisfactory, for, when so placed, the organ cannot give the necessary support to the congregation without overpowering the choir. Another objection to the choir occupying seats in the chancel is that even a minimum of movement is noticeable and distracting, especially in a building of moderate dimensions, though against this may be set the fact that large numbers of people prefer to see the choir: they really like the effect of a chancel crowded with white-robed singers, and cannot readily visualise the æsthetic and devotional value of an unobstructed view of the altar.

Again, where a choir is accustomed to sing antiphonally a chancel position is helpful, but unless there is a wide space between the two bodies of singers it is doubtful whether the effect of a double choir is noticeable more than a few feet down the nave: moreover, to obtain the proper result—unless the organ be placed upon the screen—there should be *two* organs, one to support each "side" or, at least, a divided organ with its two parts fairly evenly balanced. There is, of course, nothing to prevent a west-end choir from singing in "sides."

Where organ and choir are placed elsewhere than in the chancel there is usually a feeling of spaciousness, even in a small building, that conduces no little to its devotional atmosphere.

As to where else the organ should be placed, the west end at once suggests itself as ideal. A roomy gallery with wide and easy stairs leading directly to the floor of the nave would take both instrument and singers: alternatively, only the organ might be in the gallery while the organist and choir might occupy a position below and in front of it—possibly on a platform, architecturally treated, a few feet above floor level.

To sum up this section, whilst the chancel position for organ and choir can be entirely satisfactory, provided there is no cramping of the one nor crowding of the other, the writer's purpose will have been achieved if he has made it clear that no worthwhile tradition will have been broken should it be decided to place both, either at the west end, or in any other effective position. There is freedom of choice, and every reason for due deliberation before making it.

Appearance of the Organ

From the earliest times organs have been wholly or partly encased in order to save them from damage; and it was not very long before the woodwork used for this purpose was treated ornamentally. This woodwork, which originally enclosed the entire instrument, including (by means of folding doors or shutters) even the front pipes, is called the *case*. In practice, however, the word *case* is often used when only the *front* of it is meant: sometimes, indeed, there is nothing but the front, and this is really a screen stretching across the open end of a recess into which the organ has been packed. Excellent as some of these *screen-fronts* are, it is to be hoped that in the planning of all new churches, sufficient space will be allowed for the organ to stand quite independently, with only its back to the wall. Where the sides of an organ are exposed to view it is usually better that they should not form subsidiary fronts since these take away from the solidity of the case and, by adding to the cost, divert money from the enrichment of the main front. In those instances where the organ occupies practically the whole of a recess, its front either flush with the opening or slightly set back, it is always a good thing to make the façade less wide than the recess, to give it return ends, and to make the cornices—especially of the towers—solid-looking by returning them likewise well back into the instrument.

The front pipes

In addition to having studied the evolution of the organ case, an architect wishing to design one would find a visit to a pipemaker's shop of extreme value. For an organ front cannot be judged by reference to its woodwork alone : the displayed pipes must also be taken into consideration. This involves at least an elementary knowledge of the construction of metal pipes. Front pipes are, of course, more carefully finished off than internal ones.

A metal pipe consists of a cylindrical *body* ending in an inverted cone called its *foot*. In front, at the place where body and foot are joined by soldering, there is a horizontal slit called the *mouth*, above and below which are depressions known as the *upper and lower lips*. The length of the body, that is, from the mouth upwards, is called its *speaking length*. On either side of the mouth are narrow vertical pieces of metal that go by the name of *ears*. These may be disregarded by the architect, but lips and mouths, even when unobtrusive, form lines or curves that are important elements in the design. There is, however, little need to remind architects of these lines and curves since in many modern fronts they have made them almost dominate the design to the utter disregard of a far more important principle, namely, the proportions of each individual pipe, whatever its place in the group. This matter—a vital one—will crop up again.

Large modern pipes are sometimes fitted with *bars*—strips of metal placed horizontally between the *ears* in front of the *mouths*—these are necessary for the proper speech of certain kinds of stops, but they are disfigurements, and efforts should be made to keep such pipes inside the case where they cannot be seen.

The pitch of a pipe is determined by the length of its *body*—the longer the *body* the deeper the note. The length of the *foot* has no effect upon the pitch, so that it may be made longer or shorter as desired. From this it follows that a group of pipes may have feet of equal length, as in most of the older cases ; or proportional to their speaking lengths, which is not usually pleasing ; or inversely proportional, a practice which is also both old and effective. Examples of the first and third will be found in the cases illustrated.

Pipes gradually decrease in speaking length as they ascend the scale. There are twelve semi-tones, and therefore twelve pipes, to the octave: every thirteenth pipe has half the speaking length of the first of the series, that is, of the pipe one octave below it.

For purposes of symmetry the body of a pipe may be slightly lengthened without ill effect, but in this event a large hole is cut out of the back of the pipe near the top in order to enable it to sound its rightful note. Undue lengthening of the bodies of pipes is an unsatisfactory way of obtaining extra height: the proper method of achieving the same end is to lengthen the feet.

Pipes decrease in diameter as well as in length as they ascend the scale, but not so rapidly—the diameter is usually halved at the seventeenth pipe.

Well-made, well-shaped pipes, singly or in groups, are beautiful examples of craftsmanship, especially when of good organ metal with a polished surface or of English tin—both materials are now rarely used on account of their high cost.

Embellishment of Organs

Bright metal pipes look far better than painted ones, however elaborate their decorations. If a rich effect be desired it should be attained by gilding them or by embossing some or all: for extreme richness there is nothing that can exceed the double process, as at Tewkesbury. It is a mistake to gild only the lips of metal pipes.

The woodwork of the case lends itself to enrichment by means of gold and colour. There seems no valid reason why oak should not be painted, nor, indeed, why oak should be so extensively desired. Dr. A. G. Hill, who designed what is probably the finest of all modern cases—at Sydney Town Hall (1890)—had that case made of deal, with the carving of gilded mahogany, this being, as he said, in accordance with ancient precedent as exemplified in most Continental organs.*

It is quite possible to trace in detail the development of the front during the thousand years of the instrument's association with the worship of the church. Roughly speaking, it began with a single row of front pipes, arranged in one compartment, and enclosed in an ornamental wooden frame. Later on came the division of the front pipes into two or more compartments or *flats* by means of buttresses or uprights, and into two or more *stories* by means of transoms. Additional variety was obtained by allowing some of the larger pipes to break through the cornice in the form of flat or *quasi* towers, and these, before long, were made to project forwards as V-shaped, square, or semicircular towers. Brackets to support the towers and various kinds of structure above their cornices supplied

---

* *The Musical Standard*, August 30, 1890.

almost everything necessary: with these at his command and with the aid of skilled carvers, the designer had unlimited range for his fancy. Hundreds of examples, from Britain to Italy and from Poland to Spain, some of them exuberant and others restrained, testify to the artistry that found in the organ case an outlet of expression and a noble means of enriching the furnishing of any church.

Typical Organ Cases

In appraising the six cases here selected for illustration, the chief points to be noted are: (1) the *naturalness* of each group of pipes (almost exactly true speaking length in the foreign examples and approximately the same in the English ones); (2) the line or lines made by the pipemouths (mostly horizontal in these six instances, but where inclined the reason can easily be discerned); and (3) the treatment of the carving between the tops of the pipes and the lower edge of the cornice. (This carving, technically known as the *pipe-shades*, has an ornamental value that is here—and always should be—subservient to its purpose.) Other features of considerable interest will be noted, but these three are of primary importance.

1. Franziskaner Hofkapelle, Innsbruck. This ancient organ, made *circa* 1569, is placed over the choir stalls on the north side. Externally perfect, it is internally derelict. The smaller (*Positiv*) case is closely modelled on the larger one. The whole case is painted, with pictures on both sides of the hinged doors, and elaborate brackets supporting the overhanging sides. As a case it is entitled to be classed as perfect.

2. Hardwicke, near Gloucester. This was designed in 1938 by Mr. S. E. Dykes-Bower, who was asked to do something on the lines of the Innsbruck case, but was limited by having to use the front pipes (plain metal) of the existing instrument. The carving is heavily gilt. It stands at the west end of the north aisle: another front, facing the nave, has yet to be made.

3. Great Bardfield, Essex. This is the simplest of the six, and was probably designed by the Rev. F. H. Sutton about the year 1870, it is in 14th-century Gothic. Painted, and enlivened with gilt, it has twenty-one plain metal pipes in front arranged in three flat compartments. The whole is contained under an ornamental gable. Overhanging sides and carved wings add to its grace and charm.

4. Leighton Buzzard. This is a chancel case, designed by G. F. Bodley, and it contains only part of the instrument. (The rest is in a loft in the north transept.) There are here two double-storied *flats* connecting a V-tower in the centre with square towers on either hand: the latter are placed angle-wise and have a slight *overhang*. The pipes display approximately their true speaking lengths: this is contrived by making the lower edge of the *pipe-shades* of the towers and upper

stories of the *flats* oppose the lines made by the mouths* and by giving the lower edge of the shades in the lower stories a steeper angle. The returned ends give this front something of the effect of a true case.

5. Kloster-kirche, Muri, Canton Aargau, Switzerland. This is another perfect case enclosing an unplayable organ †. It stands in a recess over a chapel on the north side of the chancel. The organ was made in 1760, but the case may be *circa* 1620. The pipe shades of the central tower are unsymmetrically engrailed so as to allow the pipes to display their true lengths : this is in accordance with a very ancient and pleasing practice. The end flats are inclined at an angle to the main part of the case : they also overhang, though this feature is hidden by the gallery front. The angels with trumpets and the carved wings fit in delightfully.

6. Convent Church of Montorge, Fribourg, Switzerland. This fine example is probably of early 18th-century date. The centre of the case is in two stages, representing two divisions (manuals) of the organ as at Innsbruck, but here combined in one case. The carving is of extreme delicacy, with solid lower edges to screen the tops of the pipes, and open work where there is nothing to hide.

Conclusions

If the foreign cases noticed above fall into the perfect class whilst the English ones fall just short of that high mark, it is not so much because they excel in the magnificence of their carving (though this, of course, is obvious) but rather because they were made by men who worked in the closest co-operation and companionship. The carver may have been a wizard, but his work was subservient to the claims of the pipes. His purpose was to supply a fitting frame in the fullest sense of the word, and his achievement is the proof of his magic and the secret of the perfection of their joint labours.

These foreign cases are frequently of extreme richness and elaboration, yet it is difficult to imagine that such a one as that at Muri would not look well in any church, however austere its architectural style, provided it were properly placed. It should, moreover, be clear that, so long as the same proportions of wood and metal were kept, a very much simpler version could be designed that would be both graceful and stately—and even perfect.

The Contents and Cost of an Organ

During, and after, the war of 1914–18 the cost of organs was trebled, but after

* Many modern cases are ruined by making the edge of the shade run parallel with the line of the mouths : the result is groups of pipes of the same (apparent) speaking length yet of different diameters : this is meaningless and absurd.

† Its twin, similarly placed on the south side of the chancel arch is usable ; so, too, is a third and larger instrument in a case of different design, but of almost equal merit at the west end.

**REBUILT ORGAN IN THE TWELFTH-CENTURY PARISH CHURCH OF
THAMES DITTON**

The accommodation problem was resolved by making a feature of the instrument
and placing it with a new case and pipe frontages in N.E. corner of North Aisle,
with detached console in the Chancel.

J. W. Walker & Sons Ltd., Ruislip

ORGAN STOP-KEY CONSOLE OF SPECIAL DESIGN (WALKER) INSTALLED
IN ST. MARY'S ABBEY, BUCKFAST, S. DEVON, IN 1939

Approximate dimensions : Width 6 ft. ; depth (including pedal-board) 4 ft. ;
height 4 ft. 6 in.

J. W. Walker & Sons Ltd., Ruislip

a few years had elapsed prices fell till they were not more than eighty to one hundred per cent above the level of 1914. One would have expected this to result in smaller instruments, but in the main the effect was the raising of more money and the building of larger and more complete organs. There seems no reason to believe that the same thing will not happen again, except that it will take longer to get organ building properly started. Those who want new or re-conditioned organs in the immediate future will have to wait their turn, and the prices they will have to pay will be at least double those of 1939. The purchase tax, although reduced, is still a heavy charge. What is most regrettable is that stocks of seasoned timber of the kind required for organ building will be in short supply, and that many skilled men may be tempted by higher wages to stay in other jobs.

For some years the cost of building churches will limit the amount that can be spent on organs, but this will right itself in time: those who want large and expensive instruments will, in the end, contrive to obtain them.

The two factors most likely to make for smaller organs are proper placing and more thoughtful specifications, or schemes for the stops. The former will secure that neither volume nor quality is muffled, and the latter will avoid needless duplications and ensure that most of the stops chosen make a definite contribution to the *ensemble*.

Organ builders frequently make two or more organs after the same pattern—especially small ones—but since the instruments stand in different buildings they rarely sound exactly alike, even though desired by the client. Moreover, organs are usually given their final "voicing" in the church in which they stand, so that there should be no fear of standardisation on a large scale—a state of things that would be as undesirable in organs as in churches.

Extension organs

Extension organs are those in which some or all of the stops are extended by the addition of one or more octaves of pipes and then made to serve as other stops of the same quality and power but at different pitches. This certainly makes the most of any set of pipes, but the system is fundamentally defective in that the quality and power of the said stops ought *not* to be the same. Another defect is that one does not always get the exact effect one has a right to expect when playing. Thus on putting down a chord of four notes with three stops drawn, there should be twelve different pipes speaking: on an extension organ one might get only ten, or even eight, and the number would vary from chord to chord. This does not conduce to exact interpretation of the music or to pure organ part-playing. In fairness, however, it should be said that many competent organists consider these defects outweighed by the advantage above mentioned.

Electronic organs

Before purchasing one of these very wonderful contrivances possible purchasers should read *The Organ of Tradition* by the Rev. Noel A. Bonavia-Hunt. They should also demand a guarantee, not merely that the thing will work for a definite number of years, but also that it will retain its quality unimpaired for the same period.

Organ Advisory Committee

The Central Council for the Care of Churches has appointed an Organ Construction Advisory Committee whose services are available to Parochial Church Councils and other bodies without charge—except where a visit is necessary, when ordinary expenses would be required. Expert and disinterested advice *before* asking a builder to submit a scheme for a reconstruction or for a new instrument should be of great help in deciding what kind of organ would best fulfil the musical requirements of a particular church. Letters should be addressed to the Secretary of the Organ Advisory Committee, care of the Central Council for the Care of Churches, or direct to the Secretary of the Diocesan Advisory Committee in whose area the church happens to be.

In conclusion one may note that the tendency of organ experts, both professional and amateur, is to re-introduce certain characteristics that have in recent years fallen into desuetude: they should bring out of their treasure things new and old.

Church Woodwork: Pews, Pulpits,

Altar Rails and Screens By LLEWELLYN E. WILLIAMS,
A.R.I.B.A.

IN DESIGNING THE FITTINGS for a church the craftsman must hold a middle course between two extremes. On the one hand he must be aware that almost every object within the building, whether it be the altar, choir stalls, screens, font or seating, has a tradition of workmanship associated with it dating back to the Middle Ages and earlier. On the other hand modern needs differ from those of our fore-fathers and cannot be ignored. Many appliances and methods of construction available to-day, such as reinforced concrete and the power-driven saw, the medieval craftsman would have used with joy to ease the drudgery of the work. The antiquarian spirit of the 19th century did not exist in the Middle Ages when much of the best church work was being done. The old craftsman was eager to try something new, being himself something of a modernist in his time, and, para-doxically, the modern traditionalist, shy at adopting new methods and new materials, fearful to try new forms for which there is no precedent in old work, is not following the tradition of English craftsmanship at all.

An exact copy of a medieval screen made by machinery with every part identical with the old, but every surface perfectly smooth no more resembles the original than a wax effigy at Madame Tussaud's resembles a living man. The spirit that informed the old work is missing; the copy is a dead thing. But all machine work is not of necessity bad; only when the machine is master and the craftsman reduced to the level of an operative is it deadly. A modern design, no matter how labo-riously fashioned by hand, which flouts all the standards of the past in a spirit of revolt, may catch the eye by its novelty and please for a moment, but the pleasure will be ephemeral.

The good church craftsman, therefore, while he studies deeply the traditions of church art, will use it to discipline his fancy, but never allow his fancy to become a slave. The path is a narrow one and it is fatally easy to slip over on the one side or the other. That is why no commercially mass produced object is suitable for church furnishing. The church is a sanctuary, not an auditorium, and everything placed within it is an oblation man offers to God. It is man's act of creation, and creation is a personal thing.

The fittings of a cathedral or a simple parish church are in substance the same. They consist of the altar and the ornaments of the sanctuary, the choir fittings, the screens dividing off the several parts of the building, the font for baptism and

173

the seats for worshippers. Such fittings are universal, that is to say, they are common throughout the Catholic Church in all countries. Liturgical needs and local custom may modify the design or dictate different materials; the elaborate metal screens of Spain or the baldachini of Italy, for instance, are not happy on English soil, and when used have always the air of something exotic.

The most important fitting in every church is the altar. It is the symbol of the central act of Christian worship, the office of Holy Communion or the Mass, and as such must always be the dominant object in the church to which all else is subservient. Unfortunately this fact was obscured during the 17th and 18th centuries in the English Church when the sermon became the chief part of the services, and it was not until the middle of the 19th century that ecclesiologists, stirred by the works of men like Pugin, Butterfield, Street and Bodley set about recovering for our churches the beauty of the sanctuary. When they began they had no other guide than the churches of the Continent, where the old type of altar, so often seen in illuminated manuscripts and old service books, had been replaced under the stress of the Counter Reformation by baroque specimens utterly unsuitable to the English parish church. Thus it came about that new altars were raised upon steps where no steps had been, and were fitted out with shelves and gradines bearing a quantity of brass candlesticks and flower vases, while behind was set up an enormous reredos or triptych, which usually obscured more than half of the old east window. Anyone entering a church so ill-treated must feel as he looks at this army of ornaments surrounding a diminutive altar that something has gone wrong.

Modern craftsmen before the war were slowly bringing back into our new churches the traditional arrangement of the sanctuary and eliminating, often under bitter protest, the monstrosities which disfigured it. Writers such as Dr. Percy Dearmer and Dr. Armitage Day explained the reasons for the change, and guilds of craftsmen led by artists like Mr. Martin Travers and Mr. J. N. Comper produced excellent work up and down the country. Because they were in the tradition of English church craft as distinct from Continental models these altars were called English Altars, and the principles of their design, simplicity and length, are now almost universally adopted in every new church.

Where the altar is placed below a blank wall, or the sill of the east window is at a considerable height above the floor, it is better to have a low reredos, not more than three feet six inches high to emphasise the length of the altar and to fill in the space above with a contrasting curtain or plain panelling, and avoid the temptation to erect a lofty tripytch or hanging dorsal. A successful example of this treatment is the Lady Chapel at Fairford Church, by Mr. Geoffrey Webb, and another is the church of St. Thomas the Apostle, Boston Road, Hanwell, by Mr. E. Maufe.

At the Reformation stone altars were abolished and replaced by wooden communion tables. These were often of great beauty as may be seen in the City

SEVENTEENTH- AND EIGHTEENTH-CENTURY ORGAN CASES OF HISTORIC AND ARTISTIC VALUE

67. AN EARLY EIGHTEENTH-CENTURY EXAMPLE AT THE CONVENT
CHURCH OF MONTORGE, FRIBOURG, SWITZERLAND

66. A BEAUTIFUL SEVENTEENTH-CENTURY CASE AT THE KLOSTER-
KIRCHE, MURI, CANTON AARGAU, SWITZERLAND

68. CARVED OAK REREDOS AND PANELLING IN THE CHAPEL OF ST. KATHERINE'S CHURCH, MERSTHAM

Executed by the Bromsgrove Guild to a design by Llewellyn E. Williams, A.R.I.B.A.

churches built by Sir Christopher Wren, which have happily survived the fire "blitz" of the last war. But Renaissance tables with their open fronts and elaborate carving are not models to be followed in modern churches where the practice is to denote the Church's seasons by different coloured frontals. To display these often beautiful specimens of needlework the modern altar should be a plain oak structure having a top, or mensa, at least one and a half inches in thickness and projecting one and a half inches beyond the frame below on the front and two sides while the back is made flush to fit close to the wall. The frame itself should be made of plain legs four inches square, one at each corner for small altars, but with intermediate legs for those over seven feet long. These legs should be strongly framed together with four inches by one inch rails, one placed immediately below the mensa and the other about six inches above the floor. Cross bracing at the angles should be used if there is the slightest tendency for the altar to move.

Everything about the altar and the sanctuary should be brightly coloured and this especially applies to the reredos. Mosaics, marble or uncoloured wood carving have a most depressing effect when these occur below a large window filled with stained glass, becoming just ugly masses devoid of detail.

The Altar Rails

Before the Reformation altar rails were unnecessary, the altar being already fenced by screens at the entrance to the choir, although it is uncertain whether every medieval church screen was fitted with gates. After the Reformation the position of the Holy Table was for some time in dispute and was frequently removed from the east end. One reason for providing rails was stated in the Visitation of the Caroline Bishops to be to prevent profanation by dogs and there are examples still surviving to-day of the altar entirely surrounded by rails. Archbishop Laud decreed that the altar be replaced against the east wall, and the altar rails since then have become the dividing line between sanctuary and choir. In modern churches it has become a kneeling rail, and as such should be of an open pattern (69, 70). The old rails are many of them of great beauty having richly turned balusters as at Great Slaughton, in Huntingdon, and St. Stephen's, Walbrook, in London, while others have carved and pierced panels as at Farnham, in Surrey. But quite plain rails were common in small churches of which those at Great Walsingham, in Norfolk, are typical. Where these old rails have been adapted to modern needs they are frequently uncomfortably high for the communicants and it would be well to remove them altogether from the chancel to another part of the church. A modern altar rail should not be more than two feet two inches in height and should be placed about twelve inches back from the edge of the step at the entrance to the sanctuary so as to form a kneeler for the worshippers. This step must not be more than six inches in height and a second step should never be provided at this point. Between the communion rail and the step of the altar a space at least six feet wide should be left to allow the priest to move about easily when communicating the congregation. The rails should have an opening in the centre about four feet wide which can be closed by a flap or gates, and the top of the rail should be plain with a smooth upper surface. The practice of fixing newel posts which project above the top rail should be avoided. Excellent modern communion rails exist at St. Thomas the Apostle's, Hanwell Road, and at East Cosham Church, while rails of the plainest character have been provided by Mr. Martin Smith to the John Keble Memorial Church, Mill Hill. The brass contraptions of pseudo-Gothic design which disfigure so many 19th-century churches should be abolished as soon as possible.

The Pulpit

The use of pulpits in the English church dates back to the 12th century. The usual position in pre-Reformation times was against the first pier in the nave west of the chancel arch, sometimes on the north and sometimes on the south side. In modern churches since the 19th century the usual position has been on the north or Gospel side of the nave immediately outside the entrance to the chancel. In very large churches and in cathedrals the pulpit is sometimes moved farther towards the west to allow of better sound conditions, but this presents a practical difficulty, as unless the front seats are capable of being turned round the preacher is speaking to the backs of part of the congregation.

Many good examples of 15th-century pulpit designs still exist, notably at Queen's Camel, in Somerset, where a finely carved pulpit stands outside the chancel screen and another is in Dartmouth Church. At Southwold, in Suffolk, is a fine example of a medieval pulpit supported on a single post and a post-Reformation pulpit of this type is in the nave of Westminster Abbey.

In lofty churches or where acoustics were bad the pulpit was usually provided with a sounding board, but in modern churches where acoustics are now treated as a science this means of regulating the sound is less needed. These sounding boards were large flat disks supported either from the roof or framed up and cantilevered out from the back of the pulpit itself a few feet above the head of the preacher. Some fine examples of Jacobean pulpits with sounding boards perished in the fires which destroyed many of the London churches in the last war, one of the most beautiful of these being at St. Mildred's, Bread Street, now alas only to be known through photographs. A modern example may be seen in Mr. Cachemaille-Day's remarkable church of St. Saviour, Eltham.

The old pulpit was small, not more than three feet in diameter and frequently raised about four feet above the nave floor. Square pulpits are known to have existed in medieval times, but the shape soon gave place to the polygon, and there are numerous examples existing of hexagonal and octagonal pulpits. Other shapes are also found, and that Selworthy, in Somerset, is dodecagonal in plan. The polygon is not usually complete; five sides of an octagon gives room for the preacher to enter, and many early post-Reformation pulpits were provided with doors, but this is not required in a modern church.

To-day a good size for a pulpit is from three feet six inches to four feet internal diameter and the floor need not be raised more than three feet above the level of the church. The sides surrounding the preacher should not be higher than three feet six inches, and the top capping mould should be wide enough to rest a book upon. In addition an adjustable desk is usually provided, and when electric light is available, this should have a strip light with a shade to conceal it from the congregation.

The lofty pulpits of the 17th and 18th centuries have almost all been cut down and adapted to modern needs, the only reason for their existence being the galleries with which churches were furnished at that time and the undue importance given to the sermon. The high backed pews too, common at that time, required a preacher to be considerably raised up in order to see the faces of the congregation in the body of the church.

There is a tendency in some modern churches to balance the pulpit and the reading desk on either side of the choir. This is a return to the planning of the early Christian churches. A good example is the church of St. Saviour, Acton, by Mr. Edward Maufe, and St. Columba's, Liverpool, by Mr. Bernard Miller, has the same arrangement. While it gives symmetry to the chancel it is not altogether satisfactory from the liturgical point of view.

When the pulpit is built up upon a solid stone base the construction presents no special problem, but the pillar type which is a very beautiful form must be framed upon a centre post with two cross bearers at the top to support the floor. Into these bearers are framed subsidiary bearers, the whole being held together by a stout curb. It is on this curb that the pulpit sides are built up and the space between the posts filled in with panelling or tracery. The space below the pulpit floor may be filled in with wood vaulting curved back so as to appear to spring from the centre shaft. A good example of this type of pulpit may be seen at Castle-acre, in Norfolk.

The steps up to the tall 18th-century pulpits were in the nature of elaborate staircases as may be seen in St. Mary-at-Hill by the Monument in London, but in a modern church as few steps as possible should be aimed at; and these so arranged as to be invisible to the congregation. The War Memorial chapel pulpit at Rossall school, by Sir Robert Lorimer, is a charming example. Here there are four plain oak steps from the ground arranged in an inconspicuous manner.

A warning may be given against over decorating pulpits. Some examples of richly decorated and carved pulpit fronts are found in churches when the sanctuary and altar are neglected and dingy. This puts the whole scale of values in the church out of focus. Where money is short the pulpit should be of the plainest type and everything concentrated on beautifying the altar. An excellent plain pulpit of this character may be seen in St. Saviour's, Brighton, by Mr. H. S. Goodhart-Rendel.

Seating

The seating of churches has undergone many changes. Before the Reformation the congregation frequently stood or knelt in unseated churches, the only concession to age or infirmity being stone benches placed along the walls and occasionally round the bases of the piers. The earliest benches now existing date from the 13th century, but it was not till the 15th century that pewing became common, and most of the finely carved bench ends and poppy heads date from this period. In the 17th and 18th centuries the high backed pews with doors filled the body of the church and were occupied by the gentry and church-going squires like Sir Roger de Coverley of the *Spectator*. But our forefathers' ideas of comfort fell far short of ours and all old pews are extremely uncomfortable for modern worshippers, being often very low with narrow seats and vertical backs.

In modern churches the seating is provided by pews or chairs, which are placed so as to face the altar. The cruciform church plan is not suitable for normal parish needs, and where an old church of this pattern has to be seated, it is best to use only chairs in the transepts, placed so as to face towards the centre space.

Comfort depends on the spacing of the pews and the rows should not be less than three feet back to back. The seat should never be more than two feet eight inches from the ground and the back arranged with a slope of not more than one inch between the seat and the top, which latter should be finished with a capping without any moulded projection on the seat side. The seat itself should be about fourteen inches wide and may be either horizontal or designed with a slight slope towards the back. It is often a great advantage to design pewing so that the backs are open below the seat, as in this way the cleaning of the floor is made easier. In setting out a block of seating one foot eight inches must be allowed in width for each person and if the pew is not more than seven feet in length the thickness of the bench ends must be counted in addition, but in lengths of ten feet and over no additional length need be added for the ends. No pew should be longer than twenty feet, and all over ten feet long must be accessible from both ends.

In planning the seating the centre passage down the nave should never be narrower than five feet and side aisles passage not less than three feet wide. These are minimum widths and many churches with elaborate ceremonial will require both the centre and aisle passages to be considerably wider. It should be remembered that a centre aisle six feet six inches wide will accommodate for special occasions an extra row of chairs, and one eight feet wide will take two rows. It is a good rule to allow a space equal to the width of the centre aisle between the entrance to the choir and the first row of seats. Cross aisles are determined by the position of the exits, but usually a cross aisle the same width as the centre one between the north and south doors, if these exist, will prevent crowding at the end of a service, and where there is a west door the centre aisle should be continued the full width up to this exit also. The design of pews in a modern church should be as plain as possible, but the craftsman may let his fancy play with the shapes of the bench ends within moderation. Good plain pews with small turned ornaments on the bench ends have been designed in St. Alban's Church, North Harrow, by Mr. A. W. Kenyon with great success.

The floors of the naves in modern churches are usually paved with wood blocks and the seating can be placed directly upon these. But many old churches have stone floors, often damp, and it is better in such cases to lay a joist and boarded floor over the flags and to place the pews on it. This will raise the seating a few inches above the aisles, but provided that the step at the entrance to the pew is not more than three inches this is not a drawback. Such raised floors, however, must be ventilated to prevent dry rot and other fungus diseases attacking the joists, and this can be done by inserting iron gratings in the curbs on either side of the aisle.

The practice in nearly all modern churches is to substitute chairs for pews, and from every point of view this is preferable. Chairs are more flexible in their use, make cleaning easier and do not spoil the proportions of the building. The arrangement is similar to that for pews, but in selecting the chairs, which should be rush-seated for preference, it should be seen that no front cross bar interferes with kneeling. The tops of the backs of chairs should be flat and slightly hollowed, and should have a book rest affixed to them about half way between the top and the seat.

A kneeling board in front of either chairs or pews interferes with people passing along the rows and is unnecessary, as small hassocks which can be hung up when not in use are an ample provision. Box hassocks with movable lids which the Victorians used in order to incline before the Deity without damaging their clothes are not aids to devotion and should never be tolerated in a modern church.

Choir Stalls

The position of the choir in a church is a question in constant dispute between those who like a surpliced procession and those who would sacrifice all for the best musical arrangement. Acoustically the ideal position for both choir and organ is a gallery at the west end of the church where the music can reinforce the singing of the congregation, and a good modern example of this may be seen in St.

Wilfrid's Church, Brighton. This arrangement was common in the 18th century when there were no organs in many village churches, the music being provided by a village orchestra such as that described by Thomas Hardy in *Under the Greenwood Tree*.

The battle of the surplice was won by the followers of Dr. Pusey in the last century, and to-day surpliced choirs are the normal in most churches. By bringing the singers into the chancel the position of the organ was automatically shifted to a place from which the organist could control his choir and this has led to the building of organ galleries at the side of the chancel. Musically the position could not be worse, but with electrical remote control it has in some instances been possible to retain the console of the organ in the choir while removing the instrument itself to the west end of the church. In many old churches chantry chapels have been blocked up with the instruments which is an unpardonable vandalism.

Choir stalls consist of two or more rows of seating placed on either side of the choir facing inwards. Stalls in the great churches and in college chapels are often elaborate with carved canopies and enrichments. In parish churches they should be simple and unobtrusive. The general dimensions follow those of pews, but it is common to raise the rows slightly one behind the other, and the ends of the stalls are taller than the pew ends to support the book rests of the singers. These rests should be about three feet four inches high to allow the choir to sing kneeling when needed, and between eight inches and twelve inches wide in order to support the larger books used. As the front rows of choir stalls are usually occupied by boys the height of the book rests for these should not be more than three feet. Good plain choir stalls may be seen in St. Alban's Church, North Harrow.

The clergy occupy the seats immediately west of the choir and the clergy desk is usually a separate fitting, which should be designed in harmony with the stalls. The book rest should be not less than one foot six inches deep from top to bottom with a beading on the lower edge and should be the full width of the stall, that is to say, at least two feet three inches. Below the book rest there should be a shelf for books and papers which the incumbent may require for giving out notices and publishing banns. Some churches have the clergy stalls planned to face east; as in a cathedral the seats of the Dean and Precentor face east. This has been done in St. Oswald's, Preston, but the arrangement has several drawbacks especially in moderate-sized churches, where the congregation have only a back view of the priest during Matins and Evensong, and liturgically it is a great handicap during parts of the offices when the priest addresses the people.

Screens

The chancel screen was in the past considered an indispensable part of the church. From earliest times it represented the entrance to the sanctuary and replaced the solid dividing wall pierced by a narrow doorway, an example of which still remains in the Saxon church of Bradford-on-Avon. These screens in the early Middle Ages were plain and heavy, but by the 15th century they became one of the most decorative features of the parish churches, being elaborately carved with niches and canopies and invariably painted in the brightest colours.

In a medieval church the screen was a practical protection to the altar, but to-day it is rather a symbolic division between the chancel and the nave which emphasises the legal responsibility of the rector, be he lay or clerical, for the upkeep of the former. In addition to the chancel screen most medieval churches possessed minor screens dividing off chantry chapels and other parts of the church which were called parclose screens. These were also often richly carved, but the work never reached the high watermark of craftsmanship which characterised the chancel screen.

In different parts of the country the chancel screen developed in distinct forms, and the screens common in the West of England are constructed in a manner totally different from East Anglia or the North. This clear-cut division between the local types is common to all medieval crafts, and the obliteration of it through the ease of modern transport is inevitable but is to be regretted. All screens have a central doorway and are divided horizontally about three feet six inches from the ground by a rail. Below this the panels are filled in solid and above the openings between the vertical parts are ornamented with cusping and carved work. Upon the chancel screen was built the rood loft having a panelled front projecting forward into the nave of the church. Both screen and rood loft were at times carried across both aisles as well as the nave forming a truly magnificent composition. Most of the lofts were destroyed in post-Reformation times, but a number remain in the remoter parts of the country to show what skilled artists the medieval carpenters had become. Such a screen may be seen at Llangwm Ucha Church in, Monmouth, where the panels of the loft are pierced in elaborate tracery patterns, another is at Atherington, in Devon.

Very beautiful examples of modern craftsmanship are the screens at St. Cyprian's, Baker St., London, by J. N. Comper, and at St. Oswald's, Preston, by Walter Tapper, and in many of the churches designed by the late G. F. Bodley the screens are of extreme beauty.

Metal screens were not common in English churches and few remain from pre-Reformation times, but some beautiful modern screen work in this material may be seen in the Warrior's Chapel in Westminster Abbey and in the War Memorial Chapel at York Minster. One of the most extraordinary modern examples of a rood is that in the chapel of the Sacred Mission at Kelham by Curry and Thompson. This consists of a plain brick arch thrown across the sanctuary with the figures placed at the apex.

Much of the charm of medieval joinery is due to its roughness and the generous dimensions of the timbers used. Mouldings are worked by hand and the feel of the grain of the wood and the knots led to many unevennesses and waverings of the line which gave life to the work and is entirely missed in machine-made modern examples. The modern workman too often subdues his material ruthlessly, but the medieval craftsman always humoured it and here if anywhere the modern crafts-man must steer a middle course. This has been done well by Mr. James Woodford in the charming screens which form a passage between the Children's Corner and the chancel at St. Thomas the Apostle's, Boston Road, Hanwell.

The Lectern

The lectern from which the Lessons are read at Matins and Evensong has assumed almost a standard pattern. In nearly all parish churches the Bible is carried on the outstretched wings of an eagle supported on a ball and column. In the 19th century this fitting was usually a heavy brass affair with a massive base. How hideous many of these lecterns can be must be seen to be believed. Beyond the fact that the eagle is undoubtedly an old form of lectern, and that examples still exist dating back to the 14th century (one example is in Leighton Buzzard Church) there seems little to recommend its employment in a modern church. If an eagle is required it should be carved in wood and not cast in brass, but the other medieval form of lectern known as the desk lectern deserves to be a more popular shape than it is. The old desk lectern is a double-sided fitting probably used in a medieval church to support the music books in the choir as the slope of the desk is very steep. It was often richly carved and surmounted a decorated shaft. Many old lecterns of this type survive, and good examples may be seen in the parish churches at Lenham and Detling, in Kent. A modern lectern founded on this old form may be seen in the church of St. Michael and All Angels, Little Ilford, designed by Mr. Charles Spooner, and two which have been illustrated in the press by the late Sir Robert Lorimer designed for the church of St. John, Lattingtown, U.S.A., and Pittenweem, Fifeshire, are infinitely preferable to the "brass bird."

Font Covers

Font covers have a great variety. Originally no more than a flat lid padlocked over the bowl of the font to protect the consecrated water from desecration, they became in the 15th century lofty pinnacles of delicate wood carving suspended by counterbalance weights from the roof, as may be seen in Halifax Church, Yorkshire. By the early 16th century the original use of the font cover had been so far forgotten that the cover assumed the appearance of a baldachin supported on shafts from the floor. At Trunch, in Norfolk, the font stands beneath such an erection. Many modern churches are content to return to the plain lid with some modified ornament upon it by which it may be raised (72). There are one or two

A CONTRAST SHOWING THE ADVANTAGE OF THE FLAT-TOPPED ALTAR RAIL

70. JACOBEAN ALTAR RAILS AT DURNFORD CHURCH, WILTS., ADAPTED TO PRESENT USE. THE TALL NEWEL POST IS A HINDRANCE

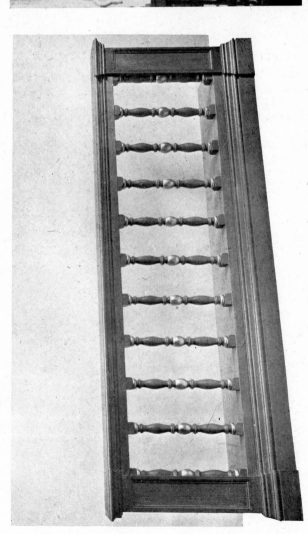

69. MODERN ALTAR RAIL AT ST. KATHERINE'S, MERSTHAM, SURREY

71. PART OF A CHANCEL SCREEN AT ST. KATHERINE'S, MERSTHAM, SURREY

Executed by the Bromsgrove Guild to a design by Llewellyn E. Williams, A.R.I.B.A.

interesting examples of a modern treatment of the pinnacled font cover, notably in the remarkable John Keble Memorial Church at Mill Hill, in St. Nicholas', Burnage, by Mr. Cachemaille-Day, and at St. Albans by W. H. Randoll Blacking (32). The font at St. Columba's, Scarborough, designed by Mr. Temple Moore is a good example of a modern treatment of the pinnacle which does not depart violently from the traditional form.

The employment of local craftsmen and the use of local materials is a matter for practical rather than sentimental considerations. When good materials are on the spot it is absurd to go to the expense of transporting others from a distance. This was the custom of the medieval builders, and it gave a distinctive character to church building in different parts of England. But even in those days of bad roads and slow movement Caen stone from Normandy was used at Canterbury Cathedral, and the timber for Westminster Hall roof was grown at Wadhurst, in Sussex. It is interesting to remember that when the Hall was repaired in 1913 by the Office of Works the oak was again brought from the same district.

Modern transport has made available materials which are grown or manufactured in all parts of the country, and in modern work full use should be made of modern methods.

The same practical considerations should govern the employment of local craftsmen. For a long time after the war there will probably be a shortage of skilled workmen as none has been specially trained during the war years. Where experts exist in a neighbourhood they should be given the first chance to do the work in the parish church, but the trend of working conditions just before the war did little to foster the survival of the country crafts, and to-day often the only real craftsman left in a village is the blacksmith. Some of the best modern church fittings have been carried out by members of guilds and craftsmen such as the Bromsgrove Guild, the St. Dominic Guild, the Wareham Guild, and best known of all the Art Workers' Guild. Fittings of all kinds can be entrusted to such guilds with complete confidence that the work will be of the best. It is the architect in charge of the building who co-ordinates the work of the various artists and craftsmen working upon it, and many modern architects have such men closely associated with them, in the same manner that Sir Christopher Wren had Grinling Gibbons, Tijou and other craftsmen providing fittings for his churches.

Shortly after many of the Wren churches had been destroyed by German bombs an association known as the Friends of the City Churches was formed to watch over and advise on the rebuilding. The association represented the considered views of many famous architects and learned societies, and their manifesto contained proposals which are applicable beyond the bounds of the City of London. It states that it is unwise "to attempt to produce replicas of ceilings or internal fittings which have vanished for ever. On the contrary it is believed," the pamphlet goes on to say, "that the right solution to this part of the problem would be for the restored churches to be furnished with the best work that contemporary craftsmen can produce."

This is sound advice, and if the present-day craftsman is humble enough to feel that he owes a debt to the craftsmen of the past, church art will develop new and living forms on the tree of tradition as inevitably as next year's blossom springs from this year's wood.

An English Church and its Surroundings   ᔋ   ᔋ

By SIR CHARLES NICHOLSON, Bt.

THE SITE OF A CHURCH is generally selected for reasons of expediency and it may often be the reverse of inspiring, particularly if it happens to be in a suburban district. But, however unattractive the surroundings may be, there is no reason why the best possible use should not be made of the ground at the disposal of the church builder. Very often, however, what happens is this. Quite wisely the first stage in the procedure is to build a parish room to serve temporarily as a Mission Church. Perhaps this is done in corrugated iron or some such temporary material; sometimes a more permanent building is put up. In either case, the architectural character is not regarded as very important and the design is entrusted to an architect who would not be likely to be employed to build the permanent church. Next, perhaps, the same or some other architect is called in to build the parsonage and, lastly, yet another is entrusted with the building of the permanent church.

It is hardly to be expected that the best possible use will be made of a site unless the whole lay-out and plan of campaign is settled in advance by a competent person and preferably carried out under his direction in all its stages. There may be cases in which two or more architects of equal ability and experience have been responsible for different buildings in a single group—as was the case with a church in North East London, by James Brooks, to which is annexed a children's hospital, designed by J. D. Sedding. The result of that experiment was most successful, but in the great majority of cases the architects of what may be regarded as the less important buildings are not so carefully selected as those employed to build the permanent churches. Often, too, a lower standard of solidity and workmanship is accepted in church halls and similar buildings than that which would be recognised as worthy of a permanent church. This tends to encourage a lowering of the standard acceptable for church work in general, since nothing in this world is so easy as to follow a bad example.

If, however, a group of buildings is well laid out, and if the buildings themselves are well designed and consistently carried out, the modern church builder is given a great opportunity and a good many instances may be recalled where such opportunities have been appreciated and made use of. The practice of building clergy houses and parish rooms and schools in connection with parish churches is a comparatively modern one. In medieval England the parish churches themselves were the only public buildings in country districts and may have been used for a variety of purposes that we should now regard as secular. The clergy lived in their rectories or vicarages which might be near the churches, but were seldom, if ever, connected with them.

The Parochial Tradition

Sometimes in the case of a large church, where there were a number of chantry priests, they may have lived together, but unless a parish church was served by a college of priests or by a community of monks there would be no domestic or secular buildings attached to it except in very rare instances. One of these is the group of buildings at Ewelme, in Oxfordshire, consisting of the parish church, a block of almshouses at its west end, the chapel of which forms the south aisle of the church, and a detached school-house, all dating from the 15th century when the almshouses and the school were founded and the church rebuilt by William de la Pole, Duke of Suffolk. There is an equally interesting collection of buildings round the church at Higham Ferrers, Northants. In this case there is a 15th-century school-house a short distance west of the church and the "bede house" with its chapel also stands in the churchyard. Archbishop Chichele, founder of All Souls' College at Oxford, was also founder of the college and probably built the school-house and rebuilt the "bede house" at Higham Ferrers.

Ewelme and Higham Ferrers are alike in one respect that each architectural group is consistent in style, and in neither case is it a collection of miscellaneous buildings. Nevertheless, in both cases the existence of the almshouses and schools in the church precincts is due to exceptional circumstances and the generality of old English parish churches stood alone in their churchyards with no other accessories except a lychgate and a churchyard cross. In this respect the parish churches of Brittany and to a less degree of Normandy contrast strongly with our old English ones. The Breton churchyards quite often contain several buildings besides the church, detached chapels, bonehouses, elaborate calvaries, fountains, imposing entrance gates dating as a rule from the 16th and 17th centuries, but these serve no secular purpose and may thus be regarded as detached portions of the church rather than as accessory buildings.

An early example of the grouping of churches with domestic and other buildings required for social and similar work is to be seen at St. Barnabas' Church, Pimlico, where the church stands between a block of school buildings and a clergy house which was planned to house a certain number of the choir boys as well as the clergy. These buildings were completed in 1850 and are well designed considering their date, but the details of the clergy house and schools are much more ecclesiastical than they would have been had they been the work of medieval builders.

The whole conception of St. Barnabas', Pimlico, was collegiate rather than parochial, and at a later date the collegiate church of St. Michael at Tenbury was founded by Sir F. Gore Ouseley who had been one of the clergy at St. Barnabas'. Tenbury is an establishment which includes a church and a school with endowed scholarships for choir boys and is built very much on the lines of an Oxford or Cambridge college, but the church itself serves also as a parish church and not merely as a college chapel.

Woodyer, the architect of Tenbury, appreciated the difference between ecclesiastical and domestic Gothic far better than Cundy, the designer of the buildings at St. Barnabas', Pimlico, but his work gives the impression of being artificial rather than spontaneous, as if he had thought more of the architectural effect of the work than of its fitness for its purpose, although it must be recognised that the domestic buildings are well planned in many respects and that their general proportions are decidedly effective. Any defects they may have are largely attributable to the fact that the style of the 14th century was chosen as the model to be followed, and so enthusiastic was the architect that the college displays a wealth of 14th-century detail such as no 14th-century architect ever attempted.

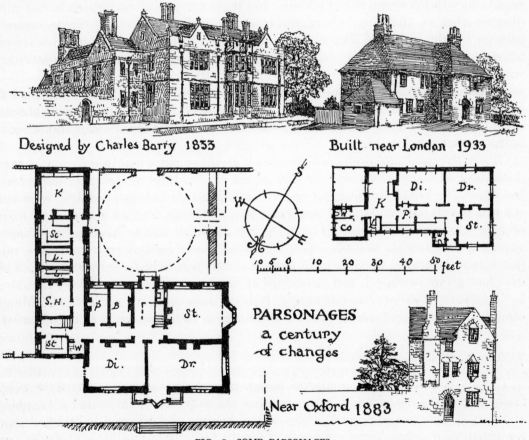

FIG. I. SOME PARSONAGES.

187

In contrast with Pimlico and Tenbury the clergy houses and school buildings attached to Butterfield's churches of All Saints, Margaret Street, and St. Alban, Holborn, are definitely straightforward buildings with very little detail of a definitely Gothic character which nevertheless harmonise extremely well with the churches. One may not wholeheartedly admire all Butterfield's work, but it must be admitted that in his secular buildings he made an honest attempt to evolve a style of domestic Gothic building appropriate to the age in which he lived.

It is true that the houses he built were sometimes uncomfortable judged by modern standards, but the reason of this was probably the fact that he was of an ascetic turn of mind himself and had no sympathy with the weaknesses of less robust mortals, especially among the clergy.

The fashion of building parsonages or clergy houses in direct connection with a church is especially favoured by Roman Catholic Church builders in England, and the great majority of Nonconformist Churches have extensive accessory buildings for social purposes either incorporated or adjacent to them. There is no special significance in these matters, they are essentially matters of convenience, but it is obvious that in churches where services are held frequently there are sound reasons for the clergy to live as close as possible to the churches in which they have to minister. It is also obviously convenient that any social work identified with the church should be centralised and that the headquarters of the church's social activities should be the church. Consequently with very few exceptions, and those generally in country districts, a complete church building scheme should include a church hall or building for social work, a parsonage or clergy house, and perhaps a school (Fig. 1).

One of the most ambitious schemes for a group of parochial buildings was prepared a good many years ago for the parish of St. John at Gainsborough, here the late J. T. Micklethwaite planned a magnificent church surrounded by ample schools, parish halls and clergy house and sexton's house and what not—very little of which has ever been built. The architectural detail was to have been a simple variety of late Gothic and the effect would no doubt have been extremely good, but it is to be feared there is little chance that it will ever be fully realised. The excellent group of church and parsonage at St. Anselm's, Davies Street, London, by Thackeray Turner, has unfortunately been destroyed as "redundant." Many church buildings in its immediate neighbourhood could better have been spared.

Vestries in Town and Country

The requirements of a medieval parish church in England must have been fairly simple: as has already been observed the majority of them had no vestries and very few contained organs, while central heating and artificial lighting, except for ceremonial lights, were unknown. Even in cathedrals and large collegiate or monastic churches there was very little provision of vestry accommodation measured by modern standards. The post-war churches must, of course, conform to modern notions with regard to such matters as these, and it is certainly conducive to orderliness that there should be a place provided for everything and that everything should be kept in its place. Most churches that are built nowadays have a couple of vestries and a lavatory, but very often no provision is made for the church cleaner or the sexton to store his things except a corner behind the organ or in the stoke-hole. Moreover, in a church of any considerable size it is an advantage if it can be managed to provide a separate sacristy as well as a couple of vestries, especially if there is a large staff of clergy or if anything like a full ceremonial is contemplated.

Lavatory provision should always, if possible, include a hot water supply, which can easily be managed if either gas or electricity is available, but in country churches where there is no public water supply it seems best as a rule to make some provision for church cleaners and for sanitation in an external building, either adjacent to or at a short distance away from the church. Then again, with regard to the heating apparatus it is remarkable how often this has the appearance of being an afterthought both in the clumsy way in which the interior of a church is disfigured by pipes and radiators and in the inadequate space allowed for the stoke-hole and for the storage of fuel. These inconveniences may sometimes be unavoidable in the case of an old church, but they are less excusable in a new one. In any case it is the reverse of edifying to find a mound of coke piled up against a church wall because there is only storage room for two tons and it is found cheaper to buy it by the truck load. However, a good deal depends upon orderly management even in the case of the coke store, for it is possible to find palatial stoke-holes in anything but palatial conditions and a stoker who takes a pride in his work can make the best of difficult conditions.

Although a good deal of post-war church building will be upon new sites or will consist of complete reconstructions of destroyed buildings there will still be cases where ancient churches have to be dealt with, and in many cases these have been without vestries or conveniences of any kind. In past years these would have been added without compunction, often causing great disfigurement to a beautiful building, at other times without offence.

Where it is felt that the addition of vestries, etc., to an existing church would be objectionable, either by darkening the interior or by concealing valuable architectural detail or by destroying the proportions or outlines of the old work, it would sometimes be best to provide vestries, etc., in a detached building connected to the church by a porch or covered way. Another good plan of adding vestries to an old church is to arrange them in a low building extending beyond the old work either eastwards or transept fashion instead of the commonplace plan of building them alongside a church wall. In any case, in an Anglican church, the vestries should be near the east end of the building and should all be kept together. Some years ago it became the fashion to build choir vestries at the west ends of Anglican churches, an arrangement that is undesirable from the point of view of discipline and dignity. Although such a plan is undesirable in a new church it may be that, in an ancient one, the only alternatives are to build a new vestry or to use the space under the west tower. In these cases it is better to put up with the inconveniences of a western vestry than to alter the outline of an old church by building an addition that is not absolutely necessary. In fact, when one is dealing with an old building every problem must be decided on its merits, no hard and fast rules can be laid down except that those responsible for the work should exercise the virtues of modesty and common sense.

In planning vestries for a new church it is usual to arrange them on the main floor level, but on a sloping site they are often provided in a basement story below the nave or the chancel. This is an economical plan, but if it is adopted it is useful to contrive some form of sacristy, not necessarily a large one, on the level of the chancel, at any rate in Anglican and Roman Catholic churches. If the bulk of the vestry accommodation is in a basement under the church it is hardly in accord with the fitness of things that lavatories and cleaners' rooms should be provided underneath a sanctuary or chapel or in a place where the necessary plumbing work is unduly prominent. The heating chamber, too, should if possible be arranged as inconspicuously as possible, but there is no need to be ashamed of a chimney or to disguise that necessary feature with a gable cross or a pinnacle.

How far cloakrooms and lavatories are desirable in new churches is a matter of opinion, but it is a matter of certainty that they are anything but desirable if they are not kept clean and tidy, and the cost of maintenance is an important matter.

Similar considerations apply where an excessive number of chapels is provided in a church. Extreme cases which illustrate the disadvantage of the multiplication of altars are very numerous on the Continent, where large churches often have an altar in every bay of its aisles, very few of which are ever used, and most of which exhibit melancholy collections of dilapidated ornaments, shabby and often dirty linen and lace, and such lumber as unwanted chairs and other furniture. In England there has been a movement in the last twenty years to refurnish the chapels in cathedrals. In nearly all cases where this has been done the chapels have all been allocated to special purposes and are in regular if not continuous use. Where this can be arranged the restoration of disused chapels and the provision of new ones is all to the good, not only in cathedrals and large churches but also in churches of quite moderate size. In fact a second altar is often of considerable use in quite a small church, because, whatever the size of the building may be, it is pretty certain that some services will be attended by larger congregations than others and provision should be made for occasions when only a few people are able to be present.

Fifty years or so ago the provision of a second altar in an Anglican church or

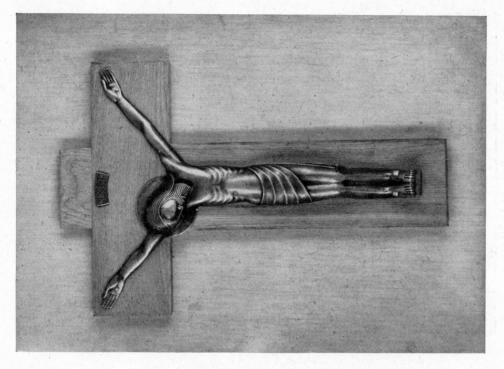

73. CRUCIFIX IN BROWN OAK
By Dunstan Pruden

72. EXECUTED IN MONKS PARK STONE, THIS MODERN
FONT HAS AN OAK COVER OF THE ANCIENT LID TYPE
By Joseph Cribb

ONE WAY OF MEETING A PROBLEM

74. ST. ANDREW, HORNCHURCH, SHOWING SANCTUARY ADDED TO A PARISH HALL

even in a cathedral, was quite exceptional; nowadays the exception has become the rule. The Roman Catholic churches built in England in the middle of the 19th century by Pugin and others did not contain a large number of altars. St. Chad's Cathedral at Birmingham and the large church built by Pugin at Derby each had a single large chapel on the Gospel side of the chancel, and apparently in both cases this was originally the only provision made for subsidiary altars on the main floor of the church, though at Birmingham there were other altars in the crypt. At St. George's Cathedral, Lambeth, there were two chapels flanking the chancel, and in Pugin's own church at Ramsgate there were altars in the south chapel and the south transept. At a much later period the same restraint has been shown in Bentley's Cathedral at Westminster where the chapels provided have each its appointed use and give no impression of display having been made for its own sake or for the sake of symmetry. Neither Pugin nor Bentley followed the Continental plan of placing side altars at right-angles to the high altar, an arrangement which may be admissible under exceptional conditions, but which has no particular advantages beyond looking Continental. These observations concerning chapels would not apply to a church built for the Eastern Orthodox Communion which allows only a single altar in one building and only sanctions chapels if they are self-contained structures, but it is possible that as time goes on the builders of Presbyterian and other Protestant churches may find that it is convenient to provide chapels in connection with their churches since there is now certainly a tendency not to emphasise the external differences between different religious bodies as was done a generation or two ago.

Besides chapels in the strict sense of the word some churches contain shrines and others Children's Corners. Such accessories are somewhat outside the province of the church builder. No doubt it is helpful to many people to say their prayers before a shrine or a statue or more especially a crucifix and it would be churlish to deny that help to those who value it. As regards such accessories, however, there seems no good reason for tolerating work which is shoddy or ostentatious.

Children's Corners, in particular, are a very modern invention and give great scope for orgies of sentimentality, sometimes going as far as a "teddy bear" upon a structure resembling an altar. Perhaps the best and most valuable form of "Children's Corner" is a properly furnished chapel, set apart especially for their use, and not an untidy nursery with chromo-lithographs by devout lady artists.

The Parish Room or Church Hall

In a confined town site it is sometimes almost necessary or at any rate convenient to build a parish room underneath a church. In the case of at least one London church the building is of several floors with the church at the top, a flat for the vicar below it and a ground floor or basement containing club rooms, etc. This particular church is not a large one and the whole of the buildings are cramped and inconvenient, which probably was inevitable, and ugly, which they need not have been. A building of this description may be better than no church at all, but can only be justified on the score of necessity. There is something just a little incongruous even in building a parish room underneath a church. No doubt the social work of a church is of great value, but there is a place for everything. Billiards and whist drives and table tennis are admirable occupations and may be instrumental in the conversion of unbelievers and the edification of the faithful, but the basement of a church is not particularly well adapted for an indoor sports' centre, often it is little better than a cellar. But apart from this fact and from any question of fitness there are some very definite advantages in having a separate building for the social side of the activities of a church. One of these is that either the church or the "church hall" can be enlarged at any time without affecting the other building. But even more important is the fact that when a new church is built in a district where the bulk of the people are indifferent to organised religion it is most desirable to begin in a small way and so to collect a group of supporters who will come in time to demand and work for a permanent church. If a ready made church is planted in the middle of an indifferent population it is apt to be looked upon with suspicion and it may be a very long time before it ceases to be ignored by the people for whose use it is built. This of course chiefly applies to churches built in newly settled districts which is the case with the majority of churches built nowadays.

The soundest policy in such circumstances is to begin church work in a room, possibly large enough to become a "parish room" or a church hall. This may at first be divided and half of it only used for church services, the other half for social purposes and Sunday school. As the influence of the church grows there will be a demand for more accommodation and a beginning may be made of the permanent church. As soon as this is ready for use the entire church hall will become available for social work, and later on either the church or the church hall can be extended as opportunity offers until both buildings have reached their full stature.

There is yet another advantage in keeping the church hall separate from the church which is that if by any chance the church gets burnt down the hall will provide alternative accommodation. This has happened in several places where churches have been destroyed by enemy action.

Assuming that it is practicable to build a self-contained church hall there will be no intrinsic incongruity in using it for any form of social work, games, dances, entertainments and so forth, and furthermore there will be nothing to prevent the building or parts of it being let for such activities to persons not identified with the organisations of the church. It is not suggested that a church hall should be built as a commercial speculation, but if it is not incorporated with the actual church building it is not unseemly that payments should be made for the amenities it provides, whereas when the crypt of a church is used for sales of work, subscription dances, whist drives and so forth there is apt to be a certain suggestion of the tables of money changers and the seats of those that sell doves.

If, however, it is anticipated that a church hall will occasionally be let to strangers or that the church authorities will use it for entertainments for which payment is made it is advisable that this should be determined before the building is planned since it will mean that a licence will have to be obtained and certain conditions with regard to the building will have to be complied with.

The ideal arrangement for such a building is to arrange the whole accommodation on one floor, but this is only possible if there is plenty of room on the site and only a limited number of activities have to be provided for. Where a church hall has to include separate quarters for Scouts, club rooms, class rooms, and so forth in addition to a main assembly hall it is generally necessary to build two or more stories. If, however, this is the case it is always advisable that the principal assembly hall should be on the ground floor and it is desirable that there should be no floor over it. Club rooms, etc., can be arranged in flats one above another.

Although it is desirable that a church hall should be a distinct and self-contained building this does not mean that a covered way connecting it with the church is undesirable, on the contrary many very excellent lay-outs provide a connected series of self-contained buildings, church, church hall, and sometimes parsonage as well. Although it is questionable whether the parsonage should be entirely detached there are no very valid reasons in favour of an entirely isolated church hall unless it is desired to use this to a great extent for letting purposes, in which event it can hardly be regarded as a church hall as distinct from a public hall owned by a Church Council. A good arrangement where space is available is to build a passage leading from the church to the church hall and for the vestries and lavatories, etc., to be accessible from this. Such an arrangement is particularly useful if the church hall is used for Sunday school purposes. And a convenience that should not be forgotten is a place for parking cycles and keeping ladders.

With regard to the style of building suitable for church halls and the like, it seems obvious that it ought not to be out of keeping with the character of the church and at the same time that it should not be definitely ecclesiastical in style. There is, however, another and less excusable error, that of building a shoddy church hall in connection with a decently constructed church. Of course, if a church has walls three or four bricks thick it does not follow that the church hall should be equally substantial. It is difficult to say exactly where extravagance ends and shoddiness begins, but an intelligent and conscientious architect or builder ought to know. A hundred years ago Pugin was very successful in differentiating between his churches and their semi-secular dependent buildings. He aimed at a consistent revival of medieval architecture, but never made his schools or presbyteries look like churches nor was he content to build them in any but a consistent Gothic manner (Fig. 2).

The task of the post-war architect is likely to be difficult in many ways, but he is not likely to be fettered by any preconceived ideas that every ecclesiastical or semi-ecclesiastical building must be "Gothic" as this adjective has been understood in the past. The danger rather is that the church hall will be built like a boiler house and that the church will follow suit.

However, the taste of the coming generation is a thing that cannot be very much influenced by the prejudices of the existing one, in fact, it is pretty certain that our successors will wonder how we can possibly have been so stupid as to admire the things we admire and produce the things we produce. Still we may plead for some shapeliness of line and some appreciation of light and shadow and some little flavour of tradition, and above all some solidity of construction in post-war work, and hope for the best.

In the years preceding the catastrophe of 1939 a certain number of new church centres were established in the diocese of St. Albans. The procedure in these undertakings was to obtain sites and in each case to build a good-sized church hall, deferring the permanent church and parsonage to a later date. The hall is divided into two parts with a solid wall and one-half is used as a temporary church and for no other purpose, the other half is used for social church work. When the permanent church is built the whole of the church hall block will become available for the social work, and of course can be added to if necessary. This arrangement seems an improvement upon the more usual one of building a hall for all purposes, with a sanctuary divided from it by means of a revolving shutter. The mistake, however, is apt to be made of putting up too slight a building and regarding it as a permanent structure, a mistake which is sure to lead to trouble in the long run. Another mistake may be made which may have quite serious results if the whole lay-out of the site is not very carefully and thoroughly thought out before the church hall is built, since, if it is built in the wrong place, it may spoil the whole arrangement of future buildings on the site—assuming, of course, that the church and the hall are to be in the same enclosure.

The combination of church and hall and possibly parsonage also is generally only possible on a new site as there are legal difficulties in building anything except a church upon consecrated ground or in a closed churchyard. In fact, in the latter case, it is only legitimate to rebuild or extend an existing church. One cannot pull down an old church and build a new one on another part of the churchyard, much less build a church hall or a parsonage there, unless one obtains a private act of Parliament for the purpose.

In many places, especially in rural districts, it is generally sufficient to provide a good-sized single hall with a small kitchen and cloakrooms and to arrange a movable partition across the hall for use when required. In town and suburban districts the social work of a church is more complex, and a church hall generally expands into a church institute with separate accommodation for different church organisations. It is not very usual and perhaps not very desirable to build such an extensive social centre in direct communication with a church though it should not be far away. If, however, the principal "institute" is in a separate building it is still useful to have one good-sized hall directly communicating with the church and distinct from the vestries. Such a room would be valuable for classes and

Presbytery: Derby
A.W Pugin 1839-40

FIG. 2. PRESBYTERY, OR PRIEST'S HOUSE, BUILT BY PUGIN.

meetings of a Church Council and for choir practices and the like; it must, however, be regarded as a luxury rather than as a necessity. In the earlier half of the 19th century nearly every church had its own schools and the school buildings were available for any social work that was carried on, so the need for church halls was not so great as it is nowadays.

Architecturally, it is a great advantage that a church should be connected with subordinate buildings provided the site is suitable and the buildings are of appropriate character, not necessarily church-like but substantial and shapely. But definite rules cannot be made; every building scheme has its own problems.

The characteristic accessories of an old English churchyard were the lychgate and the churchyard cross. It may be regarded as inconsistent to build a lychgate at the entrance to a churchyard which is not used as a cemetery, but so long as it remains customary to conduct funeral services within churches a lychgate will serve the same purpose as lychgates have always served, namely, that of providing a sheltered resting place for a coffin at the entrance to the churchyard. A church-yard cross needs no apology, but neither a cross nor a lychgate is a necessity so there is no excuse for allowing second-rate work if such accessories are included in a building scheme.

It is not often the case that a modern lychgate is very successful. Many of them are too elaborate; others look out of place, especially in built-up areas; many modern churchyard crosses, too, are unsatisfactory, sometimes because they are too small and sometimes because they are badly placed; a design which looks very well in an old country churchyard may be very disappointing if it is reproduced in different surroundings.

In London there are some suggestive pieces of Victorian work which seem to have been inspired by the old English lychgates and churchyard crosses. The most ambitious of these is the long covered way leading to St. Mary Abbott's Church, Kensington. A much simpler approach to a London church is the forecourt at All Saints', Margaret Street; here the buttress of the aisle immediately opposite the arched entrance gate of the forecourt is treated to some extent as a churchyard cross. Incidentally it is very regrettable that the very remarkable cast ironwork of the screen wall was removed as scrap metal for munition making. Another interesting entry is that on the south side of St. Albans, Holborn, where an arched gateway under the clergy house leads into a quite narrow paved yard and so into the church. In the yard are a crucifix against one of the walls and a terra cotta plaque of Della Robbia character against another, the remaining two sides of the enclosure consisting of the south aisle wall of the church and the eastern wall of one of its chapels.

None of these three pieces of work is imitative but each in its way reproduces the sense of reverent seclusion which is characteristic of the setting of a good many old English churches.

The covered way at Kensington, moreover, serves a very practical purpose and is particularly appreciated in wet weather. No doubt its architectural character is of a sort that has become unfashionable, but it cannot be denied that the work has been well and truly carried out nor can it be asserted that its design is ungraceful. Indeed it is not unlikely that if it is not destroyed by municipal enterprise in the next century or so it will be regarded with as much reverence as we now bestow upon the works of the Queen Anne and Georgian builders. An ancient church-yard that has escaped the plague of white marble and polished granite is generally an attractive setting for a church in a country village or small town, but it must be admitted that some of the old graveyards in London and other large towns are, or were in their original condition, most depressing places. In a good many cases these have been taken in hand with more or less success, but unless the operation has been fairly drastic the success has not often been very marked. Most town churchyards and a great many village ones are now closed, and if allowed to remain full of headstones and other monuments it is most difficult to keep them in order. At the same time it is not very seemly to obliterate all evidence of the existence of a burial ground after it has been closed. In some cases it may be best to clear away the individual memorials and to substitute a single one embodying some record of the individual names which it is possible to trace. In other cases the old gravestones can be preserved in the paving of churchyard paths or even in the paving of the church itself and the old graveyard levelled and turfed over, leaving perhaps a few of the more interesting gravestones undisturbed.

There are still a few London graveyards that remind one of Dickens' burial ground in *Bleak House*, but the most grisly churchyards in England are those in some of the industrial towns in the northern counties. The worst of these are in the smaller towns where the families of prosperous mill owners have competed with one another in the magnificence of their monuments. In one such case the somewhat pretentious and rather imposing church is approached through a regular avenue of monumental pomposity. In another, a forceful parish priest of the early part of the 19th century devised a standard form of headstone and allowed no other in his churchyard. In some cases the headstones have been laid flat in a manner which looks very unsightly if the site is not a level one, and in others the stones have been left standing till they fall down of their own accord, and the picture is completed with rank grass, sooty laurels, and perhaps the remains of confetti.

An old churchyard of this description round the cathedral of St. Philip at Birmingham has been dealt with quite successfully, partly by design and partly by accident. As regards design it was spoiled by the presence of a great deal of unnecessary iron fencing. As regards accident it has been transformed into a pleasant place by the patriotic sacrifice of the aforesaid ironwork for war purposes.

If a churchyard is not and has not been a burial place it will be necessary to consider how far it should be treated as a garden. It is possible to overdo this: in the case of a modern west of England church the surroundings of the sacred edifice were adorned with shrubberies and rockwork upon which ivy was planted and the walls clothed with virginia creeper—no doubt in order to bring the church into harmony with the genteel villas in which the congregation resided. Sometimes the church garden is beautifully neat with its immaculate gravel and its flower beds cut out in the turf. In other cases it is so thickly planted with shrubs that it suggests a jungle, and with the shrubs one generally finds common iron fencing, a very unpleasant combination.

There are a few places where a churchyard fence can be dispensed with as, for instance, in some cathedral closes. At Chichester the cathedral green is open to the public highway and the effect is most satisfactory. But as a rule it is considered necessary that a church site should be enclosed; in which case the best form of fence is a stone or brick wall or, in the case of a country church, a stout post and rail oak fence either left plain or painted white. And, as regards the actual gardening, turf and trees always look well, flower beds should not be overdone, paths are best if they are paved with square flagstones, and "crazy pavement" looks what it is called. Evergreen shrubs become very untidy and rubbish is apt to collect under them, but yews and box trees make a pleasant feature in a churchyard particularly if they are allowed to grow naturally. Clipped yews never seem quite in place round a church; they suggest an ungovernable desire to be quaint at all costs.

Sometimes a modern church possesses an out-door pulpit. There are ancient examples of such pulpits at Magdalen College, Oxford, and a few other places, but the British climate does not encourage experiments in open air preaching except for a very short part of the year and the steps of a churchyard cross should serve the purpose of a pulpit in case of need. It is not likely that post-war church builders will indulge in such attractions as the fountains and detached chapels and charnel houses that one finds in the churchyards of Brittany, but there have been a few instances in comparatively recent years where something of the kind has been done. At Tenbury, for instance, there is a well in the Baptistery of the church and at St. Peter's, Bournemouth, there is a mortuary chapel in the churchyard. In a Warwickshire churchyard an open air chapel was built as a memorial of the 1914–18 war and in a few churchyards seemly detached buildings have been provided for the storage of sextons' tools and garden implements. There is a very good example of such a garden building in the cathedral churchyard at Llandaff, it includes a very pretty penthouse shelter for ladders. These matters are mentioned in order to emphasise the opportunities that may be wasted if the surroundings of a church are not considered when that church is being planned. It is not always possible, but it is always desirable to determine the character of the building and of its setting as a single undertaking.

The Post-war Parsonage

It remains to consider what sort of a building will probably be suitable for the purpose of a post-war parsonage. Here we find ourselves faced with new problems of domestic economy which did not greatly trouble our predecessors. In the future the requirements of churches and halls may not greatly differ from those to which we have become accustomed, but pre-war parsonages are likely to be quite out of date in a very few years' time. A booklet published by the Incorporated Church Building Society gives useful data concerning the construction and arrangement of churches which the post-war church builder will do well to study and to follow, but the published instructions issued by the Ecclesiastical Commissioners with regard to the building of parsonages will almost certainly have to be revised when building again becomes possible. The problem is one which particularly affects the Anglican community since this is responsible for staffing every parish in the country however difficult the conditions may be, whereas other religious bodies are at liberty to select their own centres of work. It is, moreover, aggravated by the fact that since endowments exist, they are generally assumed by the laity to be sufficient for the support of the clergy, which in fact they are not even now and are still less likely to be in the future. Financial difficulties have been to a great extent overcome by the disestablished churches in Ireland and in Wales and no doubt will be overcome in England, but it is fairly obvious that Great Britain will be an impoverished country for a long time to come, and that both the clergy and the laity will have to economise in their manner of living to an extent which would have shocked the easy going gentry of the Victorian era. Perhaps two or three country parishes will be united and served by a single priest, or a group of parishes will be served by a small community of clergy living together; it is also pretty certain that a number of small parishes in towns will be united. Accordingly it is quite possible that two distinct types of residence may become recognised as appropriate for the clergy serving Anglican churches, the quasi collegiate clergy house in certain areas and the purely domestic parsonage in others.

Thus, whether parsonages are detached buildings or connected directly with churches, it will become usual to plan them on definitely labour saving lines. There will be no need to provide stabling for the rector's hunters or cellars for his port wine or a lodge for his gardener, but, on the other hand, it is possible that builders of parsonages may go to the opposite extreme and be led astray by the much-advertised nostrums of ideal home exhibitions and by too much heed to the letters in the press from housewives complaining that they have to walk three steps from the stove to the sink instead of only two.

The average diocesan authorities have often made another mistake in fixing a maximum price for a new parsonage and insisting on the provision of a number of things which can only be paid for by cramping the size of the rooms or starving the construction. It should be remembered that a fair sized room is no more difficult to keep clean than a pokey one, it is the furniture of a room that makes work. Also the multiplication of conveniences which are not in constant use is less beneficial than having a warm dry home to live in. The standard plan of a parsonage as defined by the Ecclesiastical Commissioners includes three sitting-rooms and five or six bedrooms beside kitchen, etc., and a smaller type allowed in some circumstances has only two sitting-rooms and four bedrooms. This last plan is inadequate if there is a large young family, the larger type of house is often disproportionate to the stipend of the occupant.

Certain conveniences, however, are very well worth paying for, fixed lavatories in bedrooms for instance and a drying cupboard and an accessible box room and water tank. Central heating is perhaps a counsel of perfection, but gas or electric fires are generally desirable in most rooms and for cooking. But a house may have all these conveniences and more and yet it will be unsatisfactory if it is not built well and solidly.

Years ago nothing less than a fourteen inch external wall was considered adequate for a well-built house on the scale of an ordinary parsonage.

Nowadays an eleven inch hollow wall is supposed to suffice and probably the standard will degenerate further in the future. A substantial house is likely to cost a great deal of money in the near future, and it is rather questionable whether it will be worth while to build parsonages at all if other accommodation for the clergy can be bought or rented. After all the clergy can live in houses built for the laity and it is a lesser evil that they should do so than that the church should be responsible for anything suggestive of jerry-building. Parsonages built before 1914 may not have had all the conveniences of more recent buildings, but most of them have served and continue to serve their purpose without excessive maintenance charges and are comfortable to live in though often far from beautiful to look at.

In planning a modern parsonage on an average open site it is most desirable to keep everything on two floors. It is likely that most parsonages will have to be run on strictly frugal lines and that domestic help will be on a very small scale, so the mistress of the house, whether housekeeper or wife, will have to do a good deal of house work. It will be found convenient to provide a separate small pantry for her use. And if there is a resident maid she should certainly have a room of her own to sit in, this may be separate from the kitchen but may open from it, and it should have a bright outlook and a fireplace. There is a tendency to build flat roofed houses nowadays; these are not always satisfactory or weatherproof. A better arrangement is to have a pitched roof with a boarded floor all over the roof space and to make this easily accessible for storage, water tank, and other purposes, such perhaps as a small workshop. A house built with such a roof is much warmer and more comfortable and easier to keep tidy than a house with nothing but a flat roof to keep out the cold and with no place to put things away in or no easy means of access to any storage space there may happen to be in the roof.

Regarding the architectural character of a parsonage the ideal would be that, like a church hall, it should be consistent with, and at the same time distinct from, that of the church to which it belongs. This is so even in the case of parsonages that are annexed to churches. In some cases these are so closely assimilated to the churches that one can hardly tell where the one ends and the other begins and the house is supplied with inconvenient windows, etc., which are supposed to be ecclesiastical. In many places, especially in the north of England towns, the parsonages are forbidding looking villa residences of blackened stone, with perhaps a pointed arch to the front door, which is usually "grained oak," and perhaps pointed relieving arches over the windows. There is generally a "carriage drive" almost invariably neglected and adorned with lumps of waste stone covered with ivy. There are plenty of shrubs in the garden. Inside the rooms are much too high and the finishings are all of the jerry-builders' favourite patterns and sometimes a new grate of the latest exhibition pattern has been installed in the drawing-room. Everything about such a place is so bleak and miserable looking that many people would greatly prefer to live in an ordinary non-ecclesiastical house of no pretension at all; such a house might be as ugly as the parsonage, but would probably be much more comfortable for an establishment where income was limited.

WINCHFIELD SCHOOL
Built by W. Burges

FIG. 3.—AN ATTRACTIVE 19TH-CENTURY SCHOOL.

There are, of course, plenty of modern parsonages which are very good and quite suited to financial circumstances of the time when they were built. Probably the most satisfactory ones architecturally would be described as Georgian in character and of these the best are those which are least distinctly Georgian and just plain straightforward dwelling houses with pleasant rooms inside them. But it must be confessed that some of the parsonages of the middle of the last century, generally more or less Gothic in style, are quite attractive and agreeable to live in, especially the smaller and less ambitious ones, such as one at South Benfleet, in Essex, built about 1850, and the presbytery of Pugin's church at Derby built some eight years earlier. Mention has been made elsewhere of Thackeray Turner's parsonage at St. Anselm's, Davies Street, London, now unhappily destroyed, an entirely satisfactory piece of town architecture though built on a scale that suggests men-servants and maid-servants and other things which we are warned not to covet and which perhaps we are happier without.

In contrast with this there is a very pleasant little simple presbytery built by Leonard Stokes in about 1895 at the church of St. Helen at Southend-on-Sea, and in contrast to both of the last-mentioned houses there is another presbytery adjoining a Roman Catholic Church at Leigh-on-Sea built from the designs of the priest in a style supposed to be Norman! As for the fine old rectories and vicarages up and down the country one can hope that many of them will survive, but one cannot desire to see houses on so large a scale built for households of limited income.

It is not often that in these times day schools are attached to new churches, and where this is the case there are so many demands to satisfy that there is very little chance of combining them satisfactorily with the churches themselves. During the 19th century, however, things were different and many charming village schools were built near the churches of the period and, when a site was available near old churches, where they grouped well with the other buildings.

There was a particularly attractive school building by Burges at Winchfield, Hants., but this, like many other 19th-century schools, has been much disfigured since it was built (Fig. 3). The powers that control the education of the rising generation seem to have very little appreciation of beauty and a touching faith in everything that is supposed to be practical because it is ugly, so perhaps it is as well that if church day schools are built they should not be too near the churches, besides which day schools should be kept away from traffic and churches should not be in too obscure positions.

But in north-country towns the churches often have quite extensive Sunday school buildings attached to them. These have a good deal in common with church halls and generally serve the same purposes on six days in the week, but as a rule they include a certain number of good-sized class rooms as well as a main hall. They are in many cases used for adult classes as well as for boys and girls. Unfortunately, in many cases they have been designed without very much regard for the character of the churches where these have any character, which is not always the case.

Churches built on more or less confined sites in towns do not, of course, give much opportunity of effective groupings with accessory buildings: in compensation for this they provide very interesting problems of planning. On open sites it becomes possible to combine buildings of different uses into effective architectural compositions. It is easy enough to stray from the path that leads to success whatever may be the external conditions. This book will justify itself if it has succeeded in setting up some signposts to warn the traveller of pitfalls and possibly to point the way to something that would not otherwise be perceived.